THE STORY OF WORKER SPORT

Arnd Krüger, PhD
Georg-August-University, Göttingen, Germany

James Riordan, PhD
University of Surrey, Guildford, England

Human Kinetics

Library of Congress Cataloging-in-Publication Data

The story of worker sport / Arnd Krüger, James Riordan, editors.
    p. cm
    "Collection of chapters, translated from the writings of sports scholars and historians who are natives of the countries in which worker sport played an important role"--Pref.
    Includes bibliographical references and index.
    ISBN 0-87322-874-X
    1. Sports--Social aspects--History--20th century. 2. Socialism and sports. 3. Working class--Recreation--History--20th century.
I. Krüger, Arnd. II. Riordan, James, 1936- .
GV706.5S867   1996
306.4'83--dc20
                           96-1281
                           CIP

ISBN: 0-87322-874-X

Copyright © 1996 by Arnd Krüger and James Riordan

Photos in chapter 4 courtesy of the Sport Museum of Finland.
Photos in chapter 8 reproduced by kind permission of the Workers Archive and Library, Oslo (Arbeiderbevegelsens Arkiv og Bibliotek).
Photos in chapter 9 courtesy of the Multicultural Society of Ontario.

Developmental Editor: Larret Galasyn-Wright; **Managing Editor:** Julie Marx Ohnemus; **Assistant Editor:** Anna Curry; **Editorial Assistant:** Coree Schutter; **Copyeditor:** David Frattini; **Proofreader:** Karen Bojda; **Indexer:** Barbara Cohen; **Typesetters and Layout Artists:** Julie Overholt and Tara Welsch; **Text Designer:** Judy Henderson; **Cover Designer:** Jack Davis; **Printer:** Edwards Brothers

Printed in the United States of America

10 9 8 7 6 5 4 3 2 1

Human Kinetics
Web site: http://www.humankinetics.com/

United States: Human Kinetics
P.O. Box 5076, Champaign, IL 61825-5076
1-800-747-4457
e-mail: humank@hkusa.com

Canada: Human Kinetics
Box 24040, Windsor, ON N8Y 4Y9
1-800-465-7301 (in Canada only)
e-mail: humank@hkcanada.com

Europe: Human Kinetics
P.O. Box IW14, Leeds LS16 6TR, United Kingdom
(44) 1132 781708
e-mail: humank@hkeurope.com

Australia: Human Kinetics
57A Price Avenue
Lower Mitcham, South Australia 5062
(08) 277 1555
e-mail: humank@hkaustralia.com

New Zealand: Human Kinetics
P.O. Box 105-231, Auckland 1
(09) 523 3462
e-mail: humank@hknewz.com

Contents

Preface

We compiled this book to tell a story that has never been completely told—the history of the worker sport movement. This movement, which reached its peak between World War I and World War II, became an integral part of the lives of millions of workers in Europe, and to a lesser extent involved workers in Asia and North and South America. Despite being the largest working-class cultural movement of its time, worker sport has until this point been neglected by both researchers and the mass media. This collection of chapters, translated from the writings of sports scholars and historians who are natives of the countries in which worker sport played an important role, forms the first unified story of the international worker sport movement.

As James Riordan points out in his introduction, the main goal of the worker sport movement was to provide *all* members of the working class—men, women, children, and all ethnic groups—with an opportunity to enjoy healthy, generally noncompetitive activity in a socialist environment as an alternative to bourgeois sport. As the following chapters will relate with varying levels of detail, the underlying aims and outward successes and failures of this movement were affected by conflict between socialist and communist leaders and workers, the workers' desires to blend into capitalist society, and political changes resulting from two world wars.

The Story of Worker Sport will be of special interest to sociologists, sports studies students, and historians, especially scholars interested in European and North American history from 1890 to 1949. The book comprises 10 chapters, each detailing the history of worker sport in a country in which the movement had (and in some cases still has) a prominent influence. Each chapter begins with a brief history of the country during the peak of the worker sport movement, and readers will find historical sidebars, photos, and translations of documents of the period throughout the book that depict actual events of the time. Because the breadth of the worker sport movement made it impossible to include a chapter on every country affected by the movement, we have created an appendix giving short histories of 18 additional countries important to worker sport.

This book is published at a time of radical change for many of the countries mentioned in these pages. Much of our research and writing was conducted before or during the fall of the Berlin Wall and the reunification of Germany and before the violent civil wars raging through the former republic of Yugoslavia, the splitting of Czechoslovakia, and the division of the former Soviet Union drew the world's attention to Eastern Europe and Asia. We intend *The Story of Worker Sport* to be a unique window into the histories of these and all of the countries included in this book—a look at a movement that is for the most part defunct but not forgotten. Now, at a time when many Europeans are rediscovering their cultural history and scholars around the world are delving into the past to create ties to current conflicts, the story of worker sport has once again become relevant.

Acknowledgements

For me worker sport has always been family lore. My father was a pretty good middle-distance runner, lightweight wrestler, and weightlifter for a workers' sport club in Guben, in the eastern-most part of Germany. Then his ambition led to his progress in other venues of life—a not-so-typical career going from textile apprentice to mill owner. So I understood that although putting time into athletics was good, I should not forget to transfer from running track back to real life.

I was born in the German Democratic Republic, but I emigrated early enough not to suffer much. A UCLA Bruin on a track scholarship as a half miler and miler, an Olympic semifinalist in 1968, an 11-time German champion during some of the best years for the Bayer Chemical Company's sports clubs, I earned my PhD before I was 27. I have had a very peculiar relationship to socialism; I learned from my folks, who stayed behind in Germany, to differentiate between the theory and the practice of socialism, between the dream and the reality.

So when Jim and I first talked about worker sport in the early 1980s, we came from completely different approaches. Jim, who was a card-holding communist with a degree in political science from the prestigious Higher Party School in Moscow, had played soccer for Moscow *Spartak*—a real "worker" sport team—at the same time I was doing my hill work at the Belair Country Club, running cross-country along Sunset Boulevard, and preparing for a career in the capitalist heaven next to Beverly Hills.

We readily agreed, however, that we knew only a small part of the reality and that the little we knew was not even representative. We had in common a love for athletes with their individual dreams and ambitions and an acute sense of their needs under either capitalist or socialist conditions.

Much of worker sport had disappeared in the abyss of the fascist years of Europe, and many of the athletes' dreams had evaporated under the reality of socialist governments. Yet that is what comparative sport history is about. With a network of friends around the world we wanted to know more about the specific conditions of worker sport in as many countries as possible. We were particularly interested in turning points in the history of worker sport, for we had seen the twisting and turning of the various organizations and the dependence of sport on socioeconomic conditions. This resulted in a collection of papers published in West Germany (1985) and in Japan (1988).

Had it not been for Rainer Martens and Bill Baker (*Sport in Western Society*), we would probably have called it quits after those papers, but with their encouragement and keen advice we continued to work at coming up with the world's first concise history of worker sport. Ironically, as soon as the last of worker sport became history, we started on the last leg of the relay that eventually led to the book as you see it here.

Such an effort over a 15-year period would have been impossible without the help of many friends and collaborators. It is tragic that Stephen Jones (1957-1987) cannot enjoy the final version of the book, having been killed in a car crash. Translating the chapters from many languages was not really so difficult. The various authors wrote either in English or in German; in the latter case I translated into my Germanic *Englisch*, and Jim, as the native speaker, put it into more idiomatic English.

Most people involved in the project eventually contributed to the final concise version, but of those who helped us on the way we would like to first mention the collaborators in the German compilation of essays that did not find their way into this final version: Sergij Bjeloborodov, Françoise Hache, and Günther Wonneberger—we have learned much from the discussions with them. Angela Daalmann and Swantje Scharenberg helped with many of the photos and their identification. Leena Laine not only wrote the chapter on Finland but also looked up many of the things in the TUL archives that found their way into the sidebars. We also thank the staff at Human Kinetics who assisted in the development and production of the book, especially Larret Galasyn-Wright and Julie Marx Ohnemus, who helped us through the developmental and editorial process; and Judy Henderson, Julie Overholt, and Tara Welsch, whose efforts created the layout and presentation.

If you look at the tableaux-pyramids of men or women in this book, you will see that worker sport is all about solidarity, reliability, and friendship. Our book is like one of those pyramids: It would not have been possible without relying on others in this enterprise of solidarity.

Arnd Krüger, Göttingen

Introduction

James Riordan

In 1925, a year after the Paris Olympic Games, 150,000 workers attended the first Worker Olympics at Frankfurt am Main. In 1931, one year before the Los Angeles "official" Olympic Games at which 1,408 athletes competed, over 100,000 workers from 26 countries took part in the second Worker Olympics at Vienna. More than a quarter-million spectators attended the Vienna games. Five years later, in opposition to the 1936 Nazi Olympics at Berlin, a more grand Worker Olympics was planned for Barcelona; however, it never took place. The Worker Olympics easily surpassed their rival, the bourgeois Olympic Games, in the number of competitors and spectators and in pageant, culture, and new sports records.

Only the Olympic Games, however, are commemorated in hosts of books in every town library, on radio, and in films that glorify the exploits of Nurmi, Owens, Abrahams, and Liddell; these athletes are romanticised in films such as Leni Riefenstahl's *Olympia 1936* and David Putnam's *Chariots of Fire*. The Worker Olympics and the worker sport movement are cast out of mind. Yet for millions of workers between World War I and World War II, sport was an integral part of the labour movement, and worker sport clubs or associations existed in almost every country of Europe, in the United States and Canada, and in South America and Asia. Because of a lack of space and chroniclers, we cannot, unfortunately, include the full history of worker sport in a number of countries whose workers made important athletic contributions, including Czechoslovakia, Belgium, Switzerland, and Japan. We must recognise that by 1930, worker sport united well over 4 million people, making it by far the largest working-class cultural movement.

So little is known about worker sport because just as the dominant class writes history, so that same class writes the story of sport, including the sports themselves and the rules of all the federations, clubs, and Olympics. The dominant class controls how books and mass media portray (or ignore) sports, and, as a result, worker sport has been neglected as if it never existed. Our book sets out to put the record straight and to present at least a part of the story of worker oppositional sport that, at the zenith of its existence, combined sport with socialist fellowship, solidarity, and working-class culture.

The aims of worker sport differed from country to country, as the various chapters clearly illustrate. All the countries agreed, however, that worker sport should give working people the chance to take part in healthy recreation and to do so in a socialist atmosphere. Worker sport differed from bourgeois sport because the former was open to all workers, women as well as men and black as well as white. It provided a socialist alternative to bourgeois competitive sport, to commercialism, chauvinism, and the obsession with stars and records. It replaced capitalist with socialist values and set the foundation for a true working-class culture. Worker sport, therefore, initially emphasised less-competitive physical activities, such as gymnastics, acrobatics, tumbling, pyramid-forming, mass artistic displays, hiking, cycling, and swimming.

The founders of the worker sport movement believed that sport could be *revolutionary*, that the movement was no less significant to workers than their political, trade union, and cooperative movements. Sport played a paramount role in the struggle against capitalist nationalism and militarism that pervaded the so-called "politically neutral" bourgeois sport organisations and, through them, corrupted young working people. The formation of separate worker sport organisations shielded youths from bourgeois values. While capitalism fostered mistrust among workers of different nations, the worker sport organisations banded together internationally to create peace and an international solidarity. They turned physical culture into a new international language capable of breaking down all barriers.

As Arnd Krüger shows in his chapter on Germany, a worker sport organisation, the Worker Gymnastics Association (WGA), emerged in the 1890s in conscious opposition to the nationalistic German Gymnastics Society (*Turnen*) that was to spread its considerable influence to North America with the migration of entire German communities. The WGA was followed by the Solidarity Worker Cycling Club and the Friends of Nature rambling association in 1895, the Worker Swimming Association in 1897, the Free Sailing Association in 1901, the Worker Athletics Association in 1906, the Worker Chess Association in 1912, and the Free Shooting

Association in 1926. With over 350,000 worker athletes in various clubs even before World War I, Germany became the hub of the worker sport movement.

While the worker sport movement did not take issue with much of the Coubertin idealism concerning the modern Olympic Games, it did oppose the games themselves and counterposed them with its own Olympiads, on the following grounds.

• The bourgeois Olympics encouraged competition along national lines, whereas the Worker Olympics stressed internationalism, worker solidarity, and peace. While the International Olympic Committee (IOC) barred German and Austrian athletes from the 1920 and German athletes from the 1924 games, the 1925 Worker Olympics were held in Germany under the slogan "No More War."

• While the IOC games restricted entry on the grounds of sporting ability, the worker games invited all athletes, stressing mass participation as well as expanding events to include poetry and songs, plays, artistic displays, political lectures, and pageantry.

• The IOC games were criticised for being confined chiefly to the sons of the rich and privileged because of their amateur rules and aristocratic, bourgeois-dominated Olympic committees. Baron de Coubertin himself always opposed women's participation and readily accepted the cultural superiority of whites over blacks; the longest serving IOC presidents, Baillet-Latour and Avery Brundage, both collaborated with the Nazi regime and were unabashedly anti-Semitic. By contrast, the Worker Olympics were explicitly against all chauvinism, racism, sexism, and social exclusivity; they were truly amateur, organised for the edification and enjoyment of working women and men, and they illustrated the fundamental unity of all working people irrespective of colour, creed, sex, or national origin.

• The labour movement did not believe that the Olympic spirit of true amateurism and international understanding could be attained in a movement dominated by an aristocratic, bourgeois leadership. It was, therefore, determined that the labour movement should retain its cultural and political integrity within the workers' Olympic movement.

Bourgeois society excluded workers from public life as well as from amateur sports clubs and competitions. Consequently, if workers competed locally, nationally, or internationally, they had to establish their own sports associations and contests. Such organisations were part of a far-reaching political, trade union, and cultural movement; they formed a network of worker-based organisations that could represent workers throughout their lives. The bourgeois state did all it could to obstruct this movement by introducing new laws, constantly moving the bureaucratic and administrative "goalposts," and at times resorting to brute force. The state, however, could not destroy the rapidly-growing worker movement—until Adolf Hitler's rise to power.

We must remember that worker sport did not take place in a vacuum. The problems that other branches of the labour movement faced also affected worker sport. And like these other branches of the labour movment—including trade unions, social-democratic or labour parties, the cooperative movement, and youth organisations such as the Woodcraft Folk, Young Pioneers, and Young Communist League—worker sport rose and fell everywhere almost simultaneously, reaching a peak in the 1920s and a trough in the late 1930s, and nearly fading away after World War II. National peculiarities invariably added brakes and accelerators, as the following chapters on the German and Austrian tragedies under Hitler, the peaceful demise of worker sport in the United Kingdom, Canada, and Scandinavia, and the persistence of worker sport in Israel and Finland document.

The chapters of this book confine themselves to the flourishing period of worker sport: between the two World Wars. World War II weakened—but did not defeat—the worker sport movement. It continues today, although the radically changed circumstances of the postwar world inevitably transformed the movement. In contrast with its prewar development, the movement's new role called upon its member organisations to cooperate selectively with national sports federations and clubs.

A number of factors caused this new situation. First, the Soviet Union had broken from its isolation. It emerged from the war a victor, and the Soviet Union's military and political power penetrated into Central and Eastern Europe. With the resulting international friction—the Cold War—in which two rival blocs confronted one another over a divided Europe, sport became an obvious arena for international competition, for defeating one's ideological opponent. In the Soviet Union, domestic sport was now thought potent enough to take on the world, and victories over bourgeois states, especially the United States, would evidently demonstrate the Soviet system's vitality.

Second, worker sport encouraged both the Olympic movement and bourgeois sport in general to democratise their memberships. Fewer sports and clubs were confined to middle-class white males, and the belief grew that international sport, particularly the Olympic Games, could be used for peace, democracy, and the isolation of racist regimes such as South Africa.

Third, worker sport switched its emphasis to campaigning within bourgeois organisations against commercialism and chauvinism and for sport for all, funds, playgrounds, open spaces, and facilities; for working people;

for promoting a sport that was profoundly humanistic and free; and for women's sport. As the chapter on France proves, worker sport's new goal was no longer to replace bourgeois sport but, instead, to take part in building a national sports system founded on the needs of all.

A separate worker sport movement, however, managed to survive. In 1946, immediately after the war, the socialist worker sport association in Western Europe set up the International Worker Sports Committee (IWSC) in London. Despite a peak of 2.2 million members in 14 countries, the IWSC never attained the importance of its prewar counterpart because, with the exception of Finland, France, and Austria, individual member-associations were weak. For example, the Finnish Worker Sport Association (TUL), while cooperating with the national sports association (the Finnish Gymnastics and Sports Federation [SVUL]), retains its own identity; has a membership of 450,000 (one half the SVUL membership); and promotes mass gymnastics and artistic displays, family exercise programs, cultural events, and, particularly, women's sporting activities. Its worker sport festivals held in Helsinki's Olympic Stadium attract as many as 50,000 spectators. The French Worker Sport and Gymnastics Federation (FSGT) has over 100,000 members, coordinates the activities of worker sport clubs throughout the country, organises conferences, and sponsors worker sport events such as the annual cross-country and cycling contests associated with the communist newspaper *L'Humanité* as well as the annual *Fête de l'Humanité* in which 6,000 people participated in 1981. The Austrian Worker Sports Association (ASKÖ) has similarly retained its identity and plays an important part in Austrian sport. In Israel, as Uriel Simri points out in chapter 10, *Hapoel* (The Worker) is still Israel's largest and strongest sport organisation. It is one of the few exceptions outside the socialist world where a worker sport organisation controls its country's sport.

There are several reasons why the worker sport movement is relatively weak today and why it never captured the majority of the working class within its membership. Worker sport almost always duplicated bourgeois sports, clubs, federations, and Olympics. This was not significant as long as the older organisations remained socially exclusive preserves of the bourgeoisie. But once the workers succeeded in democratising sport and once industrial firms, the church, and governments came to realise the potential of sport for social control, the duplication became problematic. Worker sport societies rarely had the prestige, facilities, or funds to compete with bourgeois teams, and they were often denied access to public funds and amenities. Similarly, media coverage of worker sport was usually confined to the socialist press and was ignored by the bourgeois media. Insofar as only a minority of workers read the socialist press, it is not surprising that only a minority of workers joined the worker sport movement or were prepared to turn their backs on the glamorous bourgeois clubs for the low-status worker sport organisations. It was common for bourgeois clubs to recruit the best worker athletes—just as they have recruited the best athletes from Africa, Asia, and Latin America—by offering athletes attractive financial inducements.

A number of problems hampered efforts to enhance the attractiveness of worker sport; these problems included the explicitly political nature of worker sport, the labour leaders' uncertain—and at times insensitive—attitude toward organised sport and competition, and the tactical differences over the role of sport in society—not to mention the socialist versus communist wrangling. Apparently, many worker sport leaders failed to understand that a sport organisation might be *more politically effective* by being *less explicitly political*.

The theoretical argument over the role of sport in society presented an obstacle to the development of worker sport. At one extreme were the proletarian culture advocates (and their supporters in the Soviet Union and parts of Scandinavia) who saw bourgeois sport as a reflection of a degenerate bourgeois culture that had to be thrown out because it was permeated by chauvinism, exploitation, and militarism; what was needed, they asserted, was a new proletarian system of physical culture based on personal fulfilment, mutual respect, and solidarity (see chapters 3, 4, and 8). At the other extreme were those like many North American and British socialists (see chapters 6 and 9) who regarded sport as one's personal affair, on the periphery of superstructural phenomena and therefore relatively apolitical—not something on which the labour movement should waste its scarce resources. Typically, both extremes resulted in the feeblest of all the worker sport movements in the industrial world.

Where the worker sport movement did flourish, it suffered from internal problems. In the early years, it emphasised noncompetitive participation, but as the 1920s and 1930s wore on, the bourgeois obsession with records, spectators, and victory infiltrated worker sport and caused the sport activities to adopt the elements of more organised competitions. It is not uncommon today for socialist and communist newspapers to devote the bulk of their sports coverage to horse racing and winning forecasts.

Recent developments have, however, opened up a number of possibilities for certain sports. There are far more opportunities for organised sports participation today than before World War II; the best athletes now are more highly skilled and have a better chance to nurture their talent to the fullest for the benefit of the individual and the community. Gifted working-class, nonwhite, and women athletes can, with dedication, reach the top of their sport. (Compare the social, ethnic, and gender composition of the British Olympic team at recent Olympic Games, for example, to the 1924 team portrayed in the film *Chariots of Fire* or to those of the more recent postwar years of Bannister, Brasher, and Chataway.)

We now have sports spectacles of unprecedented scale, grandeur, and public exposure from which working people gain considerable enjoyment. At the same time, these spectacles have subjected us to society's dominant sport values; they present a sport that the workers themselves cannot control.

The worker sport movement needed to expand if it was to fulfil its cultural and political mission, but this growth presented complex problems. Organised sport, like the working class itself, is a product of modern industrial society, and, in a bourgeois world, a large proportion of working men and women are steeped in society's dominant values. Nonetheless, the worker sport movement did try to provide an alternative experience based on the workers' culture and did inspire visions of a new socialist culture. To this end, it organised the best sporting programs it could for all athletes, whether a Sunday bike ride or a Worker Olympic Festival founded on genuinely socialist values. Its story is as much a part of the history of sport and of the labour movement as Coubertin's Olympics or trade unionism. Our book seeks to add an important chapter to both.

Chapter 1

The German Way of Worker Sport

Arnd Krüger

GERMANY

In 1933, this republic in the centre of Europe had 66.03 million inhabitants distributed over 470,545 km².

During the reorganisation of Europe at the Congress of Vienna, the numerous individual German states were unified within the *Deutscher Bund,* yet the movement for national unity that arose as a result of the war of liberation against Napoleonic France harboured small sympathies for the loose confederation of states whose few common institutions left it no room for political involvement. This disenchantment found its outlet in the revolutionary events of 1848 that resulted in democratic elections and in the formation of a German National Assembly. However, the Assembly's internal quarrels returned the initiative to the dynastic reaction. The constitution of the *Reich* formulated by the Assembly was rejected by all the important German states, and the Assembly itself was replaced by the old *Bundestag* consisting of envoys from the ruling houses. Moreover, its members became victims of vicious persecution.

After the failure of unification through the bourgeoisie, in 1871 the feudal power elite of Prussia founded the German national state and placed Bismarck at its head. The basis for this step was laid by the military solution of the Prussian-Austrian dualism in the war of 1866 and by the rekindled interest in unification resulting from the consciously sought confrontation with France. While the greater part of Europe had shown sympathy for the process of German unification, things looked different after 1890. Bismarck's successors managed to lead the *Reich* into international isolation and, ultimately, a world war with their claim to Germany's status as a world power.

The economic development of Germany was more successful. In 1834, the establishment of a customs union (*Zollverein*) produced economic unity for the greater part of the later *Reich's* territory, thus creating the basis for rapid industrialisation that developed even more quickly following the foundation of the *Reich.* These developments made Germany the most important economic power in the world after the United States.

The political structures were not seized by a similar dynamism. The government that was responsible only to the emperor, as well as the growing number of independently active military authorities, managed to act without parliamentary backing. In the face of such a demonstration of mistrust, it came as no surprise that workers' organisations were viewed with hostility. The suppressive measures introduced against the Socialist Party (SPD) in 1878 did, it is true, have to be rescinded, but this did nothing to alter the SPD's role as the enemy of the state until 1914.

The SPD's conversion to the most stable pillar of the German *Reich* took place immediately after the military's defeat and the old regime's collapse. Thus, the party's acknowledgement of parliamentary democracy allowed it to reject the soviet socialism that the communists demanded. Unfortunately, the cooperation with parts of the old elite that arose out of this acknowledgement provoked not only the split of the German workers' movement but also prevented the decisive transformation of the existing social and political conditions. Consequently, the SPD, already discredited for supporting the conditions of the Treaty of Versailles, was in a weakened position when, after the outbreak of the Great Depression, the National Socialists—with the support of groups whose survival had been guaranteed in 1919 by the SPD—sounded the charge on the parliamentary system.

Immediately after Hitler took over the government in January 1933, a policy of terror was installed that characterised Germany's national and international relations. All workers' organisations were disbanded, and their leaders were arrested. At the same time, the persecution and slaughter of the Jewish population began. With regard to foreign policy, this quick violation of the peace treaty was followed by the systematic destabilisation of the eastern neighbour states and, ultimately, aggression against almost all nations refusing to submit to Nazi rule. The terror ended with unconditional surrender in 1945 and resulted in a 45-year loss of national unity caused by the creation of two German states.

The roots of the *Turner* democratic movement reach back to the 1848 Revolution in which the *Turner* and the student organisations were particularly active. *Turnen* meant "gymnastics with apparatus," but it was also a movement that used these exercises to develop a powerful guerrilla potential (Krüger, 1975). The *Turner* meetings (*Turnfeste*) of 1842 in Mainz, 1843 in Hanau, 1844 in Gemünd, 1845 in Reutlingen, 1846 in Heilbronn, and 1847 in Heidelberg all took place in the German southwest, the home of the German democratic and radical movements. In 1847, the *Turners* (more than a thousand from over 60 different clubs) declared at their Frankfurt meeting that they would "form a union for liberty, equality and combating tyranny" (Eichel, 1965, p.121). When the first national *Turner* association was finally formed in Hanau in April of 1848, many of the founding members already bore arms ready to fight in the revolution. Soon after, the *Turners* split over the aims of the revolution. While the liberal section (including *Turnvater* Jahn) favoured a constitutional monarchy, the radicals stood for democracy. While the liberals maintained their *Deutscher Turnerbund* in Leipzig, the *Democratic Turnerbund* provided the republican armies with able soldiers throughout the German southwest.

The worker sport movement in Germany regards this *Democratic Turnerbund* as its forerunner, although it is doubtful whether any sizeable number of workers actually took part in it. Most revolutionaries left Germany after the failure of the revolution. Many went to the United States, where the forty-niners became active in spreading the notions of political liberty and physical fitness (Barney, 1984; Neumann, 1968; Ueberhorst, 1978).

At the height of the revolution there were 300 *Turner* clubs actively organising their exercises and political activities within their communities. When reduced to only gymnastics after the revolution, the number gradually diminished until about a hundred were left 10 years later. With the rising national enthusiasm after 1859, the *Turners* formed a new and rapidly growing association—the *Deutsche Turnerschaft* (DT)—that, in 1864, had as many as 1,934 clubs with 168,000 members. Insofar as the clubs were open to all, they also included leaders of the social-democratic *Allgemeine Deutsche Arbeiterverein*.

When the relatively late industrial upsurge took place in Germany, club membership also changed, and the readiness of the old members to absorb new, often working-class members decreased. Whenever there were two clubs in the same town, they normally split along the lines of what was socially acceptable to the one or the other. Associated with this was the formation of trade-specific member subdivisions, such as the student *Turnvereine*, the civil servant *Turnvereine*, a subdivision for merchants, merchant apprentices, and the like.

To counteract the influence of the social-democratic organisations, the imperial German government passed the so-called socialist laws (*Sozialistengesetze*) that prohibited many of the social organisations' activities between 1878 and 1890. During this time of illegality, these organisations often used the "Red" *Turner* clubs and the *Turner* sections of the worker educational clubs (*Arbeiter Bildungsvereine*) to maintain contacts. The apparatus became officially private property so that, if the police closed down the activity, it would not be confiscated.

Once they did receive the green light to organise after the socialist laws were revoked, it did not take long before the social-democratic *Turners* that had belonged to the clubs of the national *Deutsche Turnerschaft* and the *Turners* in the *Bildungsvereine* tried to set up their own clubs in 1891 and their own national organisation. A number of meetings in and around Berlin took place between May 1892 and late 1893 to bring together all members in this new social-democratic organisation. They even tried to ensure that all members of the new *Turner* organisation belonged to both a political party and a trade union, but this was voted down in late 1892 (Buck, 1927; Schuster, 1962; Wildung, 1911, 1929).

What were the primary aims in setting up a worker *Turner* association? There were no new intentions or forms of interior organisation, no new sports forms and

"Our *Turner* matter has become big from the moment onward when we dared to say that we are unpolitical, that we have nothing to do with political parties, but that we are in the service of the fatherland. *Turnen* evolved at a time when our fatherland was down and humiliated, and it has been involved in all the political activities of this century—but it has really started to attract a big membership, when it took up the position of *Turner* matters being completely separate from party politics. Therefore, we have been ready to fight for our fatherland like 1870 and we will—with the help of God—fight to end the shame that half of our parliament is filled with people who are not standing for the whole of our beloved fatherland—be they red or black. We *Turners* know only one thought: Great is our beloved fatherland, and those who do not love it should be thrown out!"

Dr. Goetz, Secretary General of the *Deutsche Turnerschaft,* in his official address at the *Turnfest* in Frankfurt am Main (1880). Quoted in Edmund Neuendorff, *Geschichte der Neuren Deutschen Leibesübungen* (Dresden: Limpert, vol. 4, p. 211).

Parade of worker sportsmen on the market of Leipzig.

Women's section of the worker club *ATSV Schwarzbach* performing a gymnastic display.

Gymnastic exercises of the worker club *ATSV Bischofshoven.*

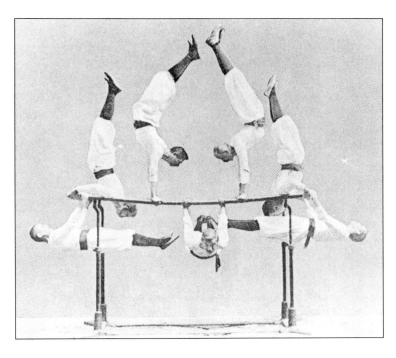

Postcard from 12 September 1916.

Illustrated report of the *ATZ* about the building up of provisional sports places by excluded worker athletes.

Caricature of the *Eulenspiegel* against Severing's plan to unite worker sport with bourgeois sport under "one hat."

Decree Concerning Political Clubs

Us Ludwig III, Arch-Duke of Hesse by the Grace of God etc. etc.

Due to the extraordinary situation, according to Art. 73 of the Constitution, to counterbalance the poisoning influences to our Archdukedom which have been caused by *political clubs*, to assure public law and order, we decree the following:

§ 1. All private clubs and private organizations which exist in our Archdukedom and the aim of which is to discuss public affairs and influence them—i.e., political clubs and organizations— are dissolved and the new foundation of such clubs and organizations is prohibited.

§ 2. Those persons who counteract this decree and continue a private political club or organization, or form such a club or organization, will be punished according to § 182 of the law:
  1. As leader or board member with imprisonment of ten days to one month,
  2. As other member with imprisonment of three to 15 days. The latter punishment is also applicable to those who become a member or seek membership.

A court of law can also rule the confiscation of papers, books etc. of such clubs or organizations.

§ 3. All subjects of our Archdukedom are prohibited to join such clubs existing or such being founded (§ 1) outside our Archdukedom.

Who is counteracting this decree will be punished according to § 183 of the law with imprisonment of one to 15 days, who is encouraging others to join such clubs or organizations with imprisonment of ten days through one month.

§ 4. As soon as a nonpolitical club also starts to pursue political ends or to include in its discussions, or as soon as a club has been determined by the appropriate authorities to be *political*, this decree is also applicable.

§ 5. This decree will be valid for six months from the day it is publicly proclaimed by being published in the Official Journal and Register (*Regierungsblatt*).

Arch-Duke of Hesse: Official Journal and Register (*Regierungsblatt*), no. 47, 3 Oct. 1850.

methods (Eichberg, 1975). Even the ideological basis was fairly fragile. Often local, immediate social conflicts seemed more important than theoretical considerations or knowledge of socioeconomic conditions.

At the official foundation, 3,500 members from 51 clubs joined the new association. Initially, one of the main concerns throughout imperial Germany was relative poverty, and this made it far more attractive to remain in a national DT club to do gymnastics (if the member wanted gymnastics). In 1897, only a dozen of the 285 worker *Turner* clubs were able to supply proper gymnasiums for their members (*Arbeiter-Turn-Zeitung*, 1898). The worker *Turner* movement originally used its meagre financial means to produce a journal, the *Arbeiter-Turn-Zeitung* (*ATZ*), that began in 1893 with a circulation of 2,000 and continued uninterrupted until 1933.

From this modest beginning, the worker *Turner* movement (*Arbeiter Turner-Bund*) grew swiftly. In 1895, it had more than 10,000 members; in 1902 more than 50,000; in 1906 over 100,000; and in 1910 in excess of 150,000. By the start of World War I, the *Turner* move-

ment had almost 200,000 members, while the bourgeois DT had 1.1 million. It should be noted that the *ATZ* continually increased its readership and reached a paid circulation of 111,000 in 1911, demonstrating that propaganda and the right "feel" for social democracy were more important than gymnastics itself (Schuster, 1962, p. 30).

Ideological Stances

Considerable debate exists in the literature as to whether these early representatives of the worker *Turner* movement were true revolutionaries in the Marxist sense. While Eichel (1965), J. Fischer and Meiners (1973), Meyer (1976), Schuster (1962), and Timmermann (1973) are convinced that they were revolutionaries and that the modest unrevolutionary tone in their journals was a tactical measure to maintain the organisation, Teichler (1980, 1987) and Ueberhorst (1973) maintain that, as with the foundation of the Social Democratic Party (SPD), it was the practical concern of direct political conflict that

"Only then do worker sports clubs have a right to exist if they move within the fight for the liberation of the working class. . . . When we consider the party and the trade union in this class war as the main block of the army, which is marching forward like the infantry and artillery, then we worker cyclists are the red hussars, the cavalry of the class war. We can reach territory which is inaccessible for the normal forces, and work for the main forces by instilling class consciousness in our members, and we can directly use our bicycles for the class struggle, by distributing pamphlets on the countryside, where ignorance still subdues the peasants. We can support the agitation for the parliamentary elections, can organize a courier service like in the recent demonstrations, to signal rapidly when the enemy is approaching. . . ."

Leader, *ATZ*, vol. 16 (15 Aug. 1910), no. 337.

Turner Movement Membership

Year	Members
1893-4	9,096
1894-5	10,367
1895-6	13,964
1897	18,523
1898	27,544
1899	32,454
1900	37,371
1901	41,779
1902	50,964
1903	61,665
1904	70,681
1905	80,147
1906	105,056
1907	120,076
1908	123,802
1909	134,104
1910	153,382
1911	169,308
1912	183,383
1913	186,958
1915	96,743

gave the organisation its basis. This was a time when, after the revocation of the socialist laws, there were still many state laws prohibiting the right of association. For example, the young worker cycling association, Solidarity, was banned and dissolved under Saxon law since it had been founded in Leipzig as a national organisation in 1893. It contained in its statutes a clause calling on its members to help agitate for the SPD. Subsequently, it reconstituted itself in Berlin with different statutes under Prussian law in 1894. This association was, however, so loose and clandestine that it did not succeed in attracting many members; at its third national congress in Fürth, Bavaria, in 1895, only four delegates represented five cities. As a result, a new organisation was called for, using the national SPD press, and this led to a fourth congress at Offenbach during the Whitsun of 1896, at which the organisation was refounded, this time under the more liberal Hesse laws that brought it within the law; in 1908 it already had a membership of 100,000 (Beduhn, 1978, 1982; K. Fischer, 1908; Frahnert, 1926).

Why did it grow so fast? In contrast to the *Turners*, it did not have the same difficulties with sports amenities. It had its own system of cycle dealers that provided the inexpensive *Frischauf* cycle through 28 full-time agents of Solidarity and 60 licensed, part-time agents by 1914. The changing attitudes towards the sport of cycling may also have played a part. While cycling still retained its upper-class appeal, gradually the well-to-do switched to motorcycles and motor cars, and the bicycle became an important means of transport and leisure for the working class (Langenfeld, 1985). It helped workers travel to work and, for the activist, helped get agitation leaflets more quickly into the street or post-boxes. Also, in contrast to the *Turners*, there was no single bourgeois association to stand against Solidarity; there were several (as many as 18) claiming to be national, though most were only regional.

Within the SPD not everyone was in favour of separate sport organisations. Up to World War I, almost every sport could be performed in a separate worker sport organisation. As Timm, an SPD member of the Bavarian state legislature, explained:

The course of the workers will be hampered more than promoted by these organisations. The strength of the comrades will be absorbed by these activities. Members of the cycling association pay 10 pfennigs a month for membership fees; there will be an annual congress, and then all those sporting exercises. Where will they get their free time for trade union and party work? How can they do their duty in the struggle for the Party? We cannot oppose too strongly the playing of club games, for it is a severe hindrance to political and trade union organisation. (Fischer, 1908, p. 10)

It took until 1908 for the SPD to accept the vanguard organisations as valuable and to declare at its annual congress that no SPD member should be allowed to be a member of a bourgeois DT club (*ATZ*, Nov. 1922, p. 2). Club culture served to strengthen the ideological hegemony and could, therefore, be used for the benefit of the bourgeoisie or the socialist movement (Denecke, 1990; Kröll, 1980).

The bourgeois *Turner* and sport clubs were convinced that they were doing a particularly patriotic job. The Latin *pro patria est dum ludere videmur* (it is for the fatherland when we seem to be playing) became their slogan prior to World War I and remained such throughout the Weimar Republic (Krüger, 1981). In 1911, the DT formally joined the *Jungdeutschland* organisation that propagated physical education in preparation for war.

Around the turn of the century, other sports began to grow in popularity (Hamer, 1989). Because most of them were arriving from England, the English rules were imported as well. Inasmuch as it was the British who often personally introduced their sports through their roles as commercial agents, engineers, merchants, students, sport journalists, and coaches, the sports tended to surface in the main cities (such as Hamburg and Berlin) that had contacts with the British (Gillmeister, 1993; Hopf, 1979).

The sports movement also brought different aims into the arena of physical exercise. While the *Turners* stood for the well-prepared, well-rounded athlete, the sports movement tended to favour record-setting and goal-breaking performances (Krüger, 1989). The *Turner* rules made it possible for many to be successful and to win; in track and field, multievents like the triathlon, pentathlon, and decathlon were popular. In 1911, the rules set the standard of 17 seconds for the 100 metres to gain 1 point, 12 seconds for a 12-point maximum; and 5 metres for 1 point in the shotput, 9.8 metres for the 12-point maximum. You gained no extra points if you ran faster or put farther (*Mittheilungs-Blatt*, 1911). So if mass participation, health, overall enjoyment, and military preparedness (or readiness for class struggle and revolution, for that matter) were the major aims, then the demonstration of personal superiority by a few could be quite frustrating to the many. In this, the *Turners*—whether bourgeois or worker—certainly agreed until 1912 (Krüger, 1985a). When the Olympic Games of 1916 were given to Berlin, the nationalist fervour was so strong that the *Turners* competed for Olympic medals. In the final vote in national parliament to provide money for the preparation of the games and Olympic athletes particularly, the social-democrats voted against; their worker

sportsmen were still suppressed, and they resented specialisation (Krüger, 1995).

Two young and growing sports—football and weightlifting—did not suffer the effects of this schism. Football began to grow from the 1870s as a school or college sport. As in the south of England, it had a similar upper-class appeal. In some areas, rugby rules were observed; in most they used Association Football rules. It was not long before soccer became the most popular game in town and country, losing its social exclusiveness; it rapidly attracted devotees from all classes. Although some attempts were made to bring worker soccer into the worker camp, on the whole, the worker clubs preferred the relatively easy access to big-time competition, gate receipts, and the notion of a relatively open society rather than class struggle (Erbach, 1965; Gehrmann, 1988; Ueberhorst & Hauk, 1989).

"The purpose of *Turnen* is the improvement of health of the inner and outer organism. It is improving the physical resistance of the individual in his struggle for survival and is suitable to balance the harmful influences of the modern one-sided modes of production.

Turnen is to be regarded as a means of educating a strong, healthy generation, it is losing its value, though, as soon as it is performed like a sport in a specialised way. Then it is sucking the strength of the individual as he is not capable—because of his material situation—to balance the use of strength neither by better food and living conditions nor sufficient rest. It is the duty of each *Turner* to keep a healthy balance and to safeguard his highest good: his health.

Individual and club competitions for points and prices, in any *Turner* event, are similar to competitions in the business world. They require giving up ideals and such *Turner* competitions require time and money—both are needed, however, by our members for more important aims. The rivalry in competitions for the honor and for prices is impeding the unity and the cooperation within and among clubs. Quarrels and dissensions are the fruits of *Turner* competitions for prices.

The 5th federal meeting of the worker *Turners* declares, therefore, that any competition for prices is illegal within the ranks of the worker *Turners* (ATB)."

5th Declaration of the German Worker Sport Congress, May 26-28, 1910, Harburg (published in *ATZ*, vol. 7, [1910], p. 116).

Worker sport postcard.

Members of the Koch school performing gymnastic exercises, 1930.

"The Worker Sportsman Is Fighting for Freedom, Unity, and Fraternity."

In weightlifting, however, workers had the competitive edge over bourgeois weightlifters by the very rules of the game. The *Arbeiter Athletenbund* had split off from the DT in 1906 to represent weightlifters and wrestlers; at first, they were the exclusive representatives of these two sports. The few nonworkers who wished to specialise in weightlifting and wrestling had to join a worker organisation (Grote, 1996).

When examining worker sport prior to World War I, we must bear in mind that working conditions put both gymnastics and other sports beyond the capabilities, interest, and concern of most workers. Those who did engage in forms of physical recreation were generally better off than the ordinary worker. They could afford a bicycle, had already been a member of a bourgeois club, and hankered after some form of club affiliation. It is very hard to distinguish between the skilled worker and petty bourgeois. With the rapid shift in industrial capacity, being a worker or being a petty bourgeois was, to some extent, a matter of the mind rather than of the relationship to the means of production.

If we study German club journals of the prewar era, we find that all *Turner* clubs, whether worker or not, covered the same themes. Nonetheless, they display not only different political interpretations of events—however covertly this had to appear in the worker press for fear of police harassment—but also a considerably different emphasis on money. While bourgeois *Turner* clubs received public subsidies after 1882, subsidies on a large scale after 1911, and support from a variety of funds after 1913, worker clubs were not subsidised and had to struggle to make ends meet. This resulted in considerable publicity being given to worker club funds; many pages of their journals were full of cash figures showing the flow of money. They displayed a certain amount of pride in making a profit on some celebration, on being able to purchase property jointly, and on hiring people. However, they also made their distrust evident, because the club was managing worker funds to a far greater extent than any individual worker could possess.

The most open organisation in this area was the ramblers association *Die Naturfreunde* (Friends of Nature), founded in Vienna in 1895 as a countermeasure to the German-Austrian *Alpenverein*. The *Alpenverein*—a rambling, climbing, and tourist organisation—had begun to become openly anti-Semitic and intolerant of social-democrat membership. It had opened lodges in the Alps to attract members and wealthy tourists. Many other regional rambling associations existed to open up the mountainous German midlands to the tourist (Denecke, 1990). Because workers found these lodges too expensive, the equipment and amenities beyond their scope, and because the wealthier tourists preferred servants around them as lackeys and not as fellow tourists, *Die Naturfreunde* rap-

"Primarily, we want to free the worker from the places of alcohol consumption, from dice and cards. We want to lead them from the narrowness of their living quarters, from the smog of the factories and pubs to the beautiful nature, towards beauty and pleasure. We will enable them to liberate their body and spirit from the dull everyday life. We want to lead them to fresh air, light, and the sun."

Georg Schmiedl (founder of the *Friends of Nature/Die Naturfreunde*) (vol. 1, no. 1 of their journal *Der Naturfreund*).

idly became popular among workers. Nonetheless, it was not in the mainstream of any socialist party; it remained relatively open, including nudists (Krüger, 1991), the *Wandervogel,* and the youth associations (which later became a base for German fascism). Their Alpine Rescue Service, however, closely cooperated with the bourgeois *Alpenverein.*

The *Wandervogel* was able to draw on the skilled-worker tradition of working for years away from home. This preindustrial tradition, when the good journeymen had still been able to become masters and teach new apprentices, was still alive within this movement. The Friends of Nature were also members of the Central Committee for Worker Sport and Physical Fitness (*Arbeitersport und Körperpflege*), the umbrella organisation of the worker sport organisation. Because it opposed competitive sport of any kind, it reinforced the position of those who favoured general fitness and opposed record-mania (Zimmer, 1984).

Sport in Wartime

With the outbreak of the world war, the results of ideological differences became obvious. Although the SPD had always favoured international cooperation and worker fraternity, it was quite unprepared for any countermeasures. It voted in favour of war credits and joined the *Burgfrieden*, the political cease-fire for the time of the war. The worker *Turner* and gymnastics association did the same (Teichler & Hauk, 1987).

There has been some discussion as to whether they did so to retain their property and prevent it being sequestered; it could well have been confiscated if they had openly opposed the war effort. But one has to ask whether the ownership of property helps to change attitudes? Did property change its role from a means to pursue sport to an end in itself?

Worker sport postcard.

Cycling postcard.

Worker sportsmen from Berlin at the departure to the national meeting of the Red Workers Sportsmen at Erfurt in 1930.

The part played by the leadership of the worker sport movement has not been thoroughly analysed. Just as the bourgeois sport clubs and the petty-bourgeois *Turner* clubs generally opted for "notables" as presidents and board members—nobility for a bourgeois club, a civil servant or other bourgeois for the *Turners*—so the worker sport organisations had men in leadership roles who were mostly connected with the SPD or the trade unions. There was generally more fluctuation in leadership than in the bourgeois clubs and more power for club employees because they were the only people with sufficient time to devote to the organisation. The contracts for printers of the party journal often served as models for the contracts of club employees. Another question to pose is whether the growing club and party bureaucracy was by its very nature in the same position as the petty bourgeoisie: Did they fear losing a privileged position and, therefore, identify with petty bourgeois role models? Rather than defending the positions of their class, did they not merely safeguard their own position and the organisation that had given them the chance of a better livelihood than their "ordinary" members had?

On 1 August 1914, 1 day after the imperial call to arms, Solidarity had its 11th Annual Congress in Cologne. As many as 25,000 cyclists from all over Germany had come on previous occasions. Would this not now have been the perfect setting for an antiwar demonstration? The leadership was there, 20 percent of the rank and file could be mobilised, and the actions toward organisational unity had already been planned. However, the 90 delegates concurred with the executive vote to call off all demonstrations. The only topic remaining on the agenda was, What can be done in the circumstances and what are the tasks of the officers? The only points debated dealt with administration, what had to be done if a person was to be called up. The distinction between patriotic and nonpatriotic organisations no longer had any meaning, for all were *pro patria*, all had the same significance.

In a letter from 6 September 1914, the *ATZ* stated:

We have emphasised that we do not have to worry about former bans on the youth *Turner*, although formally the bans have not been revoked. The basis of the ban no longer exists since we are now no longer considered *vaterlandslos* [unpatriotic]. In our agitation we shall have to avoid everything that would harm the DT; no strength should be lost in the domestic struggle. . . . Today the *Turner* brothers of both organisations are jointly fighting the foreign foe. We must not debilitate this struggle by senseless rivalry. . . . The aim is obvious, the call to arms clear!

In spite of this willingness to join the militaristic aims of the old enemies, the imperial government did not initially revoke any of the former bans. Although the workers were required to open their meetings to preconscription military drills—and did so with considerable enthusiasm and pride—the rules remained the same. After several more exchanges of letters, on 24 March 1917 the imperial government officially declared, "your organisation no longer seems to be geared to political matters, rather towards serious education of your members in physical, moral and mental matters" (Gellert & Frey, 1927, p. 101). It was finally accepted as "patriotic" (Skorning, 1952, p. 261).

Worker Sport After the War

By 1912, the various worker sport organisations had combined within the Central Committee for Worker Sport and Physical Fitness. This centralisation into a single agency helped to strengthen SPD influence and the bureaucracy. After the war, this united organisation was very influential; it had few difficulties accepting the changing emphasis that the membership put on various sports activities. This included a sizeable number of nudists who propagated the liberation of the body within a federation of the people's hygiene movement. The parallel bourgeois organisation joined the then Nazi sports movement in late 1933 (Krüger, 1991).

In the bourgeois organisations, the rivalry between *Turnen* and sports became so intense that in December 1922 the *Turners* left the *Deutscher Reichsausschuss* (DRA), their umbrella organisation and banned its members from competing with members of the bourgeois sport organisations in activities like athletics that were practised as a *Turner* skill as well as a sport (Krüger, 1989; Neuendorff, 1936).

The worker sport organisation had no such problems. The enhanced popularity of sports led to a shift in emphasis but not a split in the organisational structure. As the worker *Turner* opened their organisation to sports and began to call themselves the *Arbeiter Turn- und Sportbund* (Worker Gymnastics and Sports Association [ATSB]), they remained the strongest and most influential organisation. The Central Committee, led by the ATSB, tried to bring sports into line. Wildung, who was General Secretary of the Central Committee and, therefore, the counterpart of Carl Diem in bourgeois sport, made sure that the SPD maintained its strong influence within the organisation and did not lose ground to the communists.

Wildung followed Diem in many organisational respects: A separate worker sports school was founded in Leipzig in 1920 (*Bundesschule*), and a journal was inaugurated (*Sportpolitische Rundschau*) to provide information, the means for political agitation, and a voice for

"Every Sportsman Is Marching and Demonstrating Against the Withdrawal of Sports Places."

Jumping cloth demonstration.

Sportsmen of the *ATV Gröpelingen* circa 1910.

theoretical considerations concerning sport. The national effort was strengthened by participation in the Worker Olympics; leading positions in the respective international organisations were sought.

Bourgeois organisations were not permitted to take part in international sports competitions for several years after the war; they could participate in the Olympic Games only as late as 1928, while the international worker sport organisation in Lucerne was being reconstituted with German members as early as 1920. The newly founded Red Sport International (RSI) even had a German communist as General Secretary (Reussner). This created the paradoxical situation in which worker sport in Germany was more or less united along social-democratic lines, whereas the international communist organisation had a German, who was a member of a predominantly social-democratic organisation, as their General Secretary (Dierker, 1990).

The fight between the SPD and the communists for the domination of German worker sports has been dealt with extensively (Dierker, 1990; Nitsch, 1985a, 1985b; Teichler & Hauk, 1987). Once it was realised that sport serves as a vanguard organisation, both sides tried to use it for their own benefit. The large Berlin worker sport club, *Fichte*, was a battleground for the various factions (Dierker & Pfister, 1991). German worker sport stayed a united socialist organisation, however, as late as 1929, while the SPD and the communists split along party lines in 1917.

Theoretical Considerations of Proletarian Sport

The Leipzig School of Physical Education and Sport aimed to ensure that the worker sport movement could begin to produce theoretical literature of its own and not have to rely on material from the bourgeois DT or the DRA clubs because that literature often contained unacceptable ideological overtones. The *ATZ* publishing house also wished to use its own sales outlet to market its material. If we take a look at its publications, however, we find that they are relatively few compared to bourgeois, sport-related literature (even considering that there were about six times as many bourgeois athletes in Germany). On the whole, workers provided less of a reading market for books, but they also developed relatively few forms of their own; they did not need to have a literature of their own.

There is almost a complete lack of anything related to the theory of training and elite sport. Under the impact of the *Turners* and social democrats, sport had to serve a social end and could not be just entertaining. It had to foster a spirit of solidarity and togetherness; this obviated the need for superstars. The performances of German worker sport—as far as they were comparable—were relatively mediocre, except for weightlifting and other strength sports such as wrestling. That is not to say that workers provided poor performances, but if they were concerned with training hard and concentrating on sports, they would generally join the bourgeois organisations that provided better training facilities, more press coverage, and the chance for professional advancement with the help of bourgeois sports-club patrons.

There was a sizeable amount of literature in sociology and the politics of sport. The same authors present during the discussions on sport and politics were also active writers; Kühn (1922) and Wagner (1931) use a Marxist foundation to present interesting social analyses. However, no literature exists on the subject of natural science.

There were considerable differences between the SPD and the communists on attitudes towards competition. The former was against, the latter for competition. Braueck refers to this in an editorial for the SPD,

Proletarians Free Yourself!

Workers and Free physical culturists
  Ever more workers are realizing that free physical culture is part of socialist education.
  Workers! Your body is your only good!
  But you do not even have liberty over your own body, as your work, your living conditions, public moral, education etc. are hindering you to be yourself.
  Liberate yourself from these coercions! Liberate yourself from prejudices even towards your nude body! This will help to improve your self consciousness and you will be able to join the forces of the struggle for the liberation of the proletariat with new strengths and self assurance. Every progress has to be fought for by the working class. The individual is weak, but when we join we are strong. The workers' front must also stand together in the liberation of the body. . . .

Proletarische Lebensreform und Freikörperkultur. Propaganda Leaflet. 1927. Facsimile in Teichler & Hauk, *Illustrierte Geschichte des Arbeitersports,* 1987, p. 180.

Worker sportsmen playing ice hockey.

"Workers, Leave the Bourgeois Sport Clubs."

"Nude in the Air and the Sun"—worker sportswomen in 1924.

Member Organizations in the Social-Democratic-Oriented *Zentralkommission für Arbeitersport und Körperpflege* (1928)

Federation	Members	Clubs and Locals
ATSB	738,048	6,886
Solidarity (Cycling)	320,000	4,951
Friends of Nature	81,734	1,000
Arbeiter Athletenbund	52,000	960
Worker Chess	12,850	460
Worker Shooting	5,579	412
Free Sailing	1,660	25
Worker Angling	6,500	142
Worker Bowling	8,216	835
Worker Samaritans (First Aid)	42,757	1,209
Union for People's Health	15,393	112
Total	1,284,737	16,992

Data from H. Dierker, *Arbeitersport*, 1990, p. 259.

Sportpolitische Rundschau (Jan. 1933), complaining that the communists were even competing against bourgeois athletes. The social-democrat Paul Zobel had already pointed out in 1924, however, that 80 percent of the membership of the bourgeois sport organisations were actually workers, and that the task was not to combat them, but to convince them of their error by retaining contact with them and to show them that their true interests did not lie within the organisations with which they were involved (Ueberhorst, 1974). Furthermore, workers were flocking to the football stadiums to watch soccer and to the boxing arenas to witness professional boxing where other workers were fighting their way to a better social status for themselves rather than for their class. As Wagner (1931) argues, "where bourgeois sport takes charge of the workers it plays a role in the class struggle" (p. 96).

Worker Sport in the Weimar Republic

At the 1919 Twelfth ATSB Congress in Leipzig, the interests of the social-democrats and the communists clashed in every conference of German worker sport. Here it was a question of whether proletarian dictatorship should be included in the statutes. Later, it was the issue of whether one should remain a member of the Socialist Worker Sports International or of the communist RSI. As long as the communists were in a minority, they remained within the German worker sport movement; the movement was not only a vanguard

organisation of the social-democrats but also of the communists.

This lasted until 1928 when the SPD managed to alter the statutes so that the individual exclusion of members for political reasons was accepted. This led to the exclusion of communists on a large scale, and they took their supporters with them; as a result, the communist organisations gained strength in such places as Berlin and Halle. All members who competed with nonmembers were excluded, which resulted in some 60,000 expulsions or desertions over the expulsion of friends. The communists soon established the Interest Group for the Reunification of Worker Sport in Germany that succeeded in bringing together both communists, many nonaligned sports clubs, and even some clubs affiliated with the Socialist Worker Sports International. It also inscribed a proletarian dictatorship paragraph into its statutes to make it evident that it stood for revolution, not evolution. Because this was the time of depression, with an increase in communist electoral votes, it is not surprising that the communists had some success with their new organisation.

The shift to the right of the SPD bureaucracy of the ATSB became even more obvious in 1930 when the officers proposed that joint meetings with the DT and the right-wing veterans association, *Stahlhelm,* were to be permitted on Constitution Day. Only 4 years later, *Stahlhelm* joined the paramilitary Nazi storm-troopers (SA) and was accepted as a para-Nazi organisation. The ATSB leadership slapped a ban on any attempt to persuade workers in these organisations to abandon them and join groups of their own class. Although 244 of the

"Worker sport is in the service of the improvement of the working class. It wants to awaken the self-consciousness of the proletarians and improve on its biological components by increasing the pleasure of the body and the physical health and well being. Sport is an instrument of *class hygiene*, the strengthening of its health and resistance. It is a means of the *upbreeding of the class* (Fritz Wildung). It does not need many words to point out the relationship between the health of the proletarian class and the class struggle. Tired, weak, and sick men are poor fighters in the class struggle because of their physical condition. Strong and healthy people have the power to resist unworthy conditions. The working class needs a healthy generation for its struggle. It has to do everything to create such a healthy generation—as far as the current capitalist society with its hindering conditions gives such a chance at all. Worker sports is the movement which assures the provision of health to the proletarian youth and strengthens the chances of the proletarian class to be physically prepared for the class war."

H. Wagner, *Sport und Arbeitersport,* 1931, p. 162f.

253 delegates at the 1930 Congress were SPD members (only one communist), the proposal found only a 152:55 majority, with many abstentions (Skorning,1952, p. 321). On the other hand, the communists, in their "class against class" ideology, identified the social-democrats as "social-fascists" and maintained that they had to win the struggle against the enemy *within* the working class first, before combating the bourgeoisie in actual class struggle.

Given this anticommunist and procapitalist stand, it is hardly surprising that the ATSB rejected cooperation with communists even after the Nazis had taken over on 30 January 1933. In March of that year, the leadership warned its rank and file not of Nazi, but of any joint sports event with communists. It tried to placate the Nazis by pointing out that it was just as anticommunist as they were and that it was willing to subordinate itself to a strong national leadership in sport. While in imperial Germany the social-democratic sports organisation had been a political organisation with an interest in sport, now it was confining itself to sport alone and calling on members to refrain from political agitation, to avoid contact with the opposition, to maintain the organisation, and to keep all its property.

Highlights of Worker Sport in Weimar Germany

Depending on one's definition of the purpose of the worker sport movement, different events may be identified as highlights of the 1919-1933 period. If we take the aims of elite sport as a means of identifying and demonstrating the unity of organisation, the First National German Worker Festival in Leipzig in 1922 drew 16,000 participants in some of the major mass-gymnastic events. It had, for example, Belgian participation (*Erstes Deutsches Arbeiter-Turn- und Sportfest,* 1922), showing international workers' solidarity at a time when bourgeois sports still avoided German participation. The First International Worker Olympics in Frankfurt in 1925 is of particular importance (Gersbach, 1927; Internationaler Arbeiter-Verband, 1925; Nitsch, 1984). If we take the educational impact, the opening of the worker sports school at Leipzig in 1926 stands out. If we take international worker solidarity, the German-Soviet Sports Agreement of 1926 is of signal importance because it showed that even the SPD-controlled bureaucracy could not go against the wishes of massive popular support (Fischer, 1979).

The first Worker Olympics took place in the newly built Frankfurt stadium in front of 150,000 spectators. At the opening ceremony, a choir of 1,200 people sang, giving the sports festival a cultural content. In a festive drama presentation, 60,000 "actors" took part in the "Worker Struggle for the Earth" (Auerbach, 1925; Fischer, 1976). The winning German women's sprint relay actually beat the world record (the achievement was unratified because it was not sanctioned by the IAAF). All participants were required to take part in the cultural festivals, and all were permitted to compete in individual events to stress the performance of the general athlete rather than the specialist. This compromise position was adopted because the athletes of most countries wanted elite performances, while the athletes of some others preferred versatile participation. Athletes from 10 countries participated. All this took place 3 years before the German reappearance in the bourgeois Olympics because the aggressor of World War I had been excluded until 1928. The Finnish TUL athletes were the "stars" at Frankfurt.

The 600,000 adult members of the ATSB each paid 1 Mark extra for 2 years to fund the construction of the sports school at Leipzig. The school provided a 2-week training course for club coaches and organisers, following more informal training courses that had taken place earlier in Leipzig.

The agreement with Soviet sport came about after a successful soccer tour by a Moscow team in which it played seven matches, including a 12 to 2 victory over a

Pole long-jump by worker sportswomen.

Sail flying.

Free gymnasts at the sporting place Sonnenallee, 1930-1931.

Cologne city team in front of 70,000 spectators. It was this mass turnout of spectators that convinced the ATSB leaders that the *Russenfimmel* (*Russomania*) had to be tolerated because it provided a mass basis, even if contacts with the RSI and the Soviet Union were not very palatable.

Destruction of German Worker Sport

As soon as the Nazis took power, they banned all communist organisations. This did not, in theory, exclude communist worker sport, but in practice it meant that worker athletes, just like other communists, were hung, deported, or imprisoned. Meanwhile, the ATSB tried to keep a low profile in order to obviate its own dissolution (Bernett, 1983). With the various measures following the 23 March 1933 *Ermächtigungsgesetz* (Enabling Act), the Nazi regime gained full dictatorial power and used this in sport for a complete take-over of a state-controlled model based on Italian fascism (Krüger, 1985b). Within this type of sport, there was no room for any organisation outside the one coordinated by the *Reichssportführer*.

Considerable discussion took place in March and April of 1933 about whom Hitler would appoint leader of the newly combined sport organization. He chose Hans von Taschammer und Osten, who had made a name for himself as leader of an SA lynch gang that had murdered most worker athletes in one attack (Krüger, 1985b). The Nazis expected violent resistance to their early measures, especially from worker sport, because they assumed that worker paramilitary training would have provided sufficient drills to have made them good guerrilla fighters— as the old *Turners* had been during the Napoleonic Wars (Bach, 1981; Bernett, 1981; Ueberhorst, 1986). However, practically no resistance was forthcoming.

The ATSB and other worker sport organisations were dissolved or voluntarily disbanded by 27 June 1933, when the new Nazi sport organisation took office; all others (save religious for 2 years, and Jewish for another 5 years) were closed down, and their property confiscated—unless it was hidden in time.

The Nazis did not, however, wish to exclude worker athletes *per se* and for all time. They soon opened up their own sports clubs, so that former members of worker sport clubs could join individually. The rules did, nonetheless, stipulate that no club should take more than 10 percent (later increased to 20 percent) of those new members who had belonged to worker sport clubs, that no entire sections should be taken over, and that each erstwhile RSI club member had to produce two sworn statements by long-serving Nazis that he or she was not a Marxist. A large number of workers did, in fact, join the mainstream Nazi sport organisation through this channel.

Local sports history shows that the rules were kept in some areas more stringently than in others. The Worker Educational Association, *Peine*, played regional league soccer until the 1935-1936 season, before its teams were taken over by other clubs (Niemeyer, 1982). There were worker sport clubs that had been independent of any of the two major worker sport organisations; this was often the case when there was a balance between social-democrats and communists in the membership and when the option for either one of the national organisations would have broken up the club. These clubs succeeded in remaining solvent and joined the Nazi sport organisation *in toto*. Some of the Friends of Nature clubs left sport altogether and set themselves up as folk choral groups. The famous *Vereinigte Kletterabteilung* used its more than 300 former Friends of Nature members to cover the wooded slopes between Germany and Czechoslovakia to help comrades emigrate illegally and to bring in propaganda until Czechoslovakia was itself occupied by the Nazis in 1938 (Zimmer, 1984).

In some areas, the *Turner* and sports clubs were very willing to help workers join the official Nazi clubs, in others they were not. Where the latter was the case, the worker athletes found a different outlet: the left wing of the Nazi Party took the Italian model of *Dopo Lavoro*— the factory-run sport and leisure activity organisation— and copied it with their own *Kraft durch Freude* (Might Through Joy). It was initially named After Work, like its Italian model. This organisation had considerable difficulty in recruiting experienced personnel, because with the general sports enthusiasm prior to and following the 1936 Nazi Olympics, the majority of qualified people tended to go in for the "normal" Nazi sport. This provided opportunities for many coaches to join the *Kraft durch Freude* if they were not caught up in the general sports movement. They included conservatives such as Edmund Neuendorff who, despite being a Nazi, had resigned as DT leader over a personality clash with the *Reichssportführer* (Ueberhorst, 1985), nudism proponents like Hans Suren—who was under a cloud because of his alleged homosexual propensities (Krüger, 1991; Spitzer, 1983)—and also worker athletes who were simply needed by the movement.

During the war, all German sport diminished (Krüger, 1993), the situation deteriorated, and many imprisoned worker athletes were murdered. The case of Werner Seelenbinder may be regarded as fairly typical. A participant in the 1928 *Spartakiad* as a worker wrestler from the Worker Wrestling Association, he was integrated into Nazi sport after having produced his two sworn testimonies; he came fourth in the light-heavyweight division

Sworn Statement

I hereby swear for the purpose of becoming a member of _____ (name of sports club) that I have been a member of the following—but no other—communist or other leftist organizations or that I have been active in them:

_____ from_____ until_____

_____ from_____ until_____

_____ from_____ until_____

I have terminated any contact with these organizations if they still exist in the above or any other form. I am willing to support and further all endeavors of the national government.

At_____, date_____1933.

Name_____

Born
at_____in_____

Living at_____

I am currently a member of the following organizations

_____since_____

_____since_____

Reproduced as a facsimile with a blacked out name in F. Nitsch, *90 Jahre Arbeitersport*, 1985, p. 142.

of the Graeco-Roman wrestling bout at the 1936 Berlin Olympics. Even though he had been distributing anti-Nazi leaflets, he was not apprehended at this time; he continued to receive sports privileges until 1940. It then became clear that the next Olympic Games would not take place, and he was put back into the "production line," imprisoned for communist propaganda in 1942, and murdered in 1944. In fact, the roll call of martyrs from the worker sport organisation reads like a Who's Who of worker sport (Radetz, 1982).

Worker Sport in Postwar Germany

Günther Wonneberger has described worker sport in the Soviet occupied Zone and in the German Democratic Republic of postwar Germany that followed the RSI tradition of favouring elite sport for the purposes of encouraging mass participation and identification (Wonneberger, 1985). The situation in the U.S., British, and French zones and, later, in the Federal Republic of Germany, is far more complex (DSB, 1990).

While those worker athletes who were forced to emigrate initially favoured reviving the independent worker sport movement, it soon became evident that the resus-

citated SPD had other plans. The party leadership wanted to control all sports activities. In assuming that they would maintain a hold on the whole of the sport movement if they were to organise it themselves along noncompetitive lines and to avoid the reestablishment of the old Nazis, the SPD leaders misjudged the situation in sport. The integrative effort that took place in all social organisations successfully took over the trade unions and reduced the opposing Christian social groups to a relatively unimportant position; this, however, did not work in sport. When in May 1946, at the First Postwar SPD Congress, this general guideline was proposed as the unanimous decision of a committee of 21 members, the overrepresentation of the British Zone—where this model was already successfully practised—may have added to the erroneous judgment (Nitsch, 1976). With the appointment of John Dixon as the British control officer for sport, people like Carl Diem regained their top posts, soon to be followed by other ex-Nazis. Thus, the West German Olympic Committee in 1949 elected Karl von Halt, Hitler's last *Reichssportführer*, as its president (NOK, 1989); the newly founded combined sports movement, the *Deutscher Sportbund* (DSB), elected Willi Daume as head, whose first action was to take on Guido von Mengden, the last Nazi sports organisation chief, in the

Delegates of the Worker Cycling Congress, 25-26 May 1896.

Tug-of-war by worker sportsmen.

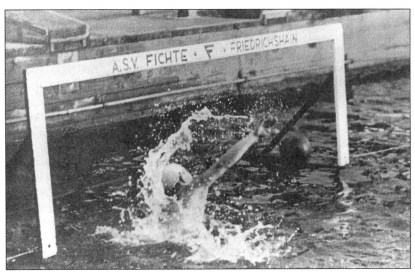

Water polo at *ASV Fichte Berlin-Friedrichshain*.

same capacity. In effect, the *ghostwriter* of the old *Reichssportführer* became the *ghostwriter* of the new president; only the title of *SA-Sturmbannführer* had to be dropped (Bernett, 1976).

Developments turned out differently for the Friends of Nature and Solidarity. Military Order No. 23 had prohibited all the old clubs, but they were able to reform and to continue business as normal. Because the property rights mainly lay with the clubs and less with the national sports organisations, the clubs were able to regain their former property fairly quickly. Insofar as the worker sport clubs possessed little property, they had little to recover by reestablishing themselves.

The Friends of Nature had had 428 buildings and ramblers' cabins when it had been dissolved; these belonged to the national association and not to individual clubs. Solidarity had lost a bicycle factory with a motorbike section, a chain store outlet for both, and 20,000 cycles and 500 motorbikes that had been manufactured yet unsold at the moment of confiscation in 1933. Military Order No. 50 ensured that all property of Nazi organisations that had previously belonged to other organisations had to be restored to their previous owners. Because the property had, in this instance, belonged to the national organisation, it was necessary to recommence both locally and nationally. The question of who exactly should be reimbursed was a source of contention among the four Allied powers. No agreement was forthcoming, so each occupying power tackled it differently in its own zone. The newly constituted Federal Republic was similarly not too keen to tackle the issue because the claim to speak for all Germany (including the GDR and the parts that had been integrated into Poland and the USSR) made it extremely difficult to substantiate any demands. Only the Federal Reclaim Law (*Bundesrückerstattungsgesetz*) of 19 July 1957 finally provided the basis for settlement and reimbursement.

Because both organisations regarded themselves as *political*, the DSB refused to accept the two even as associate members. While the Friends of Nature joined political organisations and abandoned further debate about what they were doing as *sport* (they became part of the old Easter March Movement, the ecology and peace movement), Solidarity sued the DSB in order to become an associate member. The matter went to the courts, and the German Supreme Court eventually ruled, on 19 December 1977, that the DSB had to accept Solidarity as a member. This ended the three-decade struggle for worker sport to be accepted fully in the Federal Republic of Germany—in spite of the self-imposed apolitical notion of sport, which itself became an absurdity just 3 years later with the boycott of the 1980 Moscow Olympics.

Conclusion

Some parts of the contemporary German sport movement absorbed the ideas of the old worker sport movement. The mainstream of the old movement only existed at the annual meetings of fairly venerable gentlemen, the Friends of the Worker Sports Movement. It has to be said that they are a wonderful source of oral history, but with the decisions of 1946 and 1947 that went against reconstituting a worker sport movement, they are an anachronism, an appendage to history (Nitsch, 1985b). It may be that the social-democratic tradition of most of worker sport was bound to lead to this decision, inasmuch as the historical situation of 1946 gave worker bureaucracy an opportunity to attain social respectability. These were the men and women without a Nazi past. Bourgeois athletes needed to get going again; they seemed to have respect, and they were content with that.

It should not be overlooked, however, that the border situation between the postwar political blocs, and the millions of refugees from Soviet-liberated Eastern Europe, certainly complicated the attitude of West Germans towards Marxism and worker movements in general.

When the two Germanys were finally united in 1990, East Germans left their old system in a hurry. It was not the worker sport tradition of voluntary involvement and mass participation that they tried to safeguard, but the high degree of professionalisation of their elite sport system. At the occasion of the 100th anniversary of the foundation of the German worker sport movement, the ATSB was refounded with Annemarie Renger, the former speaker of the federal parliament and daughter of Fritz Wildung, as chairperson. Again, the worker sport tradition was not to be rekindled; their property was to be reclaimed according to the *Bundes-rückerstattungsgesetz*. As most of the former sports grounds and buildings, including the *Bundesschule* in Leipzig—now choice real estate in the best downtown locations—could not be returned to their former owners by any other means, the SPD created this organisation to improve party finances. In the era of postmodernism, traditions are not only invented to create an aura of respectability; real traditions are sold to the highest bidder under the rubrics of progress and change (Levi-Strauss, 1966; Nitsch & Peiffer, 1995).

References

Arbeiter-Turn-Zeitung (ATZ). 1893-1933. (A full set is available on microfilm in the archives of the Institut für Sportwissenschaften of the Georg-August-University Göttingen).

Auerbach, A. *Kampf um die Erde. Weihespiel zur internationalen Arbeiter-Olympiade* (Frankfurt: Union, 1925).

Bach, H. "Volks- und Wehrsport in der Weimarer Republik," *Sportwissenschaft*, vol. 11 (1981), pp. 273-294.

Barney, R.K. "America's First Turnverein: Commentary in Favor of Louisville, Kentucky," *Journal of Sport History*, vol. 11 (1984), pp. 137-157.

Beduhn, R. *Chronik der Solidarität. 1896-1977* (Offenbach: RKBS, 1978).

Beduhn, R. *Die Roten Radler. Illustrierte Geschichte des Arbeiterradfahrerbundes 'Solidarität'* (Münster: Lit, 1982).

Bernett, H. *Guido von Mengden. "Generalstabschef des deutschen Sports"* (Berlin: Bartels & Wernitz, 1976).

Bernett, H. "Wehrsport—ein Pseudosport?" *Sportwissenschaft*, vol. 11 (1981), pp. 295-308.

Bernett, H. "Die Zerschlagung des deutschen Arbeitersports durch die nationalsozialistische Revolution," *Sportwissenschaft*, vol. 13 (1983), pp. 349-373.

Buck, A. *Die Arbeitersportbewegung und ihre Beziehungen zur Partei und zu den Gewerkschaften* (Leipzig: ATSB, 1927).

Bundesschulnachrichten der Zentralbildungsschule des Arbeiter-Turn- und Sportbundes. 1925-1933.

Denecke, V. *Die Arbeitersportgemeinschaft. Eine kulturhistorische Studie über die Braunschweiger Arbeitersportbewegung in den zwanziger Jahren* (Duderstadt: Mecke, 1990).

Dierker, H. *Arbeitersport im Spannungsfeld der Zwanziger Jahre. Alltagserfahrungen auf internationaler, deutscher und Berliner Ebene* (Essen: Klartext, 1990).

Dierker, H. & Pfister, G. (eds.). *'Frisch heran—Brüder, hört ihr das Klingen!' Zur Alltagsgeschichte des Berliner Arbeitersportvereins Fichte. Erinnerungen des ehemaligen Fichtesportlers Walter Giese* (Duderstadt: Mecke, 1991).

DSB (ed.). *Die Gründeriahre des Deutschen Sportbundes. Wege aus der Not zur Einheit* (Schorndorf: Hofmann, 1990).

Eichberg, H. "Alternative Verhaltensnormen im Arbeitersport?" *Sportwissenschaft*, vol. 5 (1975), pp. 69-80.

Eichel, W. (ed.). *Die Körperkultur in Deutschland von 1789-1919* (Berlin: Sportverlag, 1965), pp. 151-360.

Erbach, W. *65 Jahre Westdeutscher Fußball-Verband* (Duisburg: WSV, 1965).

Erstes Deutsches Arbeiter-Turn- und Sportfest. Festschrift (Leipzig: Arbeiter Turnverlag, 1921-1922), 6 vols.

Fenz, H. *Das erste Arbeiter-Olympia* (Graz: Kammer f. Arbeiter und Angestellte Steiermarks, 1926).

Fischer, J. "Die Olympiade der Sozialistischen Arbeitersport Internationale in Frankfurt 1925," in: H.J. Schulke (ed.), *Die Zukunft der Olympischen Spiele* (Köln: Pahl-Rugenstein, 1976), pp. 96-127.

Fischer, J. "Die Russenspiele—Einheitsfront der Arbeitersportler," in: W. Hopf (ed.), *Fußball* (Bensheim: Päd-extra, 1979), pp. 101-116.

Fischer, J. & Meiners, H.P. *Proletarische Körperkultur und Gesellschaft. Zur Geschichte des Arbeitersports* (Giessen: Achenbach, 1973).

Fischer, K. (ed.). *Handbuch für Mitglieder des Arbeiter-Radfahrer Bundes Solidarität* (Offenbach: ARS, 1908).

Frahnert, A. *Werden und Wachsen des Arbeiter-Radfahrerbundes Solidarität. Die Bundes-geschichte bis zum Jahre 1926* (Offenbach: ARS, 1926).

Gehrmann, S. *Fußball-Vereine-Politik. Zur Sportgeschichte des Reviers. 1900-1940* (Essen: Hobbing, 1988).

Gellert, C. & Frey, K. *Unser Gegner. Für die Vereine des Arbeiter-Turn- und Sportbundes*, vol. 2 (Leipzig: ATSB, 1927).

Gersbach, A. (ed.). *Die Ergebisse der sportbiologischen Untersuchungen bei der 1. internationalen Arbeiterolympiade* (Berlin: ZK, 1927).

Gillmeister, H. "English Editors of German Sporting Journals at the Turn of the Century," *The Sports Historian* (May 1993), No. 13, pp. 38-65.

Grote, C. "Die Arbeiterathleten in Niedersachsen," in: A. Krüger & H. Langenfeld (eds.), *Turnen und Sport in Niedersachsen in der Kaiserzeit* (Duderstadt: Mecke, 1996).

Hamer, E. *Die Anfänge der 'Spielbewegung' in Deutschland* (London: Arena, 1989).

Hopf, W. "Wie konnte Fußball ein deutsches Spiel werden?" in: *Fußball. Soziologie und Sozialgeschichte einer populären Sportart* (Bensheim: Päd-extra, 1979), pp. 54-80.

Internationaler Arbeiter-Verband für Sport und Körperkultur (ed.). *Erste Internationale Arbeiter-Olympiade zu Frankfurt* (Frankfurt: Union, 1925).

Kröll, F. "Vereinskultur und ideologische Hegemonie. Forschungsaspekte, Materialistische Kulturtheorie und Arbeiterkultur," in: W.F. Haug & K. Masse (eds.), Special edition of *Argument* (1980), 47, pp. 151-164.

Krüger, A. *Sport und Politik. Vom Turnvater Jahn zum Staatsamateur* (Hannover: Fackelträger, 1975).

Krüger, A. "Gesinnungsbildung durch Turnunterricht—oder pro patria est dum ludere videmur," in: R. Dithmar & J. Willer (eds.), *Schule zwischen Kaiserreich und Faschismus* (Darmstadt: Wissenschaftliche, 1981), pp. 102-124.

Krüger, A. "The rise and fall of the international worker sports movement," in: *Proceedings of the 11th HISPA Congress* (Glasgow: Jordanhill, 1985a), pp. 225-228.

Krüger, A. "Heute gehört uns Deutschland und morgen. . .? Das Ringen um den Sinn der Gleichschaltung im Sport in der ersten Jahreshälfte 1933," in: W. Buss & A. Krüger (eds.), *Sportgeschichte: Traditionspflege und Wertewandel* (Duderstadt: Mecke, 1985b), pp. 175-196.

Krüger, A. "Is there any sense in competition, specialization and the striving for records? The struggle between Turnen, sports and Swedish gymnastics in Germany," in: G. Bonhomme et al. (eds.), *La place du ijeu dans l'éducation. Histoire et pédagogie* (Paris, 1989), pp. 123-140.

Krüger, A. "There goes the art of manliness. Nudism and naturism in Germany," *Journal of Sport History*, vol. 18 (1991), pp. 135-158.

Krüger, A. "Germany and Sport in World War II," *Can. Journal of the History of Sport*, vol. 24 (1993), 1, pp. 52-62.

Krüger, A. "'Buying victories is positively degrading.' European origins of government pursuit of national prestige through sport," *International Journal of the History of Sport*, vol. 12 (1995), 2, pp. 183-200.

Kühn, F. *Die Arbeitersportbewegung. Ein Beitrag zur Klassengeschichte der Arbeiterschaft.* Diss., Rostock, 1922.

Langenfeld, H. "Aristokratischer Sport im wilhelminischen Deutschland," in: W. Buss & A. Krüger (eds.), *Sportgeschichte: Traditionspflege und Wertewandel* (Duderstadt: Mecke, 1985), pp. 63-84.

Levi-Strauss, C. *The Savage Mind* (Chicago: UCP, 1966).

Meyer, S. *Sport und Prozessunabhängige Qualifikationsmerkmale unter besonderer Berücksichtigung des Arbeitersports und des Sports im Faschismus* (Lollar: Achenbach, 1976).

Mittheilungs-Blatt des Turn-Vereins "Fichte" 16 (1911), p. 14ff.

Neuendorff, E. *Die Deutsche Turnerschaft. 1860-1936* (Berlin: Limpert, 1936).

Neumann, H. *Die deutsche Turnbewegung in der Revolution 1848/49 und in der amerikanischen Emigration* (Schorndorf: Hofmann, 1968).

Niemeyer, K.H. *70 Jahre Fußball und kein Ende. Die Geschichte des Fußballsports im Kreise Peine* (Hannover: Madsack, 1982).

Nitsch, F. "Warum entstand nach 1945 keine Arbeitersportbewegung," *Sportwissenschaft*, vol. 6 (1976), pp. 172-199.

Nitsch, F. "Die olympische Gegenbewegung—Bedeutung und Vermächtnis des internationalen Arbeitersports und seiner Olympiaden," in: M. Blödorn (ed.), *Sport und Olympische Spiele* (Reinbek: Rororo, 1984), pp. 113-137.

Nitsch, F. "Dieinternationalen Arbeitersportbewegungen," in: A. Krüger & J. Riordan (eds.), *Der internationale Arbeitersport. Der Schlüssel zum Arbeitersport in 10 Ländern* (Köln: Pahl-Rugenstein, 1985a), pp. 174-209.

Nitsch, F. *90 Jahre Arbeitersport. Bundestreffen des Freundeskreises ehemaliger Arbeitersportler.* (Münster: Lit, 1985b).

Nitsch, F. *Aspekte der Sportentwicklung nach dem 2. Weltkrieg. Traditionslinien und Brüche.* Unpubl. Diss., Göttingen, 1989.

Nitsch, F. & Peiffer, L. (eds.). *Die roten Turnbrüder. 100 Jahre Arbeitersport* (Marburg: Schüren, 1995).

NOK. (ed.). *Rückkehr nach Olympia. Nationales Olympisches Komitee für Deutschland* (München: Copress, 1989).

Radetz, W. *Der Stärkere* (Berlin: Sportverlag, 1982).

Schuster, H. *Arbeiterturner im Kampf um die Jugend. Zur Geschichte des revolutionären Arbeitersports. 1893-1914* (Berlin: Sportverlag, 1962).

Simon, H. (ed.). *Die Körperkultur in Deutschland von 1917-1945* (Berlin: Sportverlag, 1969).

Skorning, L. *Kurzer Abriß der Geschichte der Körperkultur in Deutschland seit 1800* (Berlin: Sportverlag, 1952).

Spitzer, G. *Der deutsche Naturismus* (Ahrensburg: Czwalina, 1983).

Spitzer, G. & Grote, C. "'Kraft ist, was Leben schafft.' Zur Geschichte des Arbeiter-Athletenbundes Deutschlands," in: H.J. Teichler & G. Hauk (eds.), *Illustrierte Geschichte* (1987), pp. 169-174.

Sportpolitische Rundschau. 1928-1933.

Teichler, H.J. "Arbeitersport als soziales und politisches Phänomen im wilhelminischen Klassenstaat," in: H. Ueberhortst (ed.), *Geschichte der Leibesübungen*, vol. 3/2 (Berlin: Bartels & Wernitz, 1980), pp. 443-484.

Teichler, H.J. & Hauk, G. (eds.). *Illustrierte Geschichte des Arbeitersports* (Berlin: Dietz, 1987).

Timmermann, H. *Geschichte und Struktur der Arbeitersportbewegung. 1893-1933* (Ahrensburg: Czwalina, 1973).

Ueberhorst, H. *Frisch, Frei, Stark, und Treu. Die Arbeitersportbewegung in Deutschland. 1893-1933* (Düsseldorf: Droste, 1973).

Ueberhorst, H. "Bildungsgedanke und Solidaritätsbewußtsein in der deutschen Arbeitersportbewegung zur Zeit der Weimarer Republik," *Archiv für Sozialgeschichte*, vol. 14 (1974), pp. 275-292.

Ueberhorst, H. *Turner unterm Sternenbanner* (München: Moos, 1978).

Ueberhorst, H. "Ferdinand Goetz und Edmund Neuendorff—Wirkungsgeschichte zweier Turnführer," in: W. Buss & A. Krüger (eds.), *Sportgeschichte: Traditionspflege und Wertewandel* (Duderstadt: Mecke, 1985), pp. 147-160.

Ueberhorst, H. "Nicht Mord, dem Sport gilt unser Wort! Arbeiterschützen zwischen Volks- und Wehrsport in der Weimarer Republik," in: S. Spitzer & D. Schmidt (eds.), *Sport zwischen Eigenständigkeit und Fremdbestimmung* (Schorndorf: Hofmann, 1986), pp. 145-153.

Ueberhorst, H. & Hauk, G. *Arbeitersport und Arbeiterkultur im Ruhrgebiet* (Opladen, 1989).

Wagner, H. *Sport und Arbeitersport* (Berlin: Büchergilde Gutenberg, 1931).

Wildung, F. (ed.). *Handbuch des Arbeiter-Turnerbundes* (Leipzig: ATV, 1911).

Wildung, F. *Arbeitersport* (Berlin: Bücherkreis, 1929).

Wonneberger, G. "Arbeitersport in der DDR. Zur Realisierung der Ziele und Träume deutscher Arbeitersportler im ersten deutschen Arbeiter- und Bauern-Staat," in: A. Krüger & J. Riordan (eds.), *Der internationale Arbeitersport* (Köln: Pahl-Rugenstein, 1985), pp. 14-34.

Zimmer, J. (ed.). *Mit uns zieht die neue Zeit. Die Naturfreunde* (Köln: Pahl-Rugenstein, 1984).

Chapter 2

The Worker Sport Movement in France

William Murray

FRANCE

This largest state of Western Europe covers an area of 543,965 km², and in 1931 the French population numbered 41.94 million.

After the dramatic events of 1870-1871—the defeat in the Prussian-French War and the first attempt at a socialist revolution in the form of the Paris Commune—France was generally unsympathetic toward reform. This situation did not change until the end of the century when, in the face of numerous scandals (the Dreyfus affair, in particular), a rapprochement between progressive petty-bourgeois groups and the predominantly socialist workers' movement took place. The results of this development can be seen in the support given until 1905 to the governments of the radicals by the socialists, which in turn gave the latter the beginnings of a social security system and protective labour laws. The close cooperation was, however, ended by the anti-trade union policy of the radicals and the rejection of a policy that would support bourgeois cabinets on the part of the II International. The cooperation was resumed, however, at the outbreak of World War I.

The alliance briefly survived after the war because the radicals were willing to legislate for the 8-hour day but refused demands for further reforms and for softening the peace conditions of war enemies. The left's scope of activity was further reduced by the electoral triumph of the right-wing parties at the end of 1919 and the split in the Socialist Party (SFIO) over the question of joining the Comintern into a communist majority (SFIC) and a socialist minority (SFIO) a year later. The right's insistence on the exact fulfilment of the Treaty of Versailles—which led to the invasion of the Ruhr in 1923—brought a clear electoral victory for the so-called *cartel des gauches* in 1924. However, the financial crisis brought about by the Ruhr invasion ended plans for social reform. At least the radicals, with the support of the SFIO, were able to introduce a change in foreign policy that produced the Pact of Locarno (1925) and the basis for reconciliation with Germany.

Behind the protection of high customs walls, the phase of economic stability beginning in 1926 continued beyond the outbreak of the Great Depression. When the crisis became noticeable in 1931, the results were the same as elsewhere: Mass poverty, which accompanied the rapidly rising unemployment, produced the ideal conditions for the growth of the extreme right. Yet socialists and communists had learned from their experiences in Germany. When right-wing extremists attempted a coup in 1934, it was countered by a unity of action on the left that not only removed the fascist threat but also set the scene for the election victory of the Popular Front in 1936. After this success, Blum, the leader of the SFIO, formed a government composed of socialists and radicals and tolerated by the SFIC, which introduced extensive sociopolitical reforms but lost its reputation because of its inability to combat the reappearing recession. In 1938, France once again had a nonsocialist government that repealed most of the reforms introduced by the Popular Front.

After the victory of the German troops in June 1940, the establishment of the Vichy Regime, and the expulsion of the invaders in 1944, the history of the Fourth Republic began with a new Popular Front government made up of communists, socialists, and the Catholic left; it legislated for extensive social and economic reforms. The end of the reform phase, marked by the exclusion of the communists from government in 1947, was rapidly followed by the continuous change of governments characteristic of the dissolution process of the Fourth Republic. This dissolution finally led—provoked by the intensifying Algerian War of Independence—to the nomination of de Gaulle, the French resistance leader of World War II, as head of the government, a new constitution, and the Fifth Republic. For a long time, the left was sceptical of the new order that overemphasised the position of the president. This attitude did not change until the 1970s when, with the development of closer ties between socialists and communists, the chances of a candidate from the left becoming president grew. In 1981, the socialist Mitterrand achieved this position and stayed in office until 1995, when he was succeeded by Jacques Chirac, the new president who was also from the conservative right.

Modern sport is a product of industrialisation, the change from an agricultural to an urban setting, and a pattern of time that was measured by the clock rather than the climate. Out of the Industrial Revolution came the working classes, and it was their passionate involvement that made modern sport. Modern sport became a mass phenomenon that was a spectacle, a source of income, and a leisure time pursuit—a concept hitherto restricted to the aristocrats and the rich. When the workers were fighting for reasonable working conditions and a living wage, how they spent their time while not at work was not a major issue. This changed as shorter hours and better wages allowed them to think beyond the workplace. At the same time, moralists of various persuasions became concerned about how workers would use or misuse their "idle" time, and some bosses sought to channel their workers' enthusiasm for sports to their own advantage. In this regard, the socialists and others fighting on behalf of the workers were rather slow off the mark; moreover, when they turned their attention to workers' leisure, they were often singularly inept. As late as 1937, the journal of the Comintern, *Communist International*, noted that while there were as many as 50 million active sportsmen in the chief capitalist countries alone, very few of them were in the working-class sport organisations. The socialists and communists, it pointed out, had neglected this. Consumed by the primacy of politics, they regarded sport as something that turned the worker's mind away from higher things (*The Communist International*, 1937).

This is hardly surprising. While workers embraced sport with joy, only a few became socialists and even fewer adopted both. Socialism and sport are not inherently contradictory, but socialism is an essentially intellectual pursuit, and intellectuals are notoriously arrogant in regard to sport. Fascism, on the other hand, has a basically adolescent and macho appeal that fits well with sport, and capitalism and competitive sport can be mirror images of each other (Hoberman, 1984). Above all, sport is supposed to be fun, and high-minded socialist leaders were not often noted for encouraging frivolity. When they tried to influence the leisure pursuits of their would-be flock, they were often disappointed by simple souls who would rather score goals than consider their relevance to the evils of bourgeois society and the glories of the socialist dawn to come. As their leaders, the socialists had the choice of following them or losing them (Wheeler, 1978).

In France, with its patchy industrial development and the persistence of strong centres of peasant isolation and independence, the working class was poorly organised and chronically divided. Less disciplined than the Germans and less easily bought off than the British, the French workforce was less successful in winning basic rights. It was this fragmentation, rather than a supposed preference for intellectual pursuits, that gave France the appearance of a country that was not interested in sport (Murray, 1987a). It was for these reasons, too, that the organisation of worker sport in France was not as successful as that of other economically advanced countries.

Worker Sport in France Before the Bolshevik Revolution

There were worker sport groups in France at the turn of the century: in the Nord, around Paris, and in the Gironde, in particular. It was not until 1907 that the first official clubs were formed, and another year before there was a federal organisation. The benefits gained by the workers of Germany and Britain, in the one case by Bismarck's paternalism and in the other by a highly organised trade union movement, came much later in France. It was only in 1900 that the working day was set at 10 hours and 1906 before workers were granted 1 day off per week. The 8-hour day was won in 1919, and it was only in the 1920s that most workers gained the Saturday afternoon holiday, a long time after the creation of the British "weekend."

Sport may have been controlled by the rich and the aristocratic, but it attracted the interest of common folk and the young. As a result, they were wooed by those who wanted to win them to their particular beliefs. In 1898, the Catholic *Fédération Gymnastique et Sportive des Patronages de France* (FGSPF) had its first annual meeting, and in 1903, it formally organised. With the separation of church and state in 1905, this became a major organ in the church's battle against the forces of secularism (Dubreuil, 1980; Holt, 1981). The government encouraged young people to support republicanism with a proper secular basis through its youth organisations, known as the *Petites A's*. Essentially, these were youth clubs for boys and girls who had left primary school and were unable to continue their formal education. Run by lay school teachers, they were to preserve young people from the temptations of the street, dance halls, and cabarets by offering the morally uplifting examples of visits to galleries and museums, lectures, and visits to the countryside. Their main success was to come, like that of their Catholic rivals, in following their young charges' interest in sport (Margadant, 1978).

While these two bodies fought over whether God or the state deserved ultimate loyalty, the French National Sports Council (*Conseil National des Sports* [CNS]) was formed on 23 May 1908 as the umbrella body for the various sports federations in France. This body shared the commitments to discipline and nationalism that were behind the resurgence of sport at this time. In turn, these sports bodies encouraged sport as an ideal way of preparing French youth for the defence of the fatherland at home and the spread of its virtues abroad. The socialists, being anticolonial, pacifist, and internationalist, did not seek sport as a means of combating this.

The concept of sport as military preparation is probably as old as sport, celebrated in phrases like the "playing fields of Eton" and worshipped in many of the sporting metaphors that were to accompany young men to their death in World War I. The revived Olympic Games were founded by de Coubertin with totally different ends in mind: They were to bring the youth of the world together in a festival of peace and fraternity. Yet, even the Olympics had their origins in France's defeat by Prussia in the Franco-Prussian War of 1870-1871 and the need to build up the strength of French youth. Charles Maurras, much sharper, albeit more cynical than de Coubertin, praised the first Olympics held in Athens for the nationalism they evoked rather than the love they engendered (MacAloon, 1981). The Olympic Games were to be beset from the start with the contradiction between high ideals and its often base outcomes. In 1911, the French National Olympic Committee (*Comité Olympique Français* [COF]) was formed to act within the CNS on behalf of those sports entered in the Olympics.

All these bodies, acting on behalf of God, state, or international understanding and each trying to attract the allegiance of the growing working class, claimed to be above politics. For the more militant working-class sportsmen, this was errant nonsense, and so, themselves wearing their politics on their vests, titles, slogans, or wherever they were most obvious, they set out to unmask the hypocrisy of those whose only interest in the workers was as cannon fodder or to make them into docile victims of class exploitation.

In 1908, some French workers in the Paris region, through the columns of *L'Humanité*, the organ of the French section of the Second International, founded the *Fédération Sportive Athlétique Socialiste* (FSAS) (Delétang, 1980; Ehrenberg, 1980; Moustard, 1983). The FSAS soon expanded to take in clubs from the Nord, the Aube, and other provincial regions, and in 1913 changed its name to the *Fédération Socialiste de Sport et de Gymnastique*. In that year it became, with Great Britain, Germany, Belgium, and Switzerland, a founding member of the international worker sport movement, the *Fédération Sportive Socialiste Internationale*, at a meeting in Ghent, Belgium. Despite this, and despite having founded their own newspaper, *Sport et Socialisme,* in 1910 or 1911 (Pépin, 1938), the membership of the organised worker sport movement in France barely reached 1,000. Despite this, too, they were already torturing themselves over whether their ranks should be opened to those who did not share the faith. In 1911, the

rule restricting membership to paid-up socialists and their families was dropped, but the leaders had to be members of the party (Arnaud, 1994).

The problem of the goals of worker sport was to plague the movement for most of its existence: Was it to be essentially an arm in the class war, or was it to provide a healthy diversion for the worker in his or her time of rest? Was it to be openly political at the expense of frightening away would-be members, or was it to welcome relations with the class enemy at the risk of being infected by them? Just as Lenin claimed that workers left to themselves would develop no more than "trade union consciousness," so the leaders of the worker sport movement tended to fear that workers left to go their own way in sport would follow the path to bourgeois perdition. They were both probably right, emphasising the near-insuperable odds they faced. In sport, as in life, workers left to themselves will compete, accept money for winning, and pay to see a fine sporting spectacle, but workers pushed into sport for its moral values will soon tell the proselytiser, however well meaning, what to do with homilies.

This was part of the problem of reform or revolution, brought from theory to practice when the Bolshevik Revolution of 1917 in Russia forced the socialists to choose between them. When Edmond Pépin and a few survivors of the prewar FSAS resumed their burden and reorganised the worker sport federation as the *Fédération Sportive du Travail* (FST) in 1919, they survived 4 years before splitting like the rest of the socialist world.

Worker Sport and the Class Struggle: 1917-1934

After 1917, the followers of the Bolsheviks came to be called communists, while those who believed the same ends could be achieved by peaceful means retained the name socialist or, in some countries like Germany, social democrats. The need to make this choice came when the Comintern insisted that its disciples toe the Moscow line and help foment world revolution by all means, and it gave its clear terms in the Twenty-One Conditions. The socialists, believing in the efficacy of parliamentary democracy and unwilling to subordinate themselves to a foreign power, were dismissed by the communists as class collaborators and traitors to the workers' cause. In 1921, Léon Blum led a minority out of the annual Congress of the Socialist Party at Tours, and the following year the French Trade Union movement was rent by schism. In 1923, it was the turn of the FST.

At Lucerne, Switzerland, in September 1920, the Socialist Worker Sports International (called at first the Lucerne Worker Sports International [LSI]) was founded, and in the following year, in Moscow, the Red Sports International (RSI) was created. Faced at the Montreuil Congress of the FST with the motion to pledge allegiance to the RSI, Anton Guillevic, one of the first members of the FSAS and a member of the LSI, led 30 clubs—who opposed the Moscow line—out of the meeting to form the *Union des Sociétés Sportives et Gymnastiques du Travail* (USSGT). The remaining 160 clubs retained the name FST and its newspaper, *Sport Ouvrier*. The USSGT founded its own newspaper, *Sport et Loisir*. In the daily press, *L'Humanité* reported sport from the point of view of the FST and *Le Populaire* from that of the USSGT. The various sports organisations tried hard to ignore the existence of their rivals. The socialists never mentioned the communists (Marie, 1934), and the bourgeois ignored all worker sport (Dubech, 1932; Renaitour, 1934). The FST was to prove itself to be a faithful agent of the Moscow policies that pitted worker against worker and made the job of the fascists so much easier.

For a few years in the 1920s, the rival bodies made a few attempts at reunion, but these attempts were more often the excuse for a quarrel than unity. The FST was urged by the RSI to agitate with the rank and file of the USSGT against the leaders and to join the USSGT for this purpose. At sports meetings organised by the USSGT, they would demonstrate against the "treachery" of the reformist leadership. The RSI, appealing to peasants as well as workers, openly declared that its aim was to form "resolute, courageous and combative" participants in the proletarian struggle to overthrow capitalism. The USSGT, implacably opposed to all bourgeois sport and open to all who accepted the class struggle, concentrated most of its energies on building up a workers' subculture of parades, plays, mass exercises, and sports that would form the basis of the new society when capitalism collapsed.

At the international level, the USSGT supported the Worker Olympiads organised by the LSI, while the FST promoted the *Spartakiads* organised by the RSI. The RSI encouraged its members to enter LSI-sponsored competitions in order to attack them from within, while the LSI hoped that in this way it might bring them under its own leadership. But by 1928, the LSI had abandoned all hope of reunion. At the same time the socialists gave up their attempts to win back the communists, the RSI fell into line with the "class against class" policies of the Comintern. Both bodies ran their own sports meetings, often dedicated, like their stadiums, to heroes from the socialist past, but they neither competed with nor against each other. The USSGT did its best to ignore the FST, which—faithful to the Twenty-One Conditions of communism—spent more time attacking the collaborationist brother than the class enemy. At a time when a worker could be sacked for having a copy of *L'Humanité* or *Le Populaire*, it is hardly surprising that sports events

organised by the FST as well as by the USSGT were met by obstruction from police and unsympathetic local bodies. Even these common enemies did not bring the two warring federations together. More than any other branch of the workers' movement, be it the political, trade union, or cooperative, sport had the means to bring together workers in friendly, face-to-face contact. Given the bitterness of the sectarian quarrels, the worker sport federations could only have driven them away.

While the sports organisations specifically devoted to the salvation of the workers tried to tear each other apart, those representing the evils from which they were supposed to be saved continued to consolidate themselves. The Catholic patronages, despite the annoying presence of leftist outsiders who were as concerned with the discomforts of the workers in this world as with their place alongside God in the next, maintained a consistent membership. In 1938, this amounted to 600,000 members in 76 regional unions and 3,700 societies (*Élan Social*, 1938). Their secular opponents continued to expand, and in 1927 the republican and anticlerical *Union Française des Oeuvres Laïques d'Education Physiques* (UFOLEP), which took over from the *Petites A's*, was founded. Ten years later it boasted 310,000 members and 5,000 clubs (Holt, 1981). Leaders of industry had also decided that sport could calm the passions of revolutionary ardour and that the provision of pleasant leisure pursuits might distract the worker from what some might have called exploitation or even injustice. Peugeot, Michelin, Renault, Schneider, and Pommery provided playing fields and swimming pools for their workers, and in some cases, let the workers run the facilities themselves (Holt, 1981).

After 1928, the USSGT saw some increase in its membership, while the FST fell steadily under the zeal of the self-appointed guardians of ideological purity. In 1930, they provoked another split, forcing the departure of those who did not share their dogmatism. *Sport Ouvrier* rejoiced in the unloading of this dead wood, and the FST sent its congratulations to Moscow for the way it was bringing counterrevolutionary saboteurs to book. It went on to pledge the support of France's "red sportsmen" in defence of the Soviet Union, to denounce French imperialism, and concluded by expressing its best wishes for the Five Year Plan, the Red Army, and world revolution (Ehrenberg, 1980).

A diminished but purified FST continued to follow the Moscow masters even after the advent of Hitler. As late as March 1934, it was still spitting out most of its venom at the socialists, and in April it could still find time to condemn those who had split in 1930 as seeking "tranquillity in collaboration" (*Sport*, 10 April 1938). By this time, like the French Communist Party (PCF) itself, its policies were being reflected in membership figures, which declined at the same time as interest in sport was increasing. By the 1930s, mass sport had arrived in France, and workers provided the bulk of the stars and the spectators at the three most popular sports: football, cycling, and boxing. This was reflected in the sports coverage in the daily press. *L'Auto* still maintained healthy circulation figures in the early 1930s, but its share of the sporting market was steadily decreasing by the adoption in the information press of regular sports coverage. Above all, *Paris Soir* dominated the Parisian press with sales of over 1 million. Its success, in large measure, was built on its coverage of sport, where Gaston Bénac used his imagination as much as his sense of the dramatic to build up the most mundane or even nonexistent sports event into a controversy of breathtaking proportion (Meyer, 1978; Seidler, 1964).

It was not concern for achieving its due market share that brought about a change in the policies of the FST. Such a turnaround had to come from Moscow, and it came as a result of the international political situation. Hitler was not only consolidating his power at home, he was winning praise in Germany and abroad for crushing political dissidents, particularly communists. Stalin had good reason to believe that the democracies would not stand in the way of Hitler's long-stated aim to conquer Bolshevism and win *Lebensraum* in the east at the same time. On his eastern borders, Stalin could not contemplate with equanimity the growth of an aggressive and expansionist Japan.

Already in France, the rank and file had been showing their discontent at the ruinous policies of the communist leadership, particularly after the riots of 6 February 1934, when fascist and antirepublican forces had attempted a coup against the government. In the ensuing repression, the workers suffered most from the government's bullets. The pressures from below for a union of the left in a Popular Front against fascism were growing, but they could only become a reality when word came from Moscow that the days of denouncing the socialists were over. Not only were the worker sport bodies to play a key role in this new policy, but the first working example of the Popular Front was when the FST and the USSGT came together in December 1934 to found the *Fédération Sportive et Gymnique du Travail* (FSGT) (Murray, 1987a, 1987b).

The Heroic Period: 1934-1938

The triumph of the Popular Front in France in 1936 was one of the few bright spots in a decade when the democracies dithered in economic distress and the fascists strutted the stage as the would-be leaders of the world. It was a triumph soon to dissolve in despair, but not before the seeds of hope for a new order had been planted, waiting for better times before they could come to flower. In this period, the FSGT played a major role, its policies coinciding with those of the new government, its aspirations based on a genuine concern for the lives of ordinary workers rather than the salvation of the Soviet Union (Hache, 1985).

One of the first indications of a change in policy from Moscow came when the Executive Committee of the RSI decided that rather than hold its annual *Spartakiad* in the Soviet Union, it would be held in Paris. This was to be a vast assembly of people: a *Rassemblement Sportif International* set for the following August, open to all workers without distinction of federation. As an indication of how serious the Soviets were, the July congress of the FST was blessed by the presence of the Soviet president of the Superior Council of Physical Culture and the secretary of the RSI. Here was a man presiding over a membership of 6 million honouring a federation with 13,000 members (Delétang, 1980). Soviet repentance might have come late, but it was coming with a vengeance. By the end of June, the FST was making constant appeals for sporting unity from those it was more in the habit of denouncing. The leaders of the USSGT, somewhat reluctant to embrace their new friends, politely refused their invitation to take part in the displaced *Spartakiad* but allowed their members to participate as individuals. And while they also refused the offers of help from the FST for their own sports meeting of 5 August, they again softened their refusal by inviting them to send a relay team.

The great worker sport meeting took place in August as planned. Bolstered by some of the Soviet Union's best athletes, as well as a few members of the USSGT, it was a huge success. The new ecumenism of the FST was justified in the words of Lenin: "The advance guard by itself is powerless." The USSGT, with its memories of rancorous onslaughts rather than the words of the prophet to work with, continued to react less than rapturously to the overtures of the FST. Pierre Marie in *Le Populaire* and Anton Guillevic in the USSGT were among those who expressed a certain disquiet.

In the meantime, the rank and file, less hidebound than their leadership, started to compete against and with each other. In late September, the Paris regional council of the USSGT came out strongly in favour of unity, and by the end of October, most of the loose ends had been tied up. On 10 November, the FST—and the USSGT on the following day—voted unanimously for unity, and this was duly carried out at a joint session on 23-24 December. The international wings of the worker sport movements, the RSI and the SWSI (Socialist Worker Sports International, as the LSI was now called) failed to come to an agreement and remained apart. Nevertheless, the French workers had come together, and for the next 4 years the FSGT was to exert what was probably its greatest influence on the worker sport movement: fighting for the election of a Popular Front government and formulating its policies. By their fusion in December 1934, the two worker sport federations set themselves up as an example for the political leadership to follow.

One of the major organs of unification was the newspaper of the FST, *Sport*, which became the organ of the new FSGT. Founded in October 1933 to replace the narrower *Sport Ouvrier*, *Sport* came out weekly, berating the sluggards in its own party with the same zeal as it attacked the corrupters of sport in the bourgeois press. Sales were mainly by subscription to the FSGT's own clubs, but circulation drives were now and then run to encourage new readers. Individual vendors, selling *Sport* at sports meetings, could earn a small commission; if they were particularly successful, they could look forward to seeing their picture in the paper. *Sport*, however, was caught in a perplexing dilemma. If it wanted to appeal beyond the membership of the FSGT, it had to include material more suited to the bourgeois press; if it did this, it was in danger of becoming just another commercial paper. In the excitement of the Popular Front period, it managed a nice balance of criticism and campaigning, but, by 1938, ideology and the narrow view came to predominate, and sales began to falter. In April of that year, *Sport* started to come out as a monthly, and so it remained until it folded or was forced to close down after the outbreak of war.

René Rousseau was editor of *Sport* throughout its 5-year struggle; he was one of the leading figures in the history of the worker sport movement (FSGT, 1965). Born into modest circumstances in 1906, Rousseau saw *Sport* as a weapon in the class war, and he scolded readers who told him it should be otherwise. He prided himself in his refusal to compromise with the commercial interests of professional sport or to accept bribes outright or through advertisements that were an unsavoury feature of the press in France at this time. He threw himself wholeheartedly into the spirit of the Popular Front, imprinting his paper with a fervour that embodied the success of the antifascist coalition.

The success of *Sport* at this time no doubt owed a great deal to the skills of Rousseau as editor and the loyalty of the mainly unpaid contributors. Of much greater importance, however, was the abandonment of sectarianism. Membership of the FSGT also reflected this. At its creation, the FSGT had about 30,000 members, increasing to nearly 43,000 in 1935 and leaping to nearly 100,000 with the victory of the Popular Front (a success that it retained until 1937). *Sport* claimed the figure of 135,000, and some of its enemies as many as 160,000. Whether this is accurate, the latter figure is a reflection of the success of the FSGT, and, in October 1937, the employers' federation, the *Comité de Prévoyance et d'Action Sociale*

(CPAS), put out a newspaper, *Élan Social,* to counter its influence (Trist, 1990). Even at this time of maximum impact, however, the worker sport movement still represented only a fraction of the 3.5 million organised sports people in France.

Sport continued in this time as the scourge of commercial sport, which was denounced for favouring spectacle over participation and encouraging the baser instincts of greed and competition; these, in turn, led to violence and cheating. Ambivalent about professionals—who were, after all, workers—*Sport* depicted them as little more than pawns in the hands of the promoters, degraded by the sponsor who owned them and discarded once they had served their purpose. This was epitomised in the *Tour de France*, where spectator and performer alike were duped by the only real winners: Desgrange and his corrupt clique who ruled commercial sport in France.

Desgrange, owner of *L'Auto* and sponsor of the *Tour de France*, also epitomised the nationalism that ran through bourgeois sport, from the federations of the CNS to the overtly right-wing leagues and their sporting offshoots. Even apparently innocent bodies like the Boy Scout movement were denounced by *Sport* as protofascist for their discipline and the patronage of notorious militarists. Nationalism could excite passions and sell newspapers; it also sold young men into war.

In the new spirit of expansion after the formation of the FSGT, however, *Sport* diluted its attacks on the rival bodies and sought to expand its influence beyond worker sport; it even considered affiliating with the official national body of amateur sport in France, the CNS. Ironically, it was Guillevic and the socialist influence in the FSGT that resisted these moves, although the CNS was wary of permitting its one-time antagonist to enter its ranks. Serious discussions were held with UFOLEP, which was composed mostly of radicals but nonetheless contained many workers in its membership. In the end, only the Basketball Federation (FFBB) entered into relations with the FSGT.

At this time, too, support for the Soviet Union tended to fall into the background. In its criticisms of bourgeois sport, *Sport* had offered the example of its own federations as an alternative, where events like the *Cross de l'Humanité* were conducted in an atmosphere of near sporting perfection; however, it was above all in the Soviet Union that the sport lover could find his or her vision of perfection. Here was a country that lived up to the expectations of any true sportsperson: a country where professionalism was banned, winning prized less than honest effort, and fellowship replaced national rivalry. There, under the benign influence of the government, all Soviet citizens, young and old, male and female, could take part in the sport of their choice, even tennis,

René Rousseau

René Rousseau was born into a working-class family in the Paris suburb of Butte-aux-Cailles in 1906. He was a bright child who shared a love of learning with a craze for the sporting heroes of the day: the "giants of the road," the cyclists in the *Tour de France*; boxers like Georges Carpentier; and the stars of the athletic track. But it was cycling that was his main interest, although his father was too poor to buy him a bike. As the son of a worker, too, he had to leave school at the end of his primary education, at only 12 years old. His job at the French post office required a bike, so he bought a second-hand one on credit that he repaid with his pay and the tips he received for delivering telegrams. He later became an apprentice jeweller.

Rousseau joined the FST shortly after its creation in 1920, and soon became a pacifist, sharing a political commitment with a continuing love of sport. His talents took him to the national administration of the FST, while his other skills saw him take part in and organise such major sporting events as the *Grand Prix Cycliste* and the *Cross*, both sponsored by *L'Humanité*. With Auguste Delaune he became a secretary of the FST. In 1929, he was elected secretary of the RSI, and left for Moscow that same year. Not only did he have his political commitment confirmed, but he found Lucienne, the woman who would share his future.

It was a future of struggle, but when he was appointed first editor of the new journal *Sport*, his life took on a new purpose, as he gathered around him a team of journalists who shared his ideals and enthusiasm. After the debacle of 1940, he was taken prisoner and interned in Hamburg, where he was said to have kept up the spirits of his fellow prisoners and engaged in subversive activities. After the liberation and his release from prison, he was appointed editor of *Sports*, where he remained until it folded.

Rousseau was elected president of the FSGT and remained an active member until the illness that had first struck him in 1953 brought him to a premature death in 1964, at 58 years old. At his funeral he received eulogies from sport leaders not only of the left, but from those of the bourgeois federations he had spent much energy denouncing in the 1930s, including Armand Massard, president of the French National Olympic Committee.

yachting, and other sports that were restricted to the rich in capitalist countries. *Sport* was happy to record the favourable impressions of sports heroes like Thil and Ladoumègue who visited the Soviet Union and was delighted when eventually Soviet sportsmen and women came to France to take part successfully in local competition. Here was proof of the superiority of the Soviet system, *Sport* would proclaim, exhibiting a certain fetish for achievement and love of nation that it found deplorable in the French—a tendency that would reappear in the 1960s.

The Popular Front was antifascist, and *Sport* and the FSGT were unequivocal about sporting contacts with fascist countries. The World Cup in soccer, held in Italy in June 1934, was dismissed by *Sport* as a festival of brutality, a revival of the Roman circuses with Mussolini as Caesar of the carnival, and the World Cup was compared unfavourably to the joy of the workers' *Rassemblement Sportif International* held in Paris 2 months later. *Sport* instructed the spectators how to behave when fascist teams came to play in France, chastising them for being provoked into nationalist replies (such as singing the Marseillaise) but approving the proles of *St. Ouen* who interrupted the respectful silence in memory of the king of Yugoslavia, recently assassinated in

Marseilles, with a storm of abuse (Murray, 1987a). Most of these incidents related to football matches. But while football was the most popular worker sport in France at this time, it was the campaign against holding the Olympic Games in Germany in 1936 that occupied the FSGT in its most sustained attempt to cut sporting links with a fascist country.

The political implications of the 1936 Olympics, and the immense efforts the Nazis were putting into a sporting event they had formerly despised, raised it high on the FSGT agenda. The boycott movement against holding the 1936 Olympics in Germany owed its original inspiration to intellectuals and others whose primary interest was human rights rather than sport (Brohm, 1983; Kidd, 1980). From this point of view, the FSGT and *Sport* were late starters, but from the 7 August 1935 issue of *Sport*, when it ran an editorial ending with the resounding slogan: "Pas un homme! Pas un sou pour Berlin!" ("Not a man and not a penny for Berlin!"), it presented its readers with a picture of the Nazi regime in all its inhumane horror, gave chapter and verse of the openly avowed hatred of Hitler and other Nazis for France, pointed to the militarisation of sport that was its very purpose in that regime, and, above all else, gave examples of the persecution of sportsmen and women, initially communists, liberals, and democrats, but later Jews and other groups outlawed by the Nazis. All this underlined the hypocrisy of the International Olympic Committee (IOC) in declaring that the 1936 Olympics were equally accessible to athletes regardless of race, religion, or political persuasion. While *Sport* told its readers what playing with the Nazis implied, members of the FSGT demonstrated at rallies and sports meetings, chanted anti-Nazi slogans, circulated petitions, and took part in committees like the International Committee for the Defence of the Olympic Idea. Indeed, the FSGT—and not without reason—claimed to be the saviour of the true Olympic spirit.

The campaign against the Nazi Olympics took on a new turn in May 1936 when the Spanish Popular Front government offered Barcelona as a place to hold a people's olympics—an "Olimpiada Popular" from 22 to 26 July—as a rival to the fascist festival being held in Berlin less than 2 weeks later. *Sport* and the FSGT waxed lyrical on the advantages of Barcelona over Berlin, from the climate of the Catalan capital to the friendly atmosphere that would be found when workers from around the world came together to compete in fraternity. In the event the FSGT sent the largest delegation, the Soviet Union declined to send anyone, and Franco's military putsch against the Spanish government put an end to the People's Games before they had begun.

The main activity of the FSGT in the first half of 1936, however, was the election campaigns of the Popular Front. Here it put forward a programme for a New Deal for French youth, set out in a 9-point programme and encapsulated in its brochure, "For a Strong, Happy and Healthy Youth." At the same time as it urged massive spending on a national level, the FSGT campaigned on specific local issues relating to the use of existing sports facilities (Murray, 1987b).

At the national level, the FSGT called for compulsory physical education in schools, free medical checks, the training of teachers to meet the new demand, and the creation of sports facilities. It also called on the government to provide money for playing fields, swimming pools, and basic sports facilities throughout France. *Sport* justified the expenditure by pointing to the disgraceful state of health in France, referring specifically to the high incidence of tuberculosis caused by the lack of fresh air in insalubrious working conditions and poor housing, the widespread alcoholism in the absence of suitable leisure choices, and the frightening number of deaths by drowning due to children never being taught how to swim.

At the local level, the FSGT campaigned vigorously for the better use of existing facilities, particularly where professional groups had a monopoly over municipal facilities, and for forcing the Paris municipality to keep down the price of its swimming-pool entry so that all could take advantage of it. It also stopped the Courbevoie Stadium from literally going to the dogs when the right-wing mayor granted a concession to a British entrepreneur to turn it into a greyhound racing track.

Articles and editorials in *Sport* detailed the benefits of the New Deal for French youth, and party militants arranged meetings and conducted door-to-door campaigns. They also lobbied politicians and drew up a list of approved candidates for the coming election, whose names were listed in *Sport*. It could not have been without some sardonic pleasure that the FSGT militants saw most of the bourgeois press fall in behind their campaigns. In this way, the public was being prepared for the acceptance of the widespread reforms of the Popular Front government when it came to power in May 1936.

The first problem faced by the new government was when workers in factories, department stores, and various other enterprises refused to leave their place of employment in a series of "sit-in" strikes that eventually involved over 1 million strikers. While the workers stood their ground against the bosses and a possible lack of resolution by the new leaders, members of the FSGT helped them pass their time usefully by organising games and sport exhibitions. One result of this was a rush of new recruits.

But even as the FSGT was enjoying its greatest successes, the dice were loaded against it on the international scene, and its own international contradictions came into play.

One of the first decisions facing the new government was whether to honour the subsidy granted by the previous government to the athletes going to Berlin. The decision of the new Under-Secretary for Sport and Leisure, Léo Lagrange, a firm believer in the ideals of the FSGT, pleased few people. He reduced the amount for the Berlin athletes to 1 million francs and gave 600,000 francs for the athletes going to Barcelona. The right rose up in indignation against this donation to a political cause, the communists saw it as treachery, the radicals were divided, and the FSGT was forced to accept the reality of the situation.

Unlike the Popular Olympics that ended in tragedy before a single event had been staged, the Berlin Olympics were a triumph for the Nazis (Krüger, 1972). They were not an unqualified success, however, although it could only have been bitter compensation for the FSGT when at the close of the Berlin Olympics, major sections of the French press condemned the Nazi organisation of the games for the very reasons the FSGT had said they should be boycotted (Murray, 1992). The repercussions of events in Germany and Spain were to be felt beyond mere sporting spectacles, and before the world itself paid the price for giving in to fascism, the Popular Front government in France ended in tatters, hopelessly divided by communists on the side of the angels, radicals on the

Programme of the FSGT for the 1936 Elections

Playing Areas (Terrains)

In localities with less than 20,000 inhabitants, each municipality—with the *département* and the state contributing 50%—shall set up and maintain one or several grounds where football and other sports such as running, etc. may be practised, and a gym hall.

Where there is a river or water catchment that makes it practicable, a swimming area shall be constructed.

Where communes have limited resources, these tasks should be carried out by groups of communes.

In those localities where there are more than 20,000 inhabitants, at least one swimming pool shall be constructed.

Free public admission for training will be available two days a week; on the other days and on Sundays the facilities will be shared between all the local societies.

However, in no circumstances will these concessions be granted to societies under the control of professionals or employers.

Subsidies

To assist societies in the construction and upkeep of grounds and buildings, and in the provision of sporting equipment, there will be annual subsidies to the clubs for such expenditure: 20% by the state, 20% by the department, 10% by the commune: this to be granted on presentation by the clubs of the appropriate financial statement.

These subsidies are not to be made available to clubs under the control of professionals or employers.

Committees

We demand the creation of committees with real representation by those using the sporting facilities; these committees will maintain the grounds, halls, etc., and control the subsidies.

The same will apply on the departmental level.

Medical Control

For clubs or societies exercising medical controls over their members, costs involved will be covered as follows: 40% by the state; 40% by the department; 20% by the commune.

Transport

Reduction in costs of group fares of up to 50% of return fare.

Individuals may make the return trip on their own.

Benefits of the group fare to be extended, without additional charge, on express trains and *rapides* for journeys of more than 100 kilometres.

Issue of tickets, on simple request of club, 24 hours before departure.

Suppression of passport for sporting trips abroad.

Unemployed

Free transport for training and competition.

Free access to all grounds, municipal or not, whether for training or for competition.

Soldiers

Same claims as for unemployed.

Free choice of training time each week.

Equipment to be supplied at no cost by the military.

The right to belong to the civil club of one's choice, and to participate in any sports event whatsoever.

Other Matters

Suppression of the cycling tax.

Free transport of bicycles on trains, when accompanied by the rider.

Right to camp on communal grounds and in national domains.

Exoneration from the stamp tax for posters put up by societies or clubs (as exist at present for all societies preparing for the military).

Suppression of all taxes (rights of the poor, public assistance, etc.) on functions organised by any non-professional sporting club, when the highest price of admission is less than 5 francs.

Freedom of societies or federations affiliated with or recognised by the National Sports Council to meet any society they wish, even if it is not affiliated with the CNS.

Retirement of all military officers and instructors in the clubs.

Léo Lagrange

Léo Lagrange was a man of rare integrity who carried into politics an honesty and commitment to "fair play" unusual among his colleagues. As first Under-Secretary for Sport and Leisure in the Popular Front government that came to power in May 1936, he immediately set about putting into practice the platform of the sporting idealists of the left, whose programme was largely adopted—even by the right—after France's poor showing in the 1936 Berlin Olympics (Murray, 1992). His integrity was soon made known to journalists who came for their bribes and found instead that they were shown the door. As a man of the left, he could not escape the scabrous campaigns of the right in this time, but even his most politically motivated opponents had to revise their opinions when he died at the front in 1940, a politician who could as such have escaped the call-up, but chose instead the place of honour.

Lagrange was born into a comfortable bourgeois family in Bourg-sur-Gironde, near Bordeaux in November 1900, but soon after the family moved to Paris, and, in 1905, Léo was enrolled in the Lycée Henri IV, where he would later play for the football team and become a friend of Jean Prévost. Before his 18th birthday he enlisted to serve in the last months of World War I, and, from a radical in the Jacobin tradition of the great French Revolution, he became a pacifist and a socialist. Shortly after he returned to civilian life, he enrolled for a law degree. In 1922, he joined the Paris Bar and began a doctorate in law. Lagrange joined the Socialist Party in January 1921, and, after an unsuccessful attempt to get elected as the socialist candidate for Paris IX in 1928, he was elected deputy for Fourmies in the Nord department in 1932. He was reelected in 1936.

As Under-Secretary for Sport and Leisure in the Popular Front government, Lagrange sought to make available to workers and peasants the advantages of a healthier life that had until then been the privilege of the wealthy. This he did through a series of reforms aimed at encouraging French youth to enjoy the fresh air of the countryside, and those from the countryside to visit the galleries and cultural joys of the cities.

Although a pacifist, he opposed appeasement when he saw that Hitler could be stopped only by force of arms. When hostilities broke out in September 1939, he scorned his right as a parliamentarian to keep out of uniform, enrolled in the army, and was sent to the front, where he was killed by a shell at Evergnicourt on 9 June 1940.

Today there are innumerable swimming pools and sports centres that bear his name, as well they might. Few people have better embodied the highest qualities of fair play, not only in sport but in life.

side of self-interest, and socialists who did not know what to do—and could not even if they had known.

Before the final collapse of the Popular Front, however, Léo Lagrange and the FSGT prepared the way for reforms that would be implemented when the times were more propitious. Lagrange brought the socialists Guillevic and Pierre Marie and the communist Auguste Delaune (later to be associated with more unfortunate circumstances) into his circle of advisers. Together they worked on many aspects of the FSGT programme: encouraging participation rather than spectating by providing cheap sport facilities for the masses rather than fancy facilities for the elite; by making it possible for the poor in the cities to get out into the fresh air of the country, the seaside, and the mountains to hike, swim, and ski; by providing concession tickets on the trains; and by increasing the number of youth hostels. Concerned with more than just the sound body, the new workers' government also offered popular theatre at the Arènes de Lutèce, the cinema of Jean Renoir, cheap entries to the Louvre, and an increased provision of libraries.

In education, the age to leave school was raised, compulsory sport—with free medical checks—was introduced, and three bodies were established to help bring it all to fruition: the National Sports Institute (*Institut National des Sports* [INS]), the Training College for Physical Education (*L'École Nationale Supérieure d'Éducation Physique* [ENSEP]), and a special sport council (*Conseil Supérieure des Sports*). The benefits of much of this were to be in the future and would be a focus of concern after the war for the FSGT. In March 1937, however, the *Brevet Sportif Populaire* was successfully introduced (a certificate of fitness to be awarded to school children who accomplished fairly simple and basic physical skills). It was the first serious attempt to implement some of the programmes that had been in the air before the election of the Popular Front and had become a matter for national concern after France's poor showing in athletics at the Berlin Olympics (Chappat, 1983; Murray, 1992). Although compulsory physical education, free medical checks, and the training of more physical education teachers were soon blocked—only 250 of 6,000 projects were

In the reorganisation of sport in France after the debacle of 1940, two of the socialists who had been prominent in the FSGT, Guillevic and Marie, accepted positions of authority. By accepting such positions, there was always the possibility that they could be exercised against the best interests of the conqueror, but with Guillevic this does not seem to have been the case. On the contrary, he seems to have used it against his one-time colleague, Auguste Delaune. Delaune, a close friend of René Rousseau and former secretary of the FST and the FSGT, escaped to Britain at Dunkirk, but returned to France to continue the fight. He approached Guillevic with the idea of setting up a resistance group through sport, but was repulsed; he resorted to clandestine activity for which he was allegedly denounced by Guillevic. In an escape attempt in August 1943, he was shot by the Vichy police and, while in a hospital with four bullets in his stomach, was tortured to death by the SS. He died at the end of September, the first of several martyrs, such as George André, Grousselot, and other members of the FSGT.

Delaune is credited with founding the first worker sport paper to appear in the resistance. This was *Sport*, which came out from at least September 1943 in mimeograph, produced by "A group of workers' sports leaders" ("*Un groupe de dirigeants sportifs travaillistes*"). At the same time, a "patriotic youth front" was putting out *Sport Libre* in the same style and often the same content, but without the attacks on Guillevic, concentrating instead on targets like *L'Auto* and "Kolonel" Pascot, who took over from the Basque tennis star, Jean Borotra, as *supremo* in the Vichy sport administration in April 1942 (Fieschi, 1983, p. 95ff.). *Sport Libre* seems to have been more successful than the communist-inspired *Sport* and continued into 1944 and after the liberation. In this time, it praised the swimmers who refused to compete in a national championship because Nakache, who had swum for France in the Berlin Olympics, was banned as a Jew, and it set up the example of Belgian sportspeople who went on strike rather than accept Nazi/Rexist-imposed Walloon/Flemish divisions.

With the approach of the invasion, sportsmen and women were urged to form clandestine *Sport Libre* groups within the official bodies. There they were to make life difficult for Vichy by calling for better equipment, stadiums, and swimming pools; in addition to the solidarity this encouraged in the face of the enemy, such demands would form the basis for a reorganisation of sport when the war was over. In the meantime, young French men and women were told how to use sporting events to make protests and demonstrate in favour of the victims of Vichy or the Nazis. One result of this was that while Lorraine was winning the French Cup in May 1944, a full stadium resounded to mass calls on behalf of Etienne Mattler, football hero of the prewar period then imprisoned in a Nazi cell.

realised (Hache, 1985)—it can nevertheless be considered a success.

For the most part, the people's paradise had to be postponed. The workers had gained the right to annual paid holidays—a right they would never give up—and serious inroads were made to reduce the work week to 40 hours. Problems of the economy, the hostility of the right, and the worsening situation in international affairs militated against wholesale implementation of the brave new world of decent living for all that was the aim of the FSGT. Faced by such problems, the Popular Front faded ingloriously from the political scene.

Sectarianism, War, and More Sectarianism

Prior to the outbreak of the Spanish Civil War, the most common slogans to be found around sports events organised by the FSGT were "Free Thälmann" and "Sport rouge"; thereafter, the bulk of the slogans related to "Funds for Spain." This proved to be a cause as forlorn as that of removing the Olympic Games from Germany, and as rich with omens of what was to come.

The fortunes of the FSGT were reflected in the failure of *Sport* to maintain the zest of the first months of 1936. Despite improvements in the paper that augured well for its success, its content became more and more bland as it took on a moral seriousness in the pursuit of its mission to serve the youth of France as a whole, and not just the victims of class exploitation. In 1938, the FSGT celebrated its 30th anniversary, and in an article outlining some of its achievements, it seemed most anxious to "destroy the legend that we are a political organisation." It pointed to its statutes and charter and took pride in being "pioneers of health," one big family committed to the youth of France and working in the general interest (*Sport,* 15 April 1938). In *Sport* the turpitude of bourgeois sport was ignored, to be replaced by tedious accounts of the performances of FSGT teams throughout France. The old moral outrage against the Fascists and Nazis gave way to accounts of unusual sports and how to keep healthy. Even the return to some prominence of Soviet sport was fairly muted.

At Antwerp in late July 1937, the first international worker sport meeting attended by both the RSI and the SWSI was held. In terms of spectators, performances, and receipts at the box office, it was a tremendous success, but it was the Soviet athletes who stole the show. The 170 Spanish athletes were received as heroes, the socialists from the Netherlands who refused to come because of the presence of the RSI were not missed, and the great Czech delegation outnumbered even the Soviets, although it was the latter who broke the most records.

Sport, like most of the workers' press, gave the Soviets superstar treatment, but only the Swiss federation complained about the mania for record performances and full stadiums that were more suited for bourgeois sports (Box & Tolleneer, 1988; Nitsch, 1988; Teichler, 1988). Here was a hint of the future, when the Soviets would enter the Olympic Games with the same fanatical attachment to medals and national honours as their bourgeois opponents.

In June, the same month as France hosted the World Cup in football, the main festivals of the *trentenaire* celebrations were held. The Italians had not changed their fascist approach to sport, and the German team had been swelled by the *Anschluss* of Austria, but not a word of this slipped into the columns of *Sport*. Instead, readers of the July issue could admire the front-page picture of the Soviet and Norwegian soccer team captains from the FSGT tournament shaking hands before the kick-off to their game, an example of sport and worker understanding bridging the barrier of language.

On the more extreme right, the change in emphasis of the FSGT was seen not so much as a sign of flagging enthusiasm as a cunning plot by the communists to lull France into a false sense of security. It was at this time that the CPAS, the employers' organisation, entered the leisure field to win the workers away from such influences. They founded their own tourist organisation, while in the weekly *Élan Social* a regular section on leisure warned how the communists had adopted a new profile, with pleasant and helpful individuals replacing the loud-mouthed propagandists of the past. Readers were warned of how the communists had given up their attacks on the big federations to concentrate on the small clubs. One of their tactics was to join such bourgeois bodies, concealing their political ideals and making themselves indispensable to the club so that it was too late when the club realised it had a viper in its midst (*Élan Social*, 8 December 1938).

The organ of the patronages claimed that the communists, in their well-organised plans to catch the infant in the *creche*, the child at school, and the adolescent through sport, had the bottomless bucket of Kremlin gold at their disposal (*Élan Social*, 24 February 1938). Rousseau's response to this was the rather rueful rejoinder that such claims were untrue, and raised only as a bogey to attract more funds to its own organisation. In fact, *Sport* was beset by even more serious financial troubles than usual at this time, and in his attempts to keep the paper afloat, Rousseau had accepted advertising from various manufacturers, including Suze, the alcoholic drink featured in every French paper at this time. As a result, *Sport* was criticised by its faithful readers, but its ultimate failure was in the insuperable problem of producing a commercially viable paper devoted solely to the narrow interests of worker sport. The year 1936 had been exceptional for news, with the elections, the Olympic Games, and the outbreak of the Spanish Civil War, but *Sport's* success at that time was also because it had gone beyond its class boundaries. This was not to the liking of many readers, and now it was falling into the lure of commercial advertising. Rousseau could never allow his paper to be bought off by the interests of the market, and so he saved the soul of the workers' paper at the cost of its sales.

The period of the Popular Front ended well before the outbreak of what was to become World War II, but it was dealt a conclusive blow with the signing of the Nazi-Soviet pact on 23 August 1939. In the French parliament, deputies denounced the communists, and, in the FSGT, Guillevic demanded that his communist co-workers denounce—under threat of excommunication—the Nazi-Soviet pact. Guillevic, no doubt, had many reasons to distrust the communists, but this was hardly a sporting gesture, and he would fall into further ignominy in the years ahead.

After the liberation, *Sport Libre* (later *Sports*) came out as the first of the revived sports papers, and when the problems of paper shortage were solved after the war, this was the best produced of the three sports papers of that time (Meyer, 1978). It was under the control of the communist party, claiming somewhat misleadingly to have been the sole sports paper to have come out in the Resistance and attributing its paternity to Auguste Delaune. Its director was René Rousseau, who backed up his long experience with a wide range of skilled journalists. Despite being the best presented of the sports papers, it came to a sudden end in 1948, a victim of the twin-tongued serpent of sectarianism and international politics.

The communist party emerged from the war with its pride restored as a result of its dominant role in the Resistance, and this was recognised in its success at the polls. The party took up in the spirit of the Popular Front before eventually falling back into that of the sectarian '20s, with the FSGT trying to recapture the heady days of the reforms of Léo Lagrange, now recognised as a hero by more than the left as a result of his death at the front in 1940. The FSGT called for a national reorganisation of sport, and, in a letter of 9 October 1944, asked the CNS to convoke its National Assembly. Nothing came of it. At its own National Congress in mid-1945, the FSGT proposed a series of reforms, most of which went back to those of the Popular Front, but calling, in addition, for the creation of a laic Republican Sports Federation that would lead the way as the "Federation of the Future" (FSGT, 1981).

Overwhelmingly communist, but inspired by the greater vision of the immediate postwar years, the FSGT, at its National Congress of 1946, continued to call for a complete reform of sport in France. It took up the 1938 slogan of being the "pioneers of health" and attacked the provisional government for various retrograde steps: tardiness in nominating a Director of Physical Education and Sport, cutting by half the subsidies to the sporting federations and societies, imposing a luxury tax of 18 percent on sporting goods, and banning *Sport Libre* and the sporting editions of the big dailies (FSGT, 1981, p. 16ff.).

As in the heyday of the Popular Front, the FSGT was revealing a grand vision at the same time as it addressed specific details. Again it was to fall victim to politics. In addition to calling for the democratisation of sport, the FSGT called for universal peace. What this meant in practice was not only the denunciation of the colonial wars in which the French government was engaged, but also a suspicion of all things American and a glass-eyed acceptance of all that came out of the Soviet Union. By 1948, politics was ruling—and overruling—the many fine projects the FSGT had put forward since 1944.

From 1944 to 1947, the PCF had collaborated in the tripartite government with the socialists and the moderate, catholic *Mouvement Republicain Populaire* (MPR). In May 1947, the socialist Ramadier sacked the communists in cabinet as part of a move by the middle against the two extremes. In the same year, the containment of communism by the Truman doctrine and the Marshall Plan coincided with Stalin's condemnation of communists "collaborating" in bourgeois governments. The communists, and so the FSGT, were back to the days of class against class; as always, they were in the thrall of Moscow. One of the first victims in the new Cold War was *Sports*. In Yugoslavia, Tito was making life difficult for Stalin by refusing to do what he was told, and when France played Yugoslavia in an international football match, politics decreed that it was a non-event. That was not how the public saw it, and *Sports* became a non-newspaper (Meyer, 1978, p. 125).

In 1951, the small socialist minority seceded from the FSGT to found the *Union des Sports Travaillistes* (UST), dedicated to the memory of Léo Lagrange, but it was never to be a major force. In 1952, the government subsidy to the FSGT was withdrawn. That same year, the Soviet Union entered the wide world of bourgeois sport when it took part in the Helsinki Olympics.

The Olympics, the Soviet Union, and the Problems of Prosperity

For 10 years after 1952, the FSGT, deprived of funds from the state, entered a period of introspection before returning after 1962 to the world that was opening up with hitherto unthought of wealth at the disposal of ordinary people. It was also the time of the various cultural revolutions that saw women, blacks, and other groups with grievances against prevailing prejudice successfully fight for more recognition. Throughout this time, the FSGT built on the work begun with the creation of institutions to further physical education in 1937-38, and it encouraged its members to devote more time and study to the philosophical basis of health and physical education. The work of educationalists—such as Jean Guimier and Maurice Baquet, and Robert Mérand and René Deleplace—came to fruition in 1968 with the creation of the *Conseil Pédagogique et Scientifique* (CPS) of the FSGT (Meynaud, 1966; Moustard, 1983).

In this context, the FSGT could still pursue its goals of making available "all sports to all people," fighting for the disadvantaged wherever they were (although, given the nature of things, this was no longer a specifically "working-class" appeal because it now included minority groups), and a greater emphasis on women's sport, the older age groups, and the physically disadvantaged. But there were significant changes. There was more emphasis on a "climate of success," and a willingness to measure the health of the nation by its sporting performances. The Soviet Union, whatever it preached, had never practised the principles of worker sport as put forward by the FSGT in the 1930s. Now the FSGT was prepared to accept competition, records, and individual performance, encouraging rather than dismissing elitism. Whereas before all changes had to come from the base up, now it was decided that significant change could come from the superstructure; certainly each could work on the other.

Despite the emphasis on science rather than slogans from the 1950s, and the allowance for the changes in regard to the greater prosperity that made the working class more difficult to define, much of the change within the FSGT seems to have been due to its relationship with the Soviet Union. Certainly the FSGT could claim that it was not restricted to communists and that there were more communists in other sports bodies than in the FSGT, but the coincidences of Soviet policy and FSGT practice were too close to be ignored. In 1952, the Soviet Union entered the Olympic Games, and soon the vast Soviet republic was challenging the equally vast federal republic across the ocean. The satellites of the Soviet Union, East Germany in particular, entered the Olympics with great success, successes which were hollowly trumpeted as proving the superiority of the regime that underpinned them—in the case of the GDR, medal success was serving rather as a reflection of its depravity. The FSGT, previously a supporter of "olympism" but critical of the Olympics, became one of the most whole-hearted supporters of the Olympic Games.

The FSGT did not deny its political inspiration in the postwar period, but it did try to avoid overemphasising a sport that was neither neutral nor purely political. In the 1950s, it could denounce the butchery being carried out in the name of French colonialism as not only barbaric but also as a wasteful deployment of funds that could be better spent on health or sports facilities. The problems of the Palestinians, the Cubans, and even the IRA could be assured a ready ear at the FSGT, but the problem of apartheid, the most outrageous example of political exploitation in sport since the Nazi regime, was comparatively neglected. Perhaps this was seen as a more "British" problem; certainly it was not ignored, but neither was it one of the prime concerns of the Soviet Union or the FSGT.

Support for the Soviet Union by the FSGT became most obvious when the United States and those of its acolytes it could pressure to follow suit decided to boycott the 1980 Moscow Olympics on the purely political grounds that the Soviet Union had invaded Afghanistan. Suddenly the high priests of protest against mixing politics with sport were finding that practice to their own convenience, while the Soviet Union and the FSGT came out as the champions of the Olympic Games (Brohm, 1981; FSGT, 1981).

In the 1936 boycott campaign, the FSGT and the worker sport movement in general could reasonably claim to be the true upholders of the Olympic spirit. By the 1970s, the Olympics themselves, by accepting women, blacks, and people of all political persuasions, could be said to be incorporating the spirit of free and open competition for all that was part of the Games ethic. A less dogmatic attitude toward amateurism meant that more people of restricted means could enter, although the floodgates of commercialism were also opened. The FSGT of the 1970s, however, did show an attitude different from the 1930s in its nationalism and what could be seen as a bourgeois emphasis on competition. In 1964, the FSGT even rejected as "retrograde" any measures to remove team sports, national banners, and anthems; to reducing the number of competitions; and generally to bring the games back to some simplicity (Hache, 1985, p. 80ff.). Whatever the degree of dependence of the FSGT on the Soviet Union, both had evolved over the years beyond their—and from many points of view, understandably so—narrow interests. The Soviet Union, however, was incapable of changing fast enough, and its dogmatic and overcentralised past caught up with it when reform turned into collapse.

Long before the collapse of the Soviet Union, both the victory of the Socialist Party and the election of socialist president François Mitterrand to power meant that the FSGT once more had a government in place whose ideas were basically the same as its own (Hache, 1985). By then, however, the world that had made a worker sport movement necessary no longer existed. Although the Soviet Union is gone, the FSGT still has a role to play, as has any organisation committed to the disadvantaged. That this is within the structure of existing society is less the betrayal of a past ideal than a measure of both's continuing maturity.

References

Arnaud, P. (ed.). *Les origines du sport ouvrier en Europe* (Paris, 1994).

Box, E. & Tolleneer, J. "'Hinter unserer Olympiade steckt ein anderer Gedanke.' Die III. Arbeiter-Olympiade Antwerpen 1937," *Soz. & Zeitgesch.* Sp. 2 (1988), 1, 28-42.

Brohm, J. M. "Les jeux de la honte," *Quel Corps?* vol. 7 (February 1981), no. 17/18, pp. 68-85.

Brohm, J.-M. *1936. Jeux Olympiques à Berlin* (Brussels, 1983).

Chappat, J.-L. *Les chemins de l'espoir, ou les combats de Léo Lagrange* (Paris, 1983).

The Communist International. No. 14, 8 April 1937, 579.

Delétang, B. "Le mouvement sportif ouvrier," *Éducation Physique et Sportive* (1980), No. 177, 178, 180.

Dubech, L. *Où va le sport?* (Paris, 1932).

Dubreuil, B. "La naissance du sport catholique," in: A. Ehrenberg (ed.), *Aimez-vous les stades?* (Recherches No. 43) (Paris, 1980), pp. 221-251.

Ehrenberg, A. "Notes sur le sport rouge," in: A. Ehrenberg (ed.), *Aimez-vous les stades?* (Recherches No. 43) (Paris, 1980), pp. 75-80.

Élan Social. 1938.

Fieschi, J.-T. *Histoire du sport français de 1870 à nos jours* (Paris, 1983).

FSGT (ed.). *René Rousseau, Maurice Baquet. Deux vies, deux dirigeants, deux exemples* (Paris, 1965).

FSGT (ed.). *De Moscou à Los Angeles. Olympis e et sport des travailleurs progressons ensemble* (Paris, 1981).

Gay-Lescot, J.-L. *Sport et Éducation sous Vichy. 1940-1944* (Lyon, 1991).

Hache, F. "Der Arbeitersport in Frankreich. Zwei Wendepunkte 1936 und 1981," in: A. Krüger & J. Riordan (eds.), *Der internationale Arbeitersport. Der Schlüssel zum Arbeitersport in Zehn Ländern* (Köln, 1985), pp. 64-84.

Hoberman, J.M. *Sport and Political Ideology* (London, 1984).

Holt, R. *Sport and Society in Modern France* (London, 1981).

Kidd, B. "The Popular Front and the 1936 Olympics," *Can. J. Hist. Sp. & Phys. Ed.*, 11 (1980), 1, 1-18.

Krüger, A. *Die Olympischen Spiele 1936 und die Weltmeinung* (Berlin, 1972).

MacAloon, J.J. *This Great Symbol. Pierre de Coubertin and the Origins of the Modern Olympics* (Chicago, 1981).

Margadent, T.W. "Primary Schools and Youth Groups in Pre-War Paris: Les Petites A's," *J. Contemp. Hist.*, 3 (1978), 2, 323-336.

Marie, P. *Pour le sport ouvrier* (Paris, 1934).

Meyer, G. *Les tribulations d'un journaliste sportif* (Paris, 1978).

Meynaud, J. *Sport et politique* (Paris, 1966).

Murray, W.J. "Sport and Politics in France in the 1930s: The Workers' Sports Federations on the Eve of the Popular Front," in: W. Vamplew (ed.), *Sport, Nationalism and Internationalism* (ASSH Studies in Sport History No. 2) (Adelaide, 1987a), pp. 32-90.

Murray, W.J. "The French Workers' Sports Mouvement and the Victory of the Popular Front in 1936," *Int. J. Hist. Sport*, 4 (1987b), 2, 203-230.

Murray, W.J. "France, Coubertin, and the Berlin Olympics: The Response," *Olympika. The Int. J. of Olympic Studies*, 1 (1992), 1, 46-69.

Moustard, R. *Le sport populaire* (Paris, 1983).

Nitsch, F. "Die III. Arbeiter-Olympiade 1937 in Antwerpen," *Soz. & Zeitgesch.* Sp. 2 (1988), 1, 10-27.

Pépin, E. "Comment le sport travailliste fut crée," *Sport*, June 15, 1938.

Renaitour, J.-M. *Vive le sport* (Paris, 1934).

Seidler, E. *Le sport et la presse* (Paris, 1964).

Sport. 1933-1939.

Sport. Sept. 1943-May 1944 (Bibliothèque Nationale, Paris).

Sport Libre. Sept. 1943-May 1944 (Bibliothèque Nationale, Paris).

Sports. 1946-1948.

Teichler, H.J. "Die Berichterstattung des deutschen Generalkonsulats über die III. Arbeiter-Olympiade," *Soz. & Zeitgesch.* Sp. 2 (1988), 1, 43-54.

Trist, S. *Le patronat face à la question des loisirs ouvriers: avant 1936 et après.* (Le mouvement social No. 150) (Paris, 1990).

Wheeler, R.F. "Organized Sport and Organized Labour: The Workers' Sport Movement," *J. Contemp. Hist.*, 3 (1978), 2, 191-210.

Chapter 3

Worker Sport Within a Worker State: The Soviet Union

James Riordan

SOVIET UNION

In 1931, the Eurasian multiracial state covered an area of 21,253,100 km^2 with a population of 161.23 million.

Although Czarist Russia never lost its agrarian character, it experienced increasing industrialisation after 1890 because of railway construction, a policy of protective duties, and growing foreign loans. This, in turn, created a huge industrial workforce predominantly employed in large-scale urban enterprises. The discontent of this workforce over dismal living conditions, which was further incited by numerous—mainly Marxist-orientated—revolutionary groups, the peasants' wish for land, and the growing resistance of the national minorities to the pressure of Russification, found its outlet in the revolutionary events of 1905 that caused the Czar to grant extensive civil rights. The quickly developing split between the bourgeois groups and the radical labour movement led by the Bolsheviks proffered the opportunity to rescind most of the important concessions. The home situation was once again characterised by growing tensions when the Czarist Empire entered World War I.

In 1917, military defeats and a catastrophic economic situation provoked a general workers' and soldiers' rebellion in Petrograd that culminated in the abdication of the Czar and the institution of a bourgeois government. Unwilling and unable to fulfil the wishes of a war-weary population for a rapid peace agreement and a drastic alteration in the social status quo, this government soon found itself on the defensive against the soviets (councils) made up of worker and soldier deputies that managed to gather the masses behind them the more the Bolsheviks took over the leading positions and, accordingly, the more they worked with the Leninist slogans of "Peace at Any Price" and "All Land to the Peasants." This development enabled the Bolsheviks to overthrow the government on 7 November 1917 and to prevail with their claim to absolute power against the more moderate left-wing parties.

The enemies of the Bolsheviks, supported by intervention forces of bourgeois states, launched an armed struggle against the monopolisation of power and the determination of the new government led by Lenin to begin the socialist transformation of Russian society. The civil war lasted until 1921. The conflict allowed the liquidation of secessionist efforts by Ukrainians, Georgians, and others. However, for the rapid construction of a state that acted as the sole producer and distributor of goods via a centrally directed administration, it provided the worst of all conceivable frameworks. As a consequence of the growing discontent over the deteriorating food supply, only inadequately softened by the rapid installation of a system of social security, the communists were forced, at Lenin's command, to announce a "New Economic Policy" (NEP) that would allow private economic initiatives during an interim period.

After Stalin, who was supported by the party bureaucracy, had been able to settle the inner-party disputes over the successor to Lenin (after 1924) and had established the "construction of socialism in one country" as the paramount task, the NEP, which had been very successful in improving the general supply situation, was declared finished. It was replaced by a policy of strict economic order, enhanced industrialisation, and the general collectivisation of agriculture. The new policy succeeded in developing the Soviet Union as a leading industrial power and in generating revolutionary changes at all social levels. This happened, however, at the cost of a stagnating standard of living and the physical liquidation of whole social groups, such as the free peasants (*kulaks*).

The population shouldered the burden because the further development of the Stalinist system of power based on arbitrary terror made any organised resistance impossible. Outside of the party apparatus, the terror was greatest within the ranks of the Red Army. The loss of its most competent officers was largely responsible for the military setbacks after the German attack of 1941. Nevertheless, the Red Army was ultimately responsible for the defeat of National Socialist Germany and the accompanying rise of the Soviet Union to its position as the world's second superpower.

The notion of worker sport within a worker state clearly differs from that of an oppositional sport movement within capitalism. Yet a study of the worker sport movement in Russia and the Soviet Union reveals moments apposite to the world movement. In the first place, worker oppositional sport existed prior to the October 1917 Revolution and laid its imprint on later Soviet attitudes to sport. Secondly, the early Soviet experiments in creating a new proletarian sports system are of interest in any comparative analysis. Finally, the involvement of the Communist International (Comintern) with the worldwide communist sports organisation, Red Sport International, affected the attitudes of all communist and social-democrat workers to sport and politics between the two world wars.

Russian Worker Sport Before 1917

In the west it had been the industrialists who inspired a large-scale sports movement based on the growing urban population. Having usurped the economic power of the aristocracy, the new middle classes undermined its political power and social influence, thereby transforming the social structure and introducing a new state ideology and a new pattern of culture (including sport) reflecting that new ideology.

In Russia, although urbanisation created the need for an urban pattern of recreation that differed radically from the casual, open-air, and largely unorganised rural pattern, an evolution based on the western model did not take place. That is not to say that the development of organised sport was altogether unaffected by the Russian bourgeoisie; in fact, many of the new sports clubs were set up and run by them. But just as the drive for capitalist industrialisation in Russia came predominantly from foreigners and the Russian state, so the pioneering drive in Russian sport came largely from those directions as well. The most enduring impact on the sports movement was the extensive foreign community resident in Russia. Not only did the bulk of sports then popular in their native countries come to Russia with these foreigners, the sports also served as a bond among immigrants of different nationalities: Germans, English, Scots, Belgians, and French.

Given the lack of a forceful, pioneering bourgeois influence on Russian sport, the workers themselves might have shown the way. But the outmoded social structure found little room for concessions to worker pressures for recreational facilities or a pattern of sport that reflected

Comintern and Red Sport International

The third Communist International (Comintern), set up in Moscow in March 1919, was, in intention, a single political party of which all worldwide communist parties were to be only "sections," adjusting their policies to a world revolutionary strategy determined in Moscow. Until the rise of fascism, the overall policy was for communists to prepare themselves for the overthrow of their governments and, simultaneously, to persuade those governments to maintain good relations with the Soviet Union. The Comintern was abolished in March 1943. Under Comintern tutelage, the International Association of Red Sports and Gymnastics Associations (better known as Red Sport International [RSI]) was formed in Moscow in July 1921. Its founding members were worker sport organisations from eight countries: Czechoslovakia, Finland, France, Germany, Hungary, Italy, Soviet Russia, and Sweden. The RSI was formed partly to counterbalance the social-democratic Socialist Worker Sports International, set up in 1920. RSI statutes stated: "The RSI embraces all worker and peasant sports organisations which support the proletarian class struggle. . . . Physical culture, gymnastics, games and sport are a means of proletarian class struggle, not an end in themselves."

Comintern poster by S.V. Ivanov, 1921.

The Soviets

By 1904, when war with Japan broke out, Russia was in ferment. On 9 January 1905, at least 200 peaceful demonstrators were shot dead outside the Winter Palace in St. Petersburg ("Bloody Sunday"). The unrest culminated in a general strike that paralysed the Russian empire from 7 to 17 October 1905. The strike movement was led by a *soviet* or council, that began as a central coordinating strike committee and developed into the spokesman for the entire revolutionary labour movement. By 1917, soviets existed in all major cities, in army units, and in the countryside; they formed an alternative popular government to the official regime. Upon the Bolshevik coup of 25 October 1917, the All-Russia Congress of Soviets of Worker, Soldier, and Peasant Deputies set up the Council of People's Commissars, headed by Lenin, to rule the country.

Worker sport groups were often created by the soviets in order to train workers in paramilitary skills, such as rifle shooting, unarmed combat, bomb throwing, and drill.

the needs of urban workers. Moreover, the high entrance fees and amateur regulations of existing clubs were often prohibitive for the urban poor. There was more than a hint of class contempt to justify the prevailing social apartheid in sport that kept workers out of the middle-class foreign clubs and tournaments. Consequently, they tended to organise independently of such institutions— just as they organised politically in the worker councils or soviets—in factory *druzhiny* (fraternities) and *dikie* (outlaw) groups.

The first worker sport clubs came into being at the same time as, and often under the umbrella of, the soviets during the 1905 revolutionary upsurge and general strike. The first soviet was formed at Orekhevo-Zuyevo, an industrial settlement 100 km east of Moscow; it is not surprising that it set up its own Worker Sports Club a year later (Perel, 1958, p. 5). Many of the worker sport clubs and fraternities were accused by the authorities of engaging in military and subversive training under the guise of sport. The *druzhiny* at the Obukhov Works in the capital of St. Petersburg, for example, would meet on Sundays on the banks of the Neva River and row to a deserted spot where the members could practice hand grenade and bomb throwing, unarmed and armed combat, wrestling, fencing, and military drills (Sinitsyn, 1953, p. 127). Members of the Worker Boxing Club in Rostov,

formed in 1905, also practised shooting revolvers and are said to have studied Marxist writings (Novoselov, 1950, p. 67). Similar clubs existed in factories in Moscow, Kharkov, Oryol, and the textile town of Ivanovo-Vozesensk; besides organised sports and semiclandestine training, they also included Russian folk games like *lapta* (similar to baseball) and *gorodki* (rather like skittles) in their programme.

The inability, and often unwillingness, of the tsarist authorities, the industrialists, and the church to take measures to strike a balance between the needs of the people and the availability of resources and institutions to meet those needs tended to widen the gulf between them and the urban workers. It also served to establish a dual power in the sport movement between the unregistered worker sport clubs and the official sport organisation. As a consequence, most workers were not integrated into the system through the medium of games controlled by the bourgeoisie and imbued with their values (as was to happen in Britain, for example). The unregistered worker sport clubs rapidly took on political overtones as a result of their semiclandestine nature.

The regime's failure to adequately meet the mounting needs of the urban populace for appropriate recreation may well have contributed to its demise in 1917. The British diplomat Robert Bruce Lockhart, who was in Russia during World War I, wrote that had British entrepreneurs been able to spread the passion for playing soccer more quickly in Russia, the Whites might have won on the playing fields of Moscow what they lost in the Reading Room of the British Museum (a reference to Karl Marx). He regarded the introduction of soccer by British industrialists and workers then resident in Russia as "an immense step forward in the social life of the Russian workers and, if it had been adopted rapidly for all mills, history might have been changed" (Lockhart, 1964, pp. 173-174).

Lockhart may be excused his British public-school enthusiasm for the power of sport to change the course of history, but there is little doubt that the prerevolutionary nature of Russian sport certainly predisposed the Bolshevik leaders to a functional, utilitarian, and politicised use of sport in the new worker state after the revolution. They were helped in this by inheriting a ready-made state organisation of sport that dispensed with the need to dismantle a wide-ranging structure of autonomous clubs and associations.

Initial Theorising and Experimenting After 1917

When the Bolsheviks seized power in October 1917, they found the country on the verge of collapse. Civil war

Poster advertising women's worker sport, 1935.

"Preparing for the World *Spartakiad*" in Moscow, 1934. Note Adolf Hitler and a capitalist cowering in the bottom left corner.

Worker "sport" training at a stadium in Moscow, early 1920s.

and foreign intervention accelerated and intensified the radical transformation of the country. The Bolsheviks were at war, and centralised control in the interests of war production between 1917 and 1921 was an obvious recourse.

It was against this background of war and cataclysmic events that the new sport system had to be introduced. The first steps were by no means obvious, for there was no pattern to follow. The switch from criticising capitalist institutions and sport structure to practical action in a semifeudal, 80 percent peasant country in the throes of civil war, however, presented enormous problems. What of the past was valid and useful? Was the bourgeois legacy a cancer that had to be cut out of the Russian body to make it healthy? Or, could the best of bourgeois practice be adapted to serve the requirements of the young proletarian state? Was there any social value in attempts to achieve top-class results and break records? These were the types of questions that were debated, often furiously, during the years immediately after the revolution.

Essentially, sport during 1917-1921 was geared to the war effort. The entire sports structure was handed over to the Central Board of Universal Military Training (*Vsevobuch*) which took control of all sports clubs and amenities and was responsible for the physical training of all people of recruitment (18-40) and prerecruitment (16-17) age.

This militarisation of sport led to the requisitioning of sports equipment from the existing sports clubs, and this, in turn, led to clashes with club organisers, many of whom maintained that sport should be apolitical and not used as a political or military weapon. As a result of this opposition, many sports clubs were looked upon as pockets of potential or actual counterrevolution; they were assimilated, like the old pan-slavist Sokol clubs, or forcibly disbanded, like the Boy Scout troops and the Jewish Maccabi clubs. *Vsevobuch* was given the task of "eliminating all bourgeois sports organisations and purging the sports and gymnastics clubs of all class enemies" (*Vestnik militsionnoi armii*, 1920).

At the end of 1918, *Vsevobuch* had trained 2 million people and formed 350 sport clubs based on places of work (Starovoitova, 1969, p. 40). To mark its first anniversary on 25 May 1919, it held a parade in Moscow's Red Square, reviewed by the Bolshevik leader, Vladimir Lenin; that parade is today regarded as the forerunner of the great sporting parades that were to become characteristic of Soviet festivals. In line with the policy of combining military drills and weapon handling with political and general education, as well as instruction in elementary hygiene, it was decided in 1920 to coordinate the activities of *Vsevobuch* with those of the Commissariats of Health and Education.

Having inherited a country with an inclement climate, whose population was overwhelmingly illiterate, where vital statistics (infantile mortality, birth rates, morbidity rates, and average life expectancy) tended to be far worse than those of western industrial states in 1900, where disease and starvation were common, and where most people had only the most rudimentary knowledge of hygiene, the Soviet leaders appreciated that it would take a radical economic and social transformation to substantially alter the situation. But time was short, and able-bodied and disciplined men and women were vital, first for the country's survival, then for its recovery from the ravages of war and revolution, for industrial recovery, and for defence against further probable attacks.

Regular participation in recreation was to be both one relatively inexpensive but effective means of improving health standards rapidly and a channel by which to educate people in hygiene, nutrition, and exercise. There was a health policy campaign during the Civil War under the slogans, "Help the Country with a Toothbrush," "Help the Country by Washing in Cold Water," "Help the Country by Observing the Dry [Prohibition] Law," and "Physical Culture 24 Hours a Day," meaning that "people should work, rest and sleep properly, observe the rules of hygiene and strengthen their organisms" (Semashko, 1926, p. 14). With the influx of millions of peasants into the cities, bringing with them rural habits, the significance of health through physical exercise took on a new dimension.

The ignorance that was the cause of so much disease, starvation, and misery—and hampered both military effectiveness and labour productivity—was combated by a far-reaching programme of recreation and sport. If the material facilities were lacking, then people were urged to make full use of "the sun, air, water and natural movement—the best proletarian doctors" (Podvoisky, 1919, p. 41). The therapeutic value of physical exercise was, for example, widely advertised in the intermittent, 3-day anti-TB campaigns. Moreover, it was not thought incongruous to put out a poster, ostensibly advertising physical culture, featuring a young man with a rifle and toothbrush above the caption, "Clean Your Teeth. Clean Your Rifle" (not with the toothbrush, of course!). But sport was not confined to improving *physical* health; it was regarded as vital for *social* health, for combating antisocial and anti-Soviet behaviour in town and country. If the urban youth especially could be persuaded to engage in regular physical exercise, they might develop healthy bodies *and* minds.

The Ukrainian Party Central Committee issued a resolution in 1926 expressing the hope that "physical culture would become a vehicle of the new life . . . a means of isolating young people from the baneful influence of the

Lenin and Sport

Vladimir Lenin (real name Ulyanov, 1870-1924) was the Bolshevik leader who became head of the first Soviet government.

"Young people especially need to have a zest for living and be in good spirits. Healthy sport—gymnastics, swimming, hiking, all manner of physical exercise—should be combined as much as possible with a variety of intellectual interests, study, analysis, and investigation. . . . A healthy mind in a healthy body!" (V.I. Lenin, *Polnoye sobranie sochineniy,* vol. 2, pp. 85-86).

Poster commemorating the 50th anniversary of the October revolution.

"The physical education of the younger generation is an essential element in the overall system of communist upbringing of young people, aimed at creating harmoniously developed people, creative citizens of communist society. Today, physical education also has direct practical aims: to prepare young people for work and to prepare them for military defence of Soviet power" (Resolution of the third All-Russia Congress of the Russian Young Communist League [at which Lenin spoke]).

"It is our urgent task to draw working women into sport. . . . If we can achieve that and get them to make full use of the sun, water and fresh air for fortifying themselves, we shall bring an entire revolution to the Russian way of life" (Lenin, quoted in N.I. Podvoisky, *Rabotnitsa i fizicheskaya kultura*, 1938, p. 3).

street, home-made liquor, and prostitution" (Landar, 1972, p. 13). The role assigned sport in the countryside was even more ambitious: It was "to play a major part in the campaign against drunkenness and uncivilised behaviour. . . . In the fight to transform the village, sport is to be a medium of the new way of life, a means of combating religion and natural calamities" (Landar, 1972). Sport stood for clean living, progress, good health, and rationality, and sport was regarded as an effective instrument to implement party policies.

The health-through-sport campaign could only be effective, in the opinion of *Vsevobuch* chief Nikolai Podvoisky, if the emotional attraction of *competitive* sport were to be utilised to the full—and this was at a time when "competition" and "sport" had become negative words. Certainly a number of educationalists, as we shall see later in this chapter, regarded competitive sport as debasing physical culture and inculcating nonsocialist

mores. Nonetheless, competitive sport and contests began to be organised from the bottom upwards, culminating in the All-Russia Pre-Olympiads of 1920. These were to set the stage for a national festival of sport timed to coincide with the Second Congress of the Third International (19 July through 7 August 1920). In honour of the latter, 18,000 people participated in a vast gymnastics and sports display at the new Red Stadium (formerly the Moscow River Yacht Club). The star attraction of the programme was the first Soviet international soccer match between a Russian team and foreign delegates at the congress.

Pre-Olympiads were held simultaneously in Omsk, Yekaterinburg (later Sverdlovsk), and Tashkent. The Tashkent games, which were given the prestigious title of the "First Central Asian Olympics," lasted for 10 days early in October 1920. As many as 3,000 people took part, mostly natives of Turkestan. The games included a variety of sports but, because the organised sports of Europe and North America were mostly unknown, the participants largely confined themselves to their national games. At the final ceremony, the athletes put on a display of gymnastics and folk dancing (Sholomitsky, 1964, p. 90). The significance of the sports festival in Turkestan for the Soviet national policy of the time may be judged by the fact that this was the first time in the history of Central Asia that Uzbeks, Kazakhs, Turkmenians, Kirgiz, Tadzhiks, and other local peoples, as well as Russians, Ukrainians, and Belorussians, had competed together in any sports event (and, for the first time, Moslem women also competed). As was made clear later, the authorities saw sport as a means to integrate the diverse peoples of the old Russian Empire into the new Soviet state: "The integrative functions of sport are enormous. This has great importance for our multinational state in that sport helps to cement the friendship of Soviet peoples" (*Sport v SSSR,* 1973, p. 9). Besides national integration, these and other sports competitions and festivals were also explicitly intended to further women's social emancipation through sport.

In principle, the fate of the Civil War and foreign intervention was determined by early 1921. The new state was now to enter a period of restoration and reconstruction. The end of the period of hostilities also saw the demise of *Vsevobuch* because it had outlived its usefulness. The military organisation of sports activity was no longer necessary in peacetime, and new methods had to be found that would be more in tune with the new social conditions.

The Physical Culture Versus Sport Debate of the 1920s

Just as in other fields of endeavour, sport in the 1920s was a constant subject for discussion. Controversy raged over the role of sport in a worker state and over its organisational structure as various groups contended for influence. The period, known as NEP—the New Economic Policy—was to see a completely new sport structure; the involvement of trade unions in its organisation; disputes over theory and practice involving the Young Communist League (*Komsomol*), the party, the old *Vsevobuch* leaders, the "hygienists," *Proletkultists,* and other leftist groups; and the promotion of international sports contacts.

These were the years of *physical culture* rather than sport. Competitive sport bred, in some people's minds, attitudes alien to socialism. They frowned upon the record-breaking mania of contemporary sport in the west, and

---

The New Economic Policy

The effects of the policy of "War Communism," combined with the destruction and chaos of 7 years of war, soon showed themselves in every aspect of life. Late in February 1921, Lenin submitted to the party's Central Committee a project for a new economic policy, later to be known as NEP. NEP signified, in essence, a major concession to the vast peasant majority (Russia at this time was an 80 percent peasant country) as the price of retaining power. The state retained what Lenin called the "commanding heights" of the economy, primarily the largest industrial installations, but it permitted private trade and some private production. Until 1928, by which time the economy was more or less back on its feet, there was no basic change in this mixture of competing economies.

Just as in other fields of endeavour, in sport this was a time of constant debate. Controversy raged over its role in a worker state. These were the years of *physical culture* rather than *sport*, the dividing line between the two being the presence of an element of competition: "Sport begins where the struggle for victory begins" (*Fizkultura i sport*, 1971, no. 1, p. 1).

---

they favoured noncommercialised forms of recreation that dispensed with grandstands and spectators. Doubts were cast on the social value of competitive sport, and, above all, on attempts to attain top-level results that were considered an unjustified drive to break records based on false ambitions. They charged that competitive sport distorted the "eternal ideals" of physical culture, that, instead of being universal, it led to narrow specialisation and was detrimental to health; it encouraged commercialism, demoralisation, and professionalism.

Competitive sport, it was alleged, diverted attention from the basic aim of providing recreation for the masses; it turned them into passive onlookers. Such were the views of those often influential persons who dominated the thinking on sport during the 1920s. One notion that all those working within a Marxist approach agreed upon, however, was that all work in this, as in other fields, should be subordinate to the goal of the ultimate achievement of a communist society. The question posed was: How can physical culture be employed most effectively to help secure the goals of the proletarian state? The answers to this question differed because of interest and ideological conflicts.

Members of the "agitational" team in Red Square before their ride to Leipzig to mark the 1928 Workers *Spartakiad* in Moscow.

"Young Pioneer Camp Is a Health School for the Bolshevik Reserves," 1933.

Russian friends at the inauguration of the Federation School in Leipzig, 1926. The banner reads "Workers of the World Unite. Greetings from Soviet Physical Culturists."

When the Civil War ended, a number of administrative futures were open to sport: it could remain under the aegis of *Vsevobuch* and retain a quasimilitary role, or it could be supervised by a civilian agency, a government body, the *Komsomol*, or the trade unions. Worker clubs or other cultural organisations could take over responsibility for sport. It could have either a central agency or several autonomous centres. Because of the lack of clear guidance from the party, the immediate result was, by later standards, rather chaotic as various groups jostled for position.

Vsevobuch

This military organisation now became a sports club specifically for the armed forces. For its headquarters, it was given the premises of the Moscow Ski Club and, in 1928,

it was renamed the Central House of the Red Army (it later became the Central Sports Club of the Army).

Vsevobuch also provided the nucleus for the organisation of other military or paramilitary sports organisations. For example, the *Dinamo* Sports Club was set up in 1923 on the initiative of Felix Dzerzhinsky, then head of the internal security agency. It was initially confined to border guards, internal troops, and the staff of the All-Russia Extraordinary Commission for Combating Counterrevolution and Sabotage (the *Cheka* which, in 1922, became the GPU and, in 1924, OGPU, later NKVD, and finally the KGB). As such, it had a strict training programme for service personnel. In addition to training such personnel, *Dinamo* gradually began to function as a normal sports society open to all service personnel of the internal security agency, border guards, internal troops, families of the members, and auxiliary staff.

With the substantial resources of the armed forces and the security agency, the army clubs and *Dinamo*, respectively, were able to command considerable sports facilities, and they became the largest sports organisations not only in the USSR but, until recently, in all other communist countries as well. This underlines the close relationship between sport and military training throughout Russian and Soviet history.

It is nonetheless true to say that in the "breathing space" between Civil War and the industrialisation drive of the late 1920s, sport had less association with the military than at any other time in Soviet history. The dismantling of the *Vsevobuch* and the handing of sport administration over to "civilian" bodies were accompanied, and partly motivated, by a certain antimilitarist feeling among both ordinary people, exhausted from 7 years of war, and many leaders, particularly those influential in social spheres: Education Minister Anatoly Lunacharsky; Health Minister Nikolai Semashko; Lenin's wife, Nadezhda Krupskaya, who considerably influenced social policy; and physical educationalists such as Alexander Zigmund.

Felix Dzerzhinsky and the *Cheka*

The All-Russia Extraordinary Commission for Combating Counterrevolution and Sabotage (*Cheka*) was set up, as its name implies, for national security at home and intelligence operations abroad. In addition to its secret police functions, it was also in charge of corrective labour camps, internal security troops, and press censorship. It was headed from 1917 by Felix Dzerzhinsky until his sudden death in 1926. It was his statue that stood—until pulled down in the early 1990s—outside the KGB headquarters, the Lubyanka, in Moscow.

In June 1923, on Dzerzhinsky's initiative, a sports club was established for *Cheka* staff—*Dinamo*—representing "energy, motion, and force." According to Dzerzhinsky, sport was essential to develop "strength, dexterity, courage and endurance" among his personnel. In addition to training service personnel, *Dinamo* gradually began to function as a normal sport society open to all service personnel of the internal security agency, border guards and militia, members of their families, and auxiliary staff. It later recruited top and promising athletes, gave them officer commissions, and paid them from its funds. The origins of *Dinamo* (which existed all over the communist world) were not permitted to be openly mentioned in Soviet times.

The Komsomol

The *Komsomol* had been concerned with sport during the Civil War and considered sport one of the main areas of its activity. In fact, its young members had been responsible for much of the work done under *Vsevobuch* authority: setting up clubs, getting sport going at workplaces, building sports amenities, providing much of the grass-roots enthusiasm for sports participation, and spearheading the political campaign against the old bourgeois sports clubs and movements—often with as much undiscriminating and destructive passion as the English Puritans during the English Civil War. At its Third Congress in October 1920, the *Komsomol* passed a resolution "On the Militia Army and the Physical Education of Young People" that was the most clear-cut document yet on socialist principles of physical culture and sport. Besides making it obligatory for all members to assist in the work of *Vsevobuch*, the *Komsomol* established the following principles:

> The physical culture of the younger generation is a necessary element in the overall communist upbringing of young people, intended to create a harmonious person, a creative citizen of communist society. . . . It should also serve the direct practical aims of training young people for work and for the armed defence of their country. (Chudinov, 1959, pp. 43-44)

The *Komsomol*

The Communist Youth League had come into being in 1918 and soon became a training reserve for the Communist Party; by 1927, it had a clear monopoly of young people, all other youth organisations (such as the Scouts and YMCA) having been eliminated. It recruited young people between the ages of 14 and 28; younger people were almost unanimously members of the "Young Octobrists" (7-8) and the Young Pioneers (9-14), both under *Komsomol* supervision.

The *Komsomol* had been concerned with sport from the Civil War of 1918-21 and considered it one of its principal spheres of activity. During the 1920s, the *Komsomol* led the attack on the remaining bourgeois sport clubs: "They are harmful to Soviet power and divert young people from socio-political life." It also attacked and successfully abolished the Boy Scout organisations, for which it was taken to task by Lenin's widow, Nadezhda Krupskaya: "Scouting has something that irresistibly attracts young people." She listed its attributes as study of young people's psychology, interests, and needs; use of their initiative; ceremony and ritual; and children's group feelings, as well as the employment of lively forms of activity, especially games (N.K. Krupskaya, *RKSM i boyscautizm*, 1923, p. 17).

At its Fourth Congress in the autumn of 1921, the *Komsomol* called once more for an all-out assault on the bourgeois sport societies that were now reappearing in the more relaxed atmosphere of NEP. It subsequently seized the initiative by forming its own sport societies that were open to all young people and that excluded members of the bourgeoisie.

The Party

A new direction to the controversy over sport organisation came with the findings of a special commission of the Central Committee of the Russian Communist Party (Bolsheviks), made known in March 1923. A month later, the 12th Party Congress advocated that local sport clubs should become the responsibility of factories, farms, offices, and colleges. Either they were to be run like other worker clubs for the benefit of the local community (but under trade union control) or confined to the workers and their families of a particular workplace.

The Communist Party of the Soviet Union (CPSU)

The Russian Communist Party had its origins in the Russian Social Democratic Labour Party, formed in 1898. At its conference in 1903, the party split into two separate parties—the Bolsheviks ("majority" group) and the Mensheviks ("minority" group). It was the Bolshevik Party, led by Lenin, that seized power in a coup in October 1917. It subsequently changed its name to the Russian Communist Party (Bolsheviks) and then the Communist Party of the Soviet Union. From initially being a tiny "vanguard" of professional revolutionaries, the party became, under Stalin (1879-1953), a mass organisation: from 1.3 million members in 1928 to 3.5 million in 1933.

The party came to dominate and set the policy for every area of Soviet society, including sport. All sport leaders had to be experienced party functionaries. Through its *nomenklatura* (list of party appointments), the party could control the personnel at every level of the sporting, as every other, hierarchy. Like leaders in every other walk of life, sport leaders were not exempt from the purges; at least three were executed between 1939 and 1941.

The party believed that it could best realise its objectives in sport if the sport clubs were organised on a workplace basis, where it and its auxiliary organisations—the trade unions and the *Komsomol*—were strongest, not through independent sport societies. At the same time, the party did not concur with the idea that sport should be the exclusive domain of young people and the *Komsomol*. It affirmed that in a state that enforced dictatorship by the proletariat, the trade unions were the broadest *transmission belt* from the party to the people and that it was one of their fundamental duties to educate their members, to take care of their recreational needs, and to develop their many interests.

Concerned at the continuing ambiguity in organisation, the party issued its first authoritative resolution on sport on 13 July 1925 (8 years after the revolution). From the standpoint of organisation, it instructed all party branches to ensure that its directives were followed. Their major tasks were threefold:

- Politicisation: to implement political leadership of the sport movement, to see that it combined political education with sport, and to prevent isolation from trade union and political organisations.
- Leadership: to ensure that all sports groups were effectively under party guidance and that no independent clubs should continue to exist; all sports organisations, leagues, and clubs remaining from before the revolution were to be disbanded.
- Ally-creating: to make it a mass movement that embraced peasants as well as industrial workers, old as well as young, women as well as men, and all ethnic groups.

As an umbrella organisation, it created the Supreme Council of Physical Culture attached to the government that in 1929 became an even more powerful state-controlled body responsible for the entire sports movement, the All-Union Council of Physical Culture. This was, in effect, a ministry of sport.

A controversy even greater than that concerning organisation raged throughout the 1920s over the role of physical culture in a socialist society. Some of the major proponents are interesting in that their views differ, often quite radically, from the pattern of recreation that evolved subsequently when Soviet sport became more geared to building a strong nation-state to fit the needs of labour and defence in the 1930s, and those of international recognition and prestige after World War II.

The Hygienists

Some of *Vsevobuch's* severest critics—for its alleged "militarisation" and "sportisation" (that is, emphasis on

The Hygienists

During the 1920s, much of sport's development was influenced by people who called themselves "hygienists"; they were mainly medical personnel—physiologists, anatomists, and health workers—concerned about the need to improve health standards, eliminate disease and epidemics, and reduce infant mortality and the overall mortality rate. One means they saw to make people aware of personal hygiene and bodily fitness was physical culture. The hygienists dominated the teaching of physical education at the major physical education institutes, ran the sport press, and wielded considerable authority on the Supreme Council of Physical Culture.

At this time, the average life expectancy in Soviet Russia was 28; the birth and the death rates were extremely high: births were 45.5 per 1,000 inhabitants, deaths 29.1, while infantile mortality was as high as 269 per 1,000. A number of diseases were endemic to certain areas—cholera, TB, smallpox, syphilis, trachoma, and leprosy.

There existed during the NEP period a widespread idealistic adherence to the notion of a "healthy mind in a healthy body," a feeling that physical culture could somehow be used to improve both physical and social health and to combat antisocial and anti-Soviet phenomena like prostitution, drunkenness, and even religion.

sport as competition)—were to be found among the scientists and medical personnel who had gathered round it and were later to work for the Scientific and Technical Committee attached to the Supreme Council of Physical Culture. One means they saw to make people aware of personal hygiene and physical fitness was "physical culture." To their minds, "sport" implied competition, games that were potentially injurious to mental and physical health. Such pursuits as weightlifting, boxing, wrestling, and gymnastics were, in their opinion, irrational, dangerous, and contrary to the socialist ethic, because they encouraged individualist rather than collectivist attitudes and values.

Not all supporters of the hygienists, however, were opposed to every form of competitive sport. Nikolai Semashko, Chairman of the Supreme Council of Physical Culture, himself a doctor and concurrently People's Health Commissar, was against restricting physical education to narrow medical confines and against banning competitive games: "If you keep the populace on the

Female workers taking up an aristocratic sport at the Moscow Institute of Physical Culture, 1920.

The first sports parade in Moscow against a backdrop declaring "A Healthy Mind in a Healthy Body."

Lenin (centre) with Sports Commisar Nikolai Podvoisky at the first sports parade on Moscow's Red Square, 1919.

mish-mash of hygienic gymnastics, physical culture will never gain very wide popularity" (Semashko, 1954, p. 264). Competitive sport was, he said, "the open gate to physical culture. . . . It not only strengthens various organs, it helps a person's mental development, it promotes the sort of willpower, strength and skill that should distinguish Soviet people" (Semashko, 1954).

There were others of the hygienist school who did not share his passion for competitive sport. Several members of his staff at the Health Commissariat and lecturers at the institutes of physical culture, including the Principal of the Moscow State Institute of Physical Culture, Alexander Zigmund, were firm opponents of competitive games and sports. Zigmund, in fact, drew up a list of "approved" sports that included track and field, swimming, and rowing (all against oneself and the clock, not against opponents). Nonapproved sports included boxing, wrestling, soccer, and fencing—all of which implied competition. Further, he rejected "the use of physical exercise as a spectacle for mercenary ends, narrow specialisation and professional indulgence in record-setting and record-breaking" (*Izvestiya fizicheskoi kultury*, 1925, p. 2). Because Zigmund was also chairman of the Scientific and Technical Committee, his views carried a good deal of weight. This committee was also responsible for physical education syllabi in schools and colleges. In fact, physical education was excluded from most schools, inasmuch as it was felt that it should be "an integral part of the education process and not something tacked on artificially to the curriculum. He maintained that "the existence of physical education teachers is a sign of pedagogical illiteracy" (*Vestnik*, 1925, p. 2).

Hygienists dominated the teaching of physical culture at the Moscow and Petrograd (later Leningrad) institutes; in 1924, the Moscow Institute was, for a time, renamed the Central State Institute of Physical Culture and Curative Pedology. Pedology, it should be added, was considered to be the science of child development; in their published views of sport, pedologists maintained that certain sports were harmful and encouraged selfish habits among children (in 1936 the party declared pedology a "pseudo-science" and proscribed its practice and teachings). The timetable at the physical culture institutions in the mid-1920s contained exclusively medical subjects and hygienic gymnastics; it eschewed all games and sports.

One result of pressure from the hygienists was the reduction in sport contests in the early 1920s and the exclusion from them of certain harmful sports. The First Trade Union Games, in June 1925, for example, excluded soccer, boxing, weightlifting, and gymnastics from its programme, even though these were four of the most popular sporting pursuits in the country at the time. Boxing was outlawed in the same year in the Leningrad area by order of the Leningrad Council of Physical Culture.

A change in the fortunes of the hygienist school came with the party intervention in sport mentioned earlier. Their downfall was partly caused by the changing political climate in the mid-1920s and the alleged connection of some of their leading exponents with Trotsky, whose star had been on the wane since 1924. In the "witch-hunt" of Trotskyists that took place at the end of the decade, Dr. Zigmund was labelled a Trotsky supporter and removed from all his posts (he subsequently disappeared in the purges). A more immediate reason for the party to demote the hygienists may well have been that the party (that is, Stalin) was beginning to see competitive sport (with its record breaking, individual heroes, and spectator—"bread and circus"—potential) as a valuable adjunct to its impending industrialisation campaign.

Proletarian Physical Culture

In the sphere of sport, the *Proletkultists* also had their own theories and programmes. The Proletarian Cultural and Educational Organisation had been formed in 1917 with the intention of producing a proletarian culture as an indispensable part of a socialist revolution.

The *Proletkultists* went much further than the hygienists in condemning all manner of games, sports, and gymnastics tainted by bourgeois society. In *New Games for New Children*, the *Proletkultists* advocated such innovative games as "Swelling the Ranks of Children's Communist Groups," "Rescue from the Capitalists," "Agitators," "Helping the Proletarians," and "Smuggling Revolutionary Literature Across the Frontier" (Kornileva-Radina & Radin, 1927, p. 37). The *Proletkultists* also successfully campaigned for a halt to the production of dolls "in that they help to inculcate maternal instincts."

Many theatrical spectacles were presented, often involving top stage directors such as Stanislavsky, Meyerhold, and Eisenstein; Sparrow Hills became a regular site for proletarian pageants and mock battles. The *Proletkult*, while accusing others of "sportisation" and "militarisation," itself came in for accusations of "theatricalisation" of sport.

Another proletarian event took place in August 1927 to mark the 10th anniversary of the revolution. Entitled "The Pageant of Universal October," it was intended to portray pictures of world revolution. It was a strict rule, as always at *Proletkult* events, that no one should simply be a spectator; everyone should join in, this time as British miners, American cowboys, turbaned Indians, Polish cavalry, a religious pilgrimage of émigrés, huge Chinese dragons pulling rickshaws, Red Army men, workers, and

Lenin's strategy

During this period of mass strike activity, the majority of local Social-Democratic committees in Russia are fused into the Iskra network.
Constant visits from escaped prisoners, exiles, and hundreds of letters from workers, keep Lenin well-informed.

A 'young eagle' escaped from Siberia visits Lenin in London: Lev Davidovich Bronstein, from a family of Jewish farmers in the Ukraine, union organizer in Odessa, and nicknamed Pero ('The Pen'). He is better known today as . . .

TROTSKY (1879-1940)

A MAN OF TALENT—HE WILL GO FAR!

NOTHING DOING! BESIDES, I DON'T LIKE THE WRITINGS OF THIS 'PEN'...

67 Lenin wants to place the young 'Pen' on the Iskra board, but Plekhanov won't have it!

Trotsky

Lev Davidovich Trotsky (real name Bronstein, 1879-1940) was the main architect of the Bolshevik coup in October 1917; he organised the successful Red Army in the Civil War and was the leading figure behind the Petrograd Soviet. Second only to Lenin during the revolution, he subsequently clashed with Stalin after Lenin's death and became part of the left opposition. In November 1927, he and his supporters were expelled from the party and exiled; the following year he was ejected from the USSR. During his exile in Mexico, he was murdered in 1940 by a Stalin agent.

Although he had little time to become involved in sport development, he did have a number of supporters among the hygienists and in the *Komsomol*. In his views on sport and playful activities, he maintained that they should be freely chosen and pursued for their inherent pleasure rather than for practical results: "The longing for amusement, diversion and fun is the most legitimate desire of human nature. We are obliged to give the satisfaction of that desire a higher artistic quality, at the same time making amusement a weapon of collective education, freed from the guardianship of the pedagogue and the tiresome habit of moralising" (L. Trotsky, *Problems of Everyday Life*, 1973, p. 32).

peasants—7,000 performers in all. The two sides, workers and capitalists, suddenly clash, and a radio appeal is made to the workers of the world to come to the class front. Universal October is at hand; one last onslaught and the citadels of capitalism will fall. "Now the Red Banner is flying over the entire world. Salute the Headquarters of world revolution—the Communist International" (Starovoitova, 1969).

While the hygienists admitted the possible usefulness of some bourgeois sport, the *Proletkultists* made no such concessions. For example, the hygienist V.V. Gorinevsky had described the game of lawn tennis as "ideal from the biological standpoint in enhancing harmonious development; I find it hard to say what organs and muscles are not in use" (*Krasny Sport,* 21 January 1924). The *Proletkultist* S. Sysoev, on the other hand, maintained that this game "for the white-pants brigade and the bourgeoisie exhibits no comradeship or teamwork—just the qualities that the Russian needs. Tennis is also an expen-

sive summer game . . . it should not receive as much support as other, mass games" (*Krasny Sport,* 21 January 1924).

To many *Proletkultists*, the recourse to bourgeois institutions such as sport seemed a compromise, a withdrawal from already conquered positions. They might have exerted more influence over the movement if they had followed a more well-defined programme of proletarian physical culture to replace organised sport. As it was, a number of factories did introduce production gymnastics for their workforce, and some trade union clubs confined their activities to regenerative exercises; these activities, however, tended to turn workers, especially the young, away from sport and received much criticism from the party. Lenin had earlier admonished the *Proletkult* movement, pointing out the need to draw on the cultural heritage of the past and to base further development on everything valuable that had been accumulated by humankind up to the revolution.

Sports parade on Moscow's Red Square, 1919.

The Latvian military sports company won all competition at the second Worker Olympics in Vienna.

Sports flotilla on the Moscow River accompanying the first sports parade, 1919.

"Let us set up physical culture clubs on every collective farm," 1931.

Poster advertising the launch of the national fitness programme: "We are millions in the Soviet column prepared for labour and defense," 1931.

Firefighters in Moscow demonstrating the kilometre run in full equipment as part of the national fitness programme launched in 1931.

The years of experimenting and searching in the 1920s reflect similar developments in worker sport outside the Soviet Union. They also demonstrate a contradiction fundamental to the period: that between the subjective desires of the authorities to shape society according to ideological precepts and the objective lack of the material conditions for the implementation of ideals, there can be little doubt that, because they were not based on the reality of Russia's situation, some immediate aspirations for sport were utopian and unrealistic. Despite accepting the most advanced ideas and passing resolutions and directives, despite enormous sacrifices, Soviet Russia remained a backward country economically and culturally; it stayed a largely illiterate, peasant nation. To some extent, this explains the apparent hesitations, the disputes, and the controversies in many fields. The search for a way forward in sport was accompanied by conflict over its basic role and functions that, in turn, reflected deeper political and social conflicts.

Stalin

Iosif Vissarionovich Stalin (real name Dzhugashvili, 1879-1953), the son of a Georgian shoemaker, became a full-time revolutionary in 1901; he became a member of the Bolshevik Central Committee in 1912, and from then on was one of the most prominent Bolshevik leaders inside Russia. At Lenin's death in 1924, Stalin quickly isolated his main rivals and took power into his own hands. He set about the social and economic transformation of the country: large-scale ministries and collective farms were formed, mass nationalisation was carried out, vast construction sites began to cover the countryside with towns and industry, and the repressive organs extended outwards, including the growing GULAG empire of concentration camps, forced labour camps, and transit prisons. He launched a campaign of mass repression and terror from 1936: as many as 70 percent of the party's Central Committee members elected in 1934 were executed between 1936 and 1941, including all surviving members of Lenin's old Politburo. Of total arrests, as many as 8 million people is a likely figure. Despite the madness of his methods, he did form the main elements of a modern state, brought his country through World War II, and established the structure of an industrialised state. He died at the age of 73 in 1953.

The social and political constraints on the *Kulturkampf* were certainly not merely to be found in the popular resistance of a peasant to the changing of age-old habits; they were to be located also in the growing exigencies of a leadership (rapidly becoming Stalin's one-man dictatorship) soon to be obsessed with industrialisation and economic fulfilment, a leadership that could see relatively little use in mass sport participation for its own sake but could see advantages in promoting a professional elite to entertain and distract the newly urbanised workers through competitive spectacles such as soccer, volleyball, and basketball matches. This tendency was prominent in the 1930s, but it was already discernible in the middle of the decade after the keynote party resolution on sport in July 1925.

The questions raised by certain revolutionary and health-oriented professionals are fundamentally important and relevant to any assessment of the role and function of worker sport in a socialist society. Were the proponents of such views around today, they might well wonder how Soviet sport came to support such an elaborate system of institutions, residential boarding schools, giant amphitheatres, coaches, semi- and full-time professional players, sport journalists, and even gambling establishments; they might wonder why a similar sport ideology in both the east and the west cultivated irrational loyalties and ascribed similar prominence to the winning of victories, the setting of records, and the collecting of trophies.

Red Sport International

On the assumption that world revolution was not in the distant future and that, until then, the world would be split irreconcilably into two hostile camps, the Soviet leaders initially ignored bourgeois sport organisations, refused to affiliate with their international federations, and boycotted their competitions, especially the Olympic Games (even though Russia was a founding member of the International Committee and was still represented in that body by tsarist officials). As long as the Soviet Union remained isolated and weak internationally, foreign sport relations were restricted to worker sport organisations and tended to reflect the policy of the Comintern and its sporting offspring, the International Association of Red Sports and Gymnastics Associations, better known as Red Sport International (RSI).

The RSI was set up at the First International Congress of Representatives of Revolutionary Worker Sports Organisations as an affiliate of the Comintern in Moscow on 22 and 23 July 1921, during the Comintern's Third World Congress and 2 years after the Comintern's inception. It followed a preparatory meeting of Soviet, French, and German representatives of the Comintern in June. The founding members were from worker sport organisations from eight countries—Czechoslovakia, Finland, France, Germany, Hungary, Italy, Soviet Russia, and Sweden. By 1924, it had 2,214,000 members in nine sections distributed throughout the eight countries and Bulgaria, Estonia, Norway, Uruguay, and the United States. Its first president was Nikolai Podvoisky, then concurrently head of *Vsevobuch*, and its secretary was Bruno Lieske, who, after a disagreement on tactics in regard to contacts with bourgeois teams, passed on the position to a fellow Berliner, Fritz Reussner, in August 1924.

The RSI was formed partly to counterbalance the social-democratic, Lucerne-based International Federation for Sport and Physical Culture, generally known as the Lucerne Worker Sports International (LSI, later renamed the Socialist Worker Sports International) that had been established on 12 September 1920 at the initiative of Belgian, French, and German social democrats. It was ini-

Role of German Communists in RSI Policy

A number of Russian sport historians now claim that Soviet Russia was not the moving force behind RSI's militant policies in respect to noncollaboration with representatives of either bourgeois or social-democratic sport organisations. Rather, it was the dogmatic attitude of German communists from the Berlin *Fichte* worker sport club, particularly Bruno Lieske and RSI Secretary Fritz Reussner, who were frequently at loggerheads with Soviet sport leaders keen to test Soviet sport against the best in the world. In fact, they did try to establish sports relations with the social-democratic LSI and to take part in the first Worker Olympics in Frankfurt (without success). Subsequently, sport contacts with bourgeois teams (for example, in chess and soccer) were made directly by the Soviet Supreme Council of Physical Culture and not through RSI, much to the annoyance of both Lieske and Reussner. (See D. Grantsev & N. Bugrov, in *Argumenty i fakty*, no. 7, 1992, p. 16.) This occurred after the Executive Committee of RSI "shifted to Berlin and its influence on Soviet sport ceased."

tially composed of worker organisations from those three countries as well as from Britain, Czechoslovakia, Finland, and Switzerland.

Some controversy exists among historians as to Soviet Russia's role in establishing the RSI. There is some evidence to indicate that Soviet Russia was not the moving force behind the RSI establishment or its militant policies in respect to noncollaboration with either bourgeois sport or social-democratic sport; rather, this was due to the German communists from the Berlin *Fichte* worker sport clubs, particularly Bruno Lieske.

The establishment the RSI presented socialist workers with a political choice: either the social-democratic LSI or the communist RSI. The alternatives were to split national organisations in all countries where worker sport had been established. The role of worker sport within the revolutionary worker movement, however, was as unclear and undebated as was the role of sport in Soviet Russia. In its initial phase, therefore, RSI was more of a "paper tiger" than a sport and political entity. It had no organisational apparatus until 1923, and from 1924 it was more an instrument of the German revolutionary opposition. Originally it held no sport activities, nor were there any attempts to create a sport programme separate from bourgeois sport. RSI was an ideological centre for sporting politics, not an agency for establishing sport contacts.

Relations between LSI and the RSI were hostile right from the start. The RSI accused its "reformist" rival of diverting workers from the class struggle by preaching sport neutrality and apolitical sport. It further charged the LSI with preventing its members from competing against Soviet and other communist sports bodies. In response, LSI leaders accused the RSI of being a tool of the Bolsheviks, of trying to undermine the LSI, infiltrate it, and take it over; they cited the RSI manifesto *To All Workers of the World*, in which the RSI called upon the communist parties of 47 countries to form communist cells in worker sport associations in order to conduct ideological work among worker athletes (Kozmina, 1967, p. 171).

Despite LSI opposition, until 1928 the RSI favoured open competition between athletes of the two internationals and joint opposition to all bourgeois sport bodies. Although the LSI banned Soviet and RSI athletes from its Worker Olympics in Frankfurt (1925) and Vienna (1931), it did permit its affiliates to compete with them "as long as they do not exploit the occasion for political purposes!" (*Jahrbuch der Deutschen Sozialdemokratie*, 1927, p. 379). As a result, some joint meetings occurred, and the number of international worker events in which Soviet teams participated rose— from 6 in 1922, 27 in 1923, 30 in 1924, and 38 in 1925 to as many as 77 in 1926 and 87 in 1927 (Samoukov, 1964, p. 283). That there were not more was largely due to the refusal of foreign governments to permit Soviet athletes to enter their countries. This commitment to foreign competition was a factor in persuading the Soviet authorities to promote competitive sport at home rather than to develop the noncompetitive physical culture popularised by the hygienists and *Proletkultists*.

Open competition was short-lived. In 1927, the LSI reproached RSI members with repeatedly violating the 1925 conditions and forthwith sundered all sporting ties. Subsequently, many LSI affiliates expelled all communists from their ranks.

Following the LSI-sponsored World Worker Olympics of 1925, Moscow staged its first international sporting event in August 1928: the worker *Spartakiad*. The games were intended to demonstrate proletarian internationalism as a universal worker Olympics and a counterbalance to the bourgeois Olympics held that same year in Amsterdam. At the opening ceremony, a party official explained its name and worldwide significance:

We take the word Spartakiad from Spartacus—the hero of the ancient world and leader of the insurgent slaves. . . . Both the Comintern Congress and the Spartakiad unite workers fighting for socialism and communism. They are inseparable in the common struggle for revolution—the classical physical culture of sport and the revolutionary militant culture of Marxism-Leninism. (*Pravda*,14 August 1928)

Although the *Spartakiad* was dominated by Soviet athletes, a sizeable foreign contingent arrived—in spite of the LSI ban on its members attending. Six hundred foreign athletes (about 15 percent of all participants) from 14 countries took part in the games: Algeria, Argentina, Austria, Britain (26 participants), Czechoslovakia, Estonia, Finland, France (32 participants), Germany, Latvia, Norway, Sweden, Switzerland, and Uruguay (*Pravda,* 13 August 1928). The 2-week programme included over 21 sports, more than the Amsterdam Olympic Games which had 17 sports (of the Amsterdam programme only the marathon and the 3,000-m steeplechase were missing). Although standards were not as high as those at the Amsterdam Olympics, it is claimed that "in virtually all events, the Spartakiad winners surpassed the records set at the 1925 Frankfurt Worker Olympics" (Kozmina, 1967, p. 197).

The *Spartakiad* was certainly innovative for such a novel proletarian gathering. It featured a variety of pag-

Poster advertising the August 1928 Moscow *Spartakiad*.

The First *Spartakiad*

Moscow staged its first great international sports event in August 1928: the first worker *Spartakiad*. The name was taken from the German communist Spartacus League, founded in Berlin in 1912 by Rosa Luxembourg and Karl Liebknecht (in turn named after the leader of the uprising of slaves in Rome in 73-71 B.C.). The Moscow games were dedicated to the inception of the first Five-Year Plan and the 10th anniversary of the Soviet sport movement. They were also intended as a countermeasure to the IOC-organized bourgeois Olympic Games being held that same year in Amsterdam.

Although the *Spartakiad* was largely dominated by Soviet athletes, a sizeable foreign contingent did take part—600 foreign (mostly communist) athletes from between 12 and 14 countries. The comprehensive sport programme of 21 sports (as opposed to 17 at the Amsterdam Games) covered track and field, gymnastics, swimming, diving, rowing, wrestling, boxing, weightlifting, fencing, cycling, soccer, basketball, and shooting.

eants, displays, carnivals, mass games, motorcycle and automobile rallies, demonstrations of folk games, folk dancing, and folk music. In addition there were poetry readings and mock battles between "workers of the world" and the "world bourgeoisie" in which everyone participated—there were no passive spectators for this finale. Finally, athletes put on displays of team games— rugby, tennis, and field hockey—that must have been unfamiliar to many of the spectators (*Pravda,* 22 August 1928).

The winter counterpart to the *Spartakiad* had taken place in Oslo in February 1928. This was followed by a Soviet-hosted *Spartakiad* in December 1928 in which there were 638 participants in skiing, speed skating, biathlon, and special ski contests for postal workers, rural dwellers, and border guards.

Shortly after the *Spartakiad,* the Soviet Union and the Comintern underwent a radical change in foreign policy. Concerned at the ebb of the world communist movement and convinced it was only a matter of time before the capitalist powers renewed attempts to destroy the Soviet regime, the Soviet leaders felt it vital to build up the USSR's defence capacity and to try to postpone the coming attack as long as possible in order to permit the consolidation and strengthening of Soviet defences through the country's industrialisation. Henceforward, there could be no doubt that the *Russian* revolution, not the *international* revolution, was primary. The work of the Comintern (and RSI) became defensive; they aimed to prevent or frustrate an anti-Soviet coalition rather than to foment revolution.

Not only did Soviet foreign policy alter in relation to bourgeois states; it did so towards the social democrats as well. Since 1920, communist parties abroad had been acting under the United Front slogan that indicated a readiness, at least in theory, for some sort of cooperation with other parties of the left. A new policy in regard to social democrats went into operation after the Comintern's Sixth Congress in the summer of 1928. As the British historian E.H. Carr describes:

> The manifesto issued by the Congress, ranging the Social Democrats with the Fascists, denounced them as being "on the side of the exploiters, on the side of the imperialists, on the side of the imperialist robber states and their agents," and called on the workers everywhere to fight against reformism and Fascism for the proletarian revolution. (1951, p. 99)

This new policy was applied to all areas, including sport. It was taken up immediately by the RSI, which appealed for a "relentless fight against the social-fascist [social-democratic] leaders" (*Krasny Sport,* 1929). Subsequent events—the economic depression in Europe and the growth of fascist regimes in Italy and Germany—

Period of United Fronts

Following Hitler's announcement in March 1935 of what he called "the restoration of German sovereignty," the fear of fascism became very real for the Soviet leadership, and foreign policy veered toward cooperation between social democrats and communists. In July 1935, the seventh and last Comintern congress generalised the new line: "In face of the towering menace of fascism . . . it is the main and immediate task of the world labour movement to establish a united fighting front of the working class." The defence of democracy against fascism was said to be the supreme task of labour. Sport, too, was to play its part in "safeguarding democracy and constitutional government" (*Fizkultura i sport,* 1935, no. 7, p 3).

The Soviet leaders advocated the unification of the worker sport movement; both sports internationals jointly issued an appeal for all athletes to boycott the 1936 Berlin Olympics, and Soviet and other RSI athletes were permitted to take part in the social-democratic-sponsored International Worker Olympics held in Antwerp in 1937 (following the cancelled Barcelona Worker Olympics).

witnessed a great thinning, if not complete elimination, of the ranks of both the LSI and the RSI. By the mid-1930s their feud had become an anachronism; the backbone of the LSI (the nearly 2-million-strong sport association of Germany) was broken by Hitler, and the RSI was virtually confined to the USSR.

In the early 1930s, the Soviet Union began to enter contests with bourgeois states; Soviet sport was now strong enough in selected areas to enable Soviet athletes to put up a decent showing. In the first Soviet chess venture abroad, Mikhail Botvinnik drew with the world champion from Czechoslovakia, Flohr, in 1933; 3 years later his tie for first place with his Cuban competitor, Capablanca, at the world championship held in Nottingham merited a picture and full-length, front-page article in *Pravda*. Following the signing of a mutual assistance pact between Soviet Russia and Czechoslovakia in 1935, Prague played three soccer matches against Leningrad, Moscow, and the Ukraine.

The RSI now advocated the unification of the international worker sport movement. Although the two sports internationals could not agree on a Popular Front, they did reach a measure of consensus on certain points.

Nonetheless, large areas of discord remained, notably over competition with bourgeois athletes. While the LSI leaders were opposed to such fraternisation with the class enemy, Soviet sport leaders were pressing for contacts with "all organisations opposed to the fascist danger" (*Pravda,* 27 June 1938). Soviet leaders saw the difference between the earlier United Front and the current Popular Front in that the latter extended to the anti-fascist bourgeoisie, and they now played down the class struggle against them. A few months after the outbreak of the Spanish Civil War, a Basque soccer team played nine matches in the USSR. Such competition against non-worker clubs might have continued, but international events, particularly the gathering of war clouds over Europe, were to bring to an end to the period in which the policy of popular fronts was pursued. With the signing of the Soviet-German (the Molotov-Von Ribbentropp) pact in August 1939 and the subsequent outbreak of World War II, the Comintern went into eclipse along with Red Sport International.

After the war, with the new balance of power in the world, with the USSR's desire to measure its strength against the best world opposition, and with the launching of its "peaceful coexistence" policy in 1953, the accent on competing against worker teams diminished, though it did not completely disappear. There remained sport contacts with communist and socialist sport organisations abroad, such as those with the Finnish Worker Sport Association (TUL), the French FSGT, and trade and professional associations such as the International Sports Union of Railway Workers and the International Federation of University Sport. There was, however, no serious effort to turn either communist or social-democratic sport organisations into alternatives to the existing bourgeois sport federations. Nor was any loyalty to communist sport organisations abroad permitted to interfere with Soviet foreign-policy aims: good-neighbourliness; winning friends and allies among the developing states of Africa, Asia, and Latin America; peaceful coexistence with capitalist countries; and superiority over leading capitalist sporting nations, primarily at the Olympic Games.

Conclusion

The forms of recreation that developed in Soviet society did not coincide with the predictions of socialist writers about playful activities in the worker society of the future. As far as recreation is concerned, the reasons for divergence between ideals and practice may be assumed to parallel those in other areas of life. In the early post-revolutionary period, genuine efforts were made by certain future-oriented groups to move in the direction of a new socialist pattern of physical culture, but civil war and national poverty made them impossible to bring to fruition. From the late 1920s, command over the disposal of material resources and the sources of information were in no real sense under popular control; these were controlled by members of the leading group in the ruling party that, in the absence of help from a revolution in the industrial west, was pursuing a policy of building a strong nation-state power base.

Competitive sport, with both its broad relevance to education, health, culture, and politics, and its capacity to mobilise people, seemed uniquely to foster national integration. After the war, it was also used to facilitate international relations and to achieve international recognition (even to demonstrate the superiority of Soviet communism—at least until the post-1985 Gorbachev era).

Some might argue that making a fetish of recreation in the form of competitive sport in the USSR was one of a number of temporary defects of a society in transition from a command-administrative, totalitarian state to a humanistic, socialist society "still stamped with the birthmarks of the old society from whose womb it emerge[d]" (Marx, 1904, p.12). Such "defects" might be regarded as inevitable as long as the individual still remained subordinate to the division of labour, as long as the forces of production were at too low a level to permit the development of the individual—that is, as long as the USSR remained at a low level of economic development.

It may be that given Russia's overall semifeudal backwardness in 1917, any road forward other than one of prolonged, bureaucratically enforced development was impossible, that its society was never ripe for genuinely socialist or communist human relations (including those of free recreation), and that the original social goals could hardly have remained uncontaminated (in the minds of any leaders) by the class or caste differentiation historically involved in the process of constructing a socialist state. It is here, perhaps, that we should seek the key to understanding the pattern of sport that developed in the USSR. In western society, the fetishisation of sport was a consequence of this field of human endeavour (like almost all others); it offered the possibility of making a profit, and it turned out to be a highly appropriate means of distracting workers from class-conscious politicisation. In Soviet society, the fetishisation of sport resulted from centralised planning and an administration designed to subordinate social life to the political and economic tasks of building a militarily and economically strong state. The distinction is important, not only in terms of the dynamics of the two systems, but also for any future attempt to construct a genuinely proletarian, socialist pattern of recreation.

References

Carr, E.H. *German-Soviet relations between the two world wars, 1919-1939* (London: Pelican, 1951).

Chudinov, I.D. (ed.). *Osnovnye postanovleniya, prikazy i instruktsii po voprosam fizicheskoi kultury i sporta 1917-1957* (Moscow, 1959).

Fizkultura i sport. No. 7, 1935.

Izvestiya fizicheskoi kultury. No. 3, 1925.

Jahrbuch der Deutschen Sozialdemokratie. Berlin, 1927.

K Sportu. No. 11, 1912.

Kornileva-Radina, M.A. & Radin, Y.P. *Novym detyam— novye igry* (Moscow, 1927).

Kozmina, V.P. "Mezhdunarodnoye rabocheye sport-ivnoye dvizenie posle Velikoi Oktyobrskoi sotsialisticheskoi revolyutsii," in: F.I. Samoukov and V.V. Stolbov (eds.), *Ocherki po fizicheskoi kultury* (Moscow, 1967).

Krasny Sport. No. 14, 1924.

Krasny Sport. 12 May 1929.

Landar, A.M. "Fizicheskaya kultura—sostavnaya chast kulturnoi revslyutsii na Ukraine," *Teoriya i praktika fizicheskoi kultury,* no. 12, 1972.

Leninsky sbornik XXXV (Moscow, 1945).

Lockhart, R.B. *Giants cast long shadows* (London: Methuen, 1964).

Marx, K. *A contribution to the critique of political economy* (Chicago, 1904).

Novoselov, N.P. "Fizicheskaya kultura v period russkoi revolutsii, 1905-1907," in: *Ocherki po istorii fizicheskoi kultury* (Moscow, 1950).

Perel, A. *Football in the USSR* (Moscow, 1958).

Podvoisky, N. *O militsionnoi organizatsii vooruzhonnykh sil Rossiyskoi Sovetskoi Federativnoi Sotsialisticheskoi Respubliki* (Moscow, 1919).

Pravda. 13 August 1928.

Pravda. 14 August 1928.

Pravda. 22 August 1928.

Pravda. 27 June 1938.

Samoukov, F.I. (ed.). *Istoriya fizicheskoi kultury* (Moscow, 1956).

Samoukov, F.I. (ed.). *Istoriya fizicheskoi kultury* (Moscow, 1964).

Semashko, N.A. *Puti sovetskoi fizkultury* (Moscow, 1926).

Semashko, N.A. "Fizicheskaya kultura i zdravo-okhranenie v SSSR," in: *Izbrannye proizvedeniya* (Moscow, 1954).

Sholomitsky, Y. "Fizicheskaya kultura i sport v sovetskom Uzbekistane," in: *Ocherki po istorii fizicheskoi kultury* (Moscow, 1964).

Sinitsyn, S.D. (ed.). *Istoriya fizicheskoi kultury narodov SSSR,* vol. I (Moscow, 1953).

Sport v SSSR. No. 5, 1973.

Starovoitova, Z. *Polpred zdorovya* (Moscow, 1969).

Vestnik fizicheskoi kultury. No. 3, 1925.

Vestnik militsionnoi armii. No. 10, 1920.

Chapter 4

TUL: The Finnish Worker Sport Movement

Leena Laine

FINLAND

In 1930, the republic in northeast Europe covered a territory of 388,217 km² with a population of 3.63 million.

After almost 600 years under Swedish rule, Finland was incorporated in 1809 by Russia into the Czarist Empire as an autonomous Grand Duchy. The union of unequal partners was rather harmonious in the first decades. The Russian authoritarian government, carried out by a Finnish bureaucracy, was largely indifferent to the predominantly rural population. Moreover, concessions made by Czar Alexander II managed to appease Finnish displeasure before it could properly develop. Hence, during his rule, the first steps were taken to promote the official status of the Finnish language, and a decree established the regular convening of the *Lantdag* (1869).

A serious national movement did not occur until, under Nicholas II, measures were introduced to reduce Finnish autonomy and to increasingly Russianise the country. This movement was organised, on the one hand, by liberal, middle-class groups and, on the other, by the Social Democratic Party (SDP), founded in 1899 and closely linked to the ideas of Kautsky, a Marxist. During the period of revolutionary confusion in Russia in 1905, both groups organised mass national strikes that caused the Czar to institute a complete reform of the parliamentary system, replacing the representation of estates with a unicameral parliament elected by equal and universal suffrage. The success of the SDP in the 1907 elections, however, was of little significance because the czarist regime very quickly succeeded in restoring the pre-1905 conditions in Finland.

1917 and 1918 were eventful years for Finland. The overthrow of the Czar in March 1917 meant a return to a state of autonomy; only weeks after the October revolution, Finland declared its independence (6 December 1917). An outbreak of civil war followed, in which, after several months of bitter fighting, the nonsocialist forces supported by Germany succeeded in retaking the urban centres of southern Finland from the revolutionaries and in establishing a strong presidential republic.

The policy of reconciliation followed by the first president, Ståhlberg, ensured that moderate groupings amongst the party defeated in the civil war were soon able to join the conservative political life of the country that was still only approaching industrialisation. A clear sign of this was the 1926 assumption of power by the now strictly reformist SDP. The consequences of the world economic crisis also aggravated the climate of national politics in Finland. Not only were communists denied any public activity in 1930, but they also increasingly saw themselves exposed to the terror of the Lappo-Movement. The right-wing extremists, who could count on the strong support of bourgeois circles, did not fall from grace until they extended their terror to other political opponents and attempted a coup in 1932.

World War II began for Finland on 30 November 1939 when, after Finland rejected the Soviet Union's territorial claims, the Red Army crossed Finland's borders and strategically annexed important areas of southeast Finland after 100 days of fighting. The Soviets took on a more conciliatory tone after World War II. Though Finland had joined the German aggression in June 1941, they were content with a confirmation of the 1940 territorial cessions.

Learning from the past, Finland decided on a postwar foreign policy that—despite the frequent animosity of western governments—successfully considered the vital interests of the neighbouring superpower that had also become its most important trading partner. War consequences in the economic sphere—war reparations and the integration of 300,000 refugees—and the final steps toward becoming an industrialised country were successfully addressed.

Worker Sport to 1900: Roots in National Movements

Finland became an autonomous Grand Duchy of the Russian Empire in 1809, bringing Swedish rule to an end. All the same, the country remained isolated until after the Crimean War (1853-56), when it proved itself a trustworthy ally of Russia and benefited from Russia's policy of post-1861 reform. The year 1878 saw the formation of the Finnish national army, and it was at this time that modern physical exercise gained a larger foothold in the country. Physical education reforms and the nation's growing links with the rest of Europe played important roles in this development.

The initial sports journals were published in the 1880s, and a national gymnastics festival was held in 1886. The 1880s were notable for physical education and sport; clubs formed for the major sports, shooting and skiing competitions took place for ordinary people, and educational societies started to preach the benefits of exercise.

Modern physical exercise gradually became part of the life of the industrial working class. The first steps were taken in the 1870s when a few large factory communities arranged socials for workers. These events invariably included shooting and displays of strength. Before long, hunting and sailing societies also put on such festivals. Ultimately, the tradition of popular contests became established, and workers and peasants competed against one another in sports such as shooting, rowing, and skiing. The contests frequently offered large purses in order to attract participants, and their fundamental objective was to establish a military reserve.

Besides this military training, another factor in the popularising of sport was the battle for leadership between the aristocratic Swedish-speaking establishment and the incipient Finnish-speaking civil service. The latter, known as the *Fennomaniac*, wished to gain the support of both the peasant farmers and the more prosperous sections of the urban working class. The *Fennomaniacs* used the temperance movement to mobilise the working class and further their cause.

The gymnastics clubs associated with the temperance movement made the first steps in the Finnish worker sport movement. The principal club, *Helsingin Ponnistus* (Helsinki Endeavour), was founded in 1887 and is regarded as Finland's first worker sport club. Endeavour attracted skilled workers, especially printers and craftsmen. Its policies combined the aims of the *Fennomaniac*-controlled temperance movement with the ideals of the rising labour movement. The major channels for promoting physical recreation among the working class were the printing of the workers' own periodical and the social-democrat newspaper *Työmies* (Working Man), es-

tablished in 1895. Both periodicals saw sport as a weapon in the campaign against the physical decrepitude of the working class (Lahti, 1948; Laine, 1984).

What is significant about the early evolution of Finnish sport is that the country's unique conditions made for sport's swift democratisation. The well-to-do upper class was small, and opportunities for elitist sport were few. The country's political situation, coupled with the rapidity with which it moved along the path to capitalism and formed bourgeois interest groups, opened up opportunities for unusually broad strata (Laine, 1987).

In general, the first prerequisite for the birth of independent worker sport is the existence of a proletariat and its large-scale concentration. Such conditions had come to exist in Finland by the turn of the century. Over one half of Finnish enterprise employed more than 100 workers by the early 1900s. Then, as now, the nation's economy was dominated by the timber and wood-processing industries; consequently, most industrial plants sited themselves in the country near lakes and rivers. The newly populated centres had a far-reaching cultural impact on their surroundings—especially in the countryside.

Workers in the employ of large industrial concerns were the first to secure living conditions that made physical recreation possible. This is borne out by the way in which workers in a few industries—the iron and steel industries—accounted for the bulk of the membership in the earliest sport clubs. Although the work day was not reduced to below 10 hours before the 20th century, sport clubs became much more common once the sub-10-hour day was introduced.

The advent of an independent worker sport movement also presupposed freedom, an end to working people bound to employers. When the old estate system began to disintegrate, the ruling class tried to halt workers' growing independence by forming patriarchal patron organisations, like the original temperance organisation. The workers liberated themselves from such patriarchal snackies after 1896, known as the Red Strike Year.

The Finnish Labour Party (*Suomen Työväen Puolve*) was founded in 1899. By the 1890s, there were gymnastics and sports clubs in the towns and cities that catered to working people, clerical employees, and the lower echelons of the civil service. Most of the working-class sport clubs formed before 1900 were not directly linked to the political labour movement. Gymnastics was organised according to class rather than political boundaries. The emerging Finnish-speaking gymnastics movement and the instinctive "workers-versus-bosses" attitude of the clubs joined forces to combat the new enthusiasm for sports competition in 1897 when a move was made to establish a worker gymnastics federation.

The move was launched by Viktor Damm, founder of Helsinki Endeavour. He also published two booklets in

1897 and 1898, "Establish Gymnastics Clubs" (*"Perustakaa Voimisteluseuroja"*) and "A Worker Book of Gymnastics for Clubs" (*"Tvöväen Voimistelukirja Seuroja Varten"*) that came to provide the practical and methodological basis for the worker sport movement. Damm also planned an alternative for competitions and medals, a complicated pin system. This system was the forerunner of programme sport, further developed and discussed in the country between 1900 and 1905. Conservative sport circles were alarmed at the prospect of a merger between the Labour Party and the worker sport movement, and they foiled its realisation by founding in 1900 with Damm an all-embracing Finnish-speaking gymnastics federation (Laine, 1984; 1987).

From Worker Sport Clubs to the Worker Sports Federation: 1902-1917

The foundation for an independent Finnish worker sport movement was finally laid in 1902. It consisted of the gymnastics and sports sections of worker societies affiliated with the labour movement. At first, however, this development was associated with voluntary military mobilisation resulting from Finland's oppression by czarist Russia and the dissolution of the Finnish army in 1901. The sport sections and worker societies themselves had identical political views and aims; indeed, all members of sport sections were obliged to belong to a worker society. This practice was directed against the ideology of neutrality that pervaded the conservative sport movement.

The worker and the conservative sport movements first found themselves in political opposition in 1905 when a general strike was called and members of worker sport societies formed themselves into Red Guards to protect the working class. While this split many sport clubs that had not clearly aligned themselves either with the labour or the establishment camp, the rift was not complete. A large number of strong worker sport clubs affiliated with the new Finnish general sports body, the Finnish Gymnastics and Sports Federation (SVUL) that came into existence in 1906. SVUL was the country's first mass organisation for competitive sport, and it evolved into a modern integrating body. It concentrated on the ideologically important mass sports events. Sport was held to be neutral, but, for example, during the depression of 1907-1909, the question of the treatment of strike breakers brought clubs into conflict, causing some to boycott competitions. This and other issues inevitably brought political controversy into sport. There was also dissension within SVUL. In 1912, the Swedish-speaking sports

associations broke away from SVUL and set up a body of their own. Especially after the Olympic success in 1912, SVUL came to be strongly nationalist, and worker athletes felt themselves increasingly out of place within it. The smaller worker sport clubs, in particular, felt that it was time a worker sport federation was formed.

Even though there were various noncompetitive mass sport events—especially on Labour Sports Day after 1911—and inter–trade union galas with trophies for team events, the worker sport movement focused attention on competition from its very inception. Competition was quickly becoming the most salient aspect of Finnish sport. From the labour viewpoint, the runner's and wrestler's victories symbolised the physical superiority of the proletariat and were seen as ideological weapons.

The upper echelons of SVUL's administration admittedly paid scant attention to the opinions of worker sport clubs; yet, the achievements of worker athletes could not be overlooked. The Finnish national hero of the 1912 Stockholm Olympic Games, Hannes Kolehmainen, like many other runners, was a member of a worker sport club, and Finland's best wrestlers (winning four out of six of the Olympic gold medals in Stockholm) also came from the working class.

It was, in fact, the achievements of working-class athletes that hindered the establishment of a separate worker sport federation that was discussed between 1912 and 1914 and again in 1917. SVUL was Finland's sole representative in the various international sport organisations, so affiliation to a worker sport federation would have to bar members of worker sport clubs from international competition. Lucerne Worker Sports International cooperated internationally as of 1913 but was not seen as an alternative, particularly because it could not compete after the inception of World War I in 1914. Consequently, the worker sport clubs were against forming a labour-controlled central organisation, taking the view that SVUL should be made more democratic by "working from within" (Laine, 1984, p. 519). There were 127 divisions attached to Labour Societies in SVUL in 1917, accounting for 20 percent of all SVUL divisions; about 10,000 or 22 percent of SVUL's membership consisted of worker athletes. The worker sport movement did, nonetheless, begin publication of a journal in 1915.

Very soon afterwards, matters took an entirely different course with the Russian revolution and Finland's independence in 1917. Independence made the class conflict far more virulent. In 1918, civil war broke out, some worker athletes fighting for the Red Guards and some members of conservative sport clubs fighting in the White Guards. The SVUL leadership supported the Whites and, after the war, worker athletes and clubs that had fought for the Reds were excluded from the organization.

The first course for female leaders of the TUL in Helsinki, 1921, here training in gymnastics in the TUL women's uniform. Of the membership of TUL in the 1920s and 1930s, women comprised 14% to 16% and girls about 12%.

The Festival March through the heart of Helsinki (40,000 participants) at the IU Federation Jamboree, 1954.

The "small boys group" in Pietarsaaris Voima Club, 1922. TUL worked very intensively with children; the boys' sections gathered hundreds of boys for gymnastics, wrestling, skiing, etc. A monthly journal for boys was even distributed in the late 1920s.

TUL's Formative Years: 1919-1927

The structure of TUL was generally a mirror image of SVUL. In addition to its rapidly formed network of regional organisations and the various divisions responsible for coaching various sports, TUL also acquired an independent committee and secretary for women's affairs, a section for education, and a youth section. The federation had a periodical of its own and a separate publication for women (Hentilä, 1982). Festivals, organised every third year, formed a large celebration of worker sport.

Membership soon surpassed 20,000. Indeed, for a period of 2 years, TUL had more members than SVUL (Table 4.1). TUL focused on competitive sport; this was regarded as paramount insofar as the TUL had to compete against the conservative sport organisations for the loyalty of working-class youth. TUL trained numerous top-class wrestlers, boxers, track and field athletes, and soccer players, and, on occasion, produced outstanding athletes in other areas as well (see Table 4.2 for a list of sports sections within TUL). One fact that testifies to the prowess of TUL athletes is that many athletes who left TUL during its crisis years in the late 1920s immediately won SVUL championships. Half the Finnish soccer team at the 1936 Olympics consisted of former TUL players, and TUL protégés won many of Finland's Olympic medals. Apart from TUL's crisis, the tide of "defections" was also due to economic depression and mass unemployment. Athletes who transferred to SVUL were assured of work!

The extensive TUL youth sections in clubs—sometimes over 2,000 strong—ensured a steady influx of new talent. Women also took part in competition, emulating their sisters in Germany and the USSR. All the same, they concentrated mainly on noncompetitive gymnastics and sports (Laine, 1989).

Organisational development was rapid. TUL even outpaced SVUL, the older body losing half its members to its rival. SVUL's membership was decimated by Finland's newly developing conditions: the working class had been defeated in the civil war and leading labour movement figures were either in exile or languishing in jail. The first TUL chairman, Eino Pekkala, who held office from 1919 to 1927, spent part of that period in prison. The Finnish establishment's view of the world was dominated by the threat posed to the country by its neighbour, Soviet Russia. The Communist Party of Finland, founded in 1918, was accordingly outlawed, and a host of other parties and organisations supporting it were likewise proscribed. In fact, the labour movement split, and the only organisations to preserve unity until the late 1920s were the Central Federation of Trade Unions and the worker sport federation.

Worker communities were transformed into tight-knit, militant centres of counterculture, spanning politics,

Table 4.1   Evolution of the Membership of TUL and SVUL: Selected Years, 1919–1982

Year	TUL	SVUL
(1917)	—	(43,100)
1919	11,300	(25,000)
1921	24,300	22,400
1924	28,000	34,100
1926	26,000	40,800
1928	38,700	39,000
1930	30,300	43,600
1935	39,200	83,800
1940	44,600	115,000[1]
1945	93,600	148,000
1950	230,300	320,000
1955	209,200	418,000
1965	321,500	605,000
1970	340,100	744,100
1980	491,600	949,400
1982	517,700	1,046,000[2]

[1]SVUL's membership rose as reorganisation caused a few specialised associations to join. In 1934, Finland had 49 associations for various sports with a membership of about 280,000 in 3,000 affiliated clubs.

[2]SVUL had some 44 affiliated associations in 1980; TUL, correspondingly, had 33 divisions. In 1982, 43% of TUL's members were men, 24% women, 14% girls, and 13% boys.

work, and the arts (Hentilä, 1991). The local sport clubs acted as bridges: the communities retained a strong awareness of being embroiled in class conflict; the idea of even one sphere of life—sport—being divorced from the overall solidarity movement was not to be entertained. Some initiatives of cooperation were made by boxers and wrestlers of SVUL who had lost their best teammates, but SVUL's leadership took a totally unresponsive attitude towards those attempts (Häyrinen & Laine, 1989).

International contacts were vital for competitive sport. TUL was a founding member both of the Lucerne Worker Sports International (LSI), taking an active part in its work, and simultaneously of Red Sport International (RSI). TUL had demanded that Soviet Russia be admitted to LSI from the outset, and, subsequently, it made a wide range of proposals for cooperation between the two internationals. When RSI was banned from the first Worker Olympics, TUL almost withdrew in protest. TUL kept close watch on the evolution of relations between LSI and RSI (Hentilä, 1982; Laine, 1978). Part of the reason for the rapid links forged between TUL and RSI

Table 4.2 Sports Sections[1] in TUL (With Founding Years) From 1919 to 1979

1919	Wrestling
	Track and field
	Gymnastics (separate sections for men and women[2])
	Skiing, ski jumping
	Swimming, diving
	Ball games (football[3], bandy, water polo in 30s)
1922	Boxing
1925	Cycling
1927	Sailing
1929	Skating
1930	Finnish baseball
1938	Weightlifting
1941	Basketball
	Motorsport (motorcyling)
1943	Handball
1945	Orienteering
	Ice hockey
1947	Women's track and field (to 1972)
1948	Paddling
1951	Volleyball
	Table tennis
1959	Hiking (to 1975)
	Sport for all ("Popular sports") (to 1967)
1967	Team and conditioning gymnastics (to 1971)
1972	Slalom
1974	Conditioning motion
	Chess
1978	Bowling
1979	Judo[4]
	Karate
	Rhythmic gymnastics
	Badminton
	Tennis

Data from Hentilä, 1982, 1984, 1987.

[1]Many sports had been trained in TUL, even as TUL championship sports, before the section was founded.

[2]Since 1924, women's activities were led by the Women's Committee, who took care of women's gymnastics and sports.

[3]Since 1957, the football and bandy competitions in Finland were organised and controlled by the Finnish Ball Federation.

[4]Basically the TUL member clubs had been "all-around sports clubs"; the only exceptions might be sailing, swimming, and football clubs. Since 1970 the new sports brought with them "single-sport clubs," such as judo, karate, tennis, etc.

was that many Finnish clubs had a close relationship with Soviet Russia; several Finnish athletes had moved to the USSR after the war. Finland, moreover, lay within the "competition zone" of Scandinavian and northeastern European worker sport; the latter included Soviet Rus-

sia, and the region's traditions were clearly different from those of central Europe. The countries TUL most often competed with were the USSR, Sweden, Norway, and the three Baltic states. For as long as the Paris Agreement remained in force, TUL had sufficient room for manoeuvre, even when relations between LSI and RSI became strained. TUL took part very successfully in the first Worker Olympics in Frankfurt (1925) and in all other Worker Olympics.

TUL Under Assault From the Right: 1927-1934

The 1927 TUL conference signalled the end of the organisation's peaceful evolution. The conference preparations were marked by considerable strife between social democrats and communists. The social democrats secured a slight majority of delegates and elected a new TUL leadership composed exclusively of their supporters (Hentilä, 1982).

International issues also played a part in bringing matters to a head. In LSI's view, TUL had continued to support the rival international for long enough. It could hardly have been a coincidence that the 1927 LSI conference was held in Helsinki and hosted by TUL; it was this LSI gathering that decided to permanently sever its relationship with RSI. Nevertheless, the Finnish organisation was against the decision and in favour of taking part in the 1928 Moscow *Spartakiad* (*News of the Fourth Helsinki Congress*, 1927, quoted in Hentilä, 1982).

The TUL council reconsidered taking part in the Moscow games 1 year later, and its leadership resolved by a small majority that no Finnish team would be sent. The opposition first demanded a general federation ballot on the matter, but failed to have its own way; it then selected an 80-strong team that was dispatched to Moscow. The athletes who competed in the *Spartakiad* were subsequently expelled from TUL, and the organisation terminated its relations with the USSR (Hentilä, 1982; Laine, 1978).

The 1929 TUL conference proved incapable of reunifying the organisation, and the minority continued to act as it had previously acted. TUL forbade participation in any events where RSI-affiliated bodies were represented, yet clubs such as the Helsinki *Jyry* maintained ties with communist worker sport bodies in the USSR, Norway, Sweden, Estonia, and the corresponding minority in German worker sport circles. The outcome was the expulsion of *Jyry* from TUL in August 1929. Later, all clubs that continued to cooperate with *Jyry* were also expelled (Hentilä, 1982; Laine, 1978).

In late 1929, the expelled clubs and 100 additional clubs that were still TUL members founded the Committee for the Unification of Worker Sports (*Työläisurheilun Yntenäisyys-komitea* [TYK]). The committee's task was

Franzen, winner of "putting the weight" at the second
Worker Olympics in Vienna, 1931.

The Finnish worker sport
delegation at the Moscow
Spartakiad, 1928.

Lehtinen, winner of the high jump at the second Worker Olympics in Vienna, 1931.

Lainen, winner of the long jump at the second Worker Olympics in Vienna, 1931.

Franzen, winner of the ballsling at the second Worker Olympics in Vienna, 1931.

to bring the expelled clubs back into TUL; the underground Communist Party that had contacts with the TUL opposition was strongly against establishing a new worker sport organisation. TYK proved to be short-lived. The extreme right in Finland had grown in strength and was able to force the authorities to take action to ban the supposedly communist-infiltrated organisations. In June 1930, the authorities closed the TYK office and imprisoned prominent committee members. Shortly afterwards, they prosecuted several other labour organisations and declared them illegal; several of TUL's founding members were among those outlawed—at least 157 clubs in the 1930-1934 period were now considered illegal. The social-democratic factions of TUL's leadership were relatively satisfied with this turn of events inasmuch as they now found themselves able to work in peace with the communists gone (Hentilä, 1982; Laine, 1978).

Worker Sport and National Unity

Between 1918 and 1944, the Finnish constitution precluded the left-wing labour movement from participating in politics. Members of the movement were effectively deprived of their civil rights (Kosonen, 1979, p. 400). As far as TUL was concerned, matters came to a head in the late 1920s when the federation's left-wing faction was banned. Finland's parliamentarism, narrow though its scope was, was also thrust into crisis by the mobilisation of the extreme right. In 1932, there was an attempted coup d'etat. Once the crisis was over, a general demand was voiced that the state be strengthened under the banner of national unity (Kosonen, 1979, p. 396; Laine, 1986).

The consolidation of the state involved binding various institutions closer to it. This manifested itself in sport as a call for the reunification of sport organisations and for stronger links among them, the armed forces, and the schools. The Diet and state bodies played an active part in seeking to reconcile SVUL and TUL.

The late 1930s saw the reformist Social Democratic Party emerge as a major force in these moves towards national unity. The party also accepted the idea of a national "sports settlement," evolving its own "sports policy" and maintaining that this policy was a party matter, while sport itself was TUL's affair (Hentilä, 1982, p. 391).

The attitude of the leaders of SVUL towards TUL in the 1920s was quite complicated: negative and eventually abstaining itself from it altogether. They criticised TUL for being too overtly political and for refusing to cooperate in international sport. In fact, the few approaches that had been made towards TUL in the 1920s could not be considered serious. Indeed, SVUL had more

than enough to do in consolidating its own organisation. In 1932, SVUL became a more forthright central body when it replaced its old sections for different sports by specialist associations. An additional objective was to place most of the independent associations under SVUL jurisdiction, and this was broadly accomplished. The Swedish-language organisations, some elite sport branches, and the women's gymnastic federation were virtually the only ones to remain outside the new structure (Häyrinen & Laine, 1989).

A new generation emerged in the SVUL leadership, one that included strong advocates of integration. Urho Kekkonen (formerly a prominent high jumper, later to become president of Finland), chairman of the Finnish Track and Field Federation, was one of these new leaders, and he was the first to offer TUL cooperation with SVUL on a basis of true equality (Häyrinen & Laine, 1989; Hentilä, 1982). SVUL's hard-liners nevertheless continued to make their presence felt, and they received backing from the extreme right in the Diet. It was because of them that TUL lost state financial support in 1932. The Diet had made state support contingent upon TUL members being freely allowed to join Finnish teams in international competition, a proviso to which TUL could not comply. The terms for state support were modified 2 years later, in 1934: TUL was told not to encroach upon "state affairs" (Hentilä, 1982, pp. 340ff.).

The Social Democratic Party was prepared to accept these terms; the orientation was compatible with the SDP's own policy towards TUL. The TUL leadership, furthermore, had agreed to purge the 1934 federation's festival of all overtly political slogans and colours, even though this generated widespread dissatisfaction amongst the rank and file membership. Perhaps the most conspicuous result of TUL's neutralisation was that the Berlin Nazi Olympics aroused no opposition movement in Finland, in contrast to all other countries with a strong socialist movement.

In 1935, a central sport federation committee came into being at the instigation of the Ministry of Education. The committee (with two TUL appointees) represented a first step towards reuniting sport. Its main task was to ascertain the feasibility of founding a central body to act as a liaison, a specialist body, and a centre for sports agitation. The recommendations of the committee were rejected by most of the important sporting bodies. A similar venture for a central and unified organisation had been launched unsuccessfully, somewhat earlier, by the extreme right, including the so-called Freeworker Sports Federation (*Vapaa Työväen Urheiluliitto*, established 1934), the defence forces, and the National Board of General Education (Häyrinen & Laine, 1989).

Once the depression was over and TUL had recovered from the split in its ranks, it proved strong enough to respond to the new proposal for a central organisation. The strategy clearly had to be altered. In 1937, the SDP came to share government with the leading farmers' party and began to seek to restore harmony in Finnish sport by demanding cooperation in competition. SDP and TUL leaders had a common view; they held that the labour movement was responsible not merely for sports unification, but for the welfare of the entire country. The road to "Scandinavian democracy" was opened by employing sport as a means to bridge the gap between the workers and the rest of the nation (*TUL: n jäsenille,* 1937). The demand for cooperation was, evidently, associated with the government's goals (Hentilä, 1982).

It is important to note that there was no popular democratic front behind the SDP's rise to office or the budding cooperation between TUL and SVUL. It is true that the idea of a popular front had been broached in 1936, but no more than overtures had ever really been made. The Communist Party had adopted the popular front tactic in 1935, and two or three years earlier sections of the Finnish intelligentsia had founded a body to watch over civil rights (that, perhaps, contained the germ of a popular front). But the SDP had other ideas, and in 1936 and 1937, before it entered office, the SDP expelled those of its members who had supported the notion (Hentilä, 1982).

Interestingly enough, when cooperation between the two sports bodies was promoted, the assessments made by SDP and TUL leaders of both TUL and SVUL had serious shortcomings. TUL had become far stronger, yet it was nevertheless claimed that TUL was falling apart. Problems were exaggerated and it was even argued that TUL was nothing more than an economic burden on the labour movement. In reality, only one difficulty mentioned constituted a genuine obstacle: the paralysis of LSI elsewhere in Europe. SVUL received an even more cursory evaluation. Virtually the sole issue raised was the "unwholesome" aspect of the conservative body—that is, its covert professionalism. It was held that the presence of TUL would help to eliminate unsavoury professionalism. Cooperation was made subject to the condition that discrimination against TUL athletes must cease. But there was no mention of the conservative sport organisation's ties with Nazi Germany, and neither was any decision taken on how the close ties between SVUL and the far-right defence associations (home guards) should be regarded. On the other hand, there were such persons among the SVUL leadership who actively worked against the right-wing extremist, Urho Kekkonen (Häyrinen & Laine, 1989).

In 1939, the TUL Federation Congress agreed in principle to cooperate with SVUL in international matches, competitions between the two federations, and Olympic representation. The agreement was hard to secure. As before, TUL's rank and file was strongly against cooperation. What was new, however, was that the cooperation proposal put before the 1939 TUL conference was supported by a group of left-wingers close to the Communist Party in order to advance the course of the popular front (Hentilä, 1982).

Nonetheless, the agreement between the two federations was finally rejected by SVUL. The 1940 Olympic Summer Games were due to be held in Helsinki, but not even the Olympics could bring the two sides together. Meanwhile, the special sport associations and TUL started bilateral cooperation. Because the sides wanted the games themselves to be a success, however, it was decided that each would issue a declaration of its own. The TUL statement said:

> Were the Federation to refuse to take part in the Olympic Games, this would be interpreted as failure in the present orientation of our state and would be the worst possible advertisement for our nation. . . . The issue concerns more than the relationship between Finland's two sports organisations, it concerns society as a whole. (*TUL Council Minutes,* 1939)

The TUL statement was designed to provide backing for the government policy of the social democrats. The 1940 Olympics were not held because of the outbreak of World War II. Finland and the Soviet Union became military foes in November 1939. TUL had associated itself with the cause of national defence even before the war had been declared; it had arranged first-aid courses and travelling reviews for reservists on military exercises (Hentilä, 1982; *TUL Council Minutes,* 1939). It also played an active part in the first stage of the war between Finland and the Soviet Union, the so-called "Winter War," and was then involved in military propaganda during the interim truce of 1940-1941. When Finland, in 1941, once more took up arms to fight as Nazi Germany's ally, TUL stood in the forefront of that fight—evidently as the only worker sport organisation to be part of the fascist front anywhere in the world (*TUL Annual Reports*, 1940-1944; *TUL Journal*, 1939-1944).

TUL Since 1944: A Strong Worker Sport Body

TUL found itself with much greater freedom of action once the war was over. All organisations associated with the labour movement, including the Communist Party, were legalised; the SDP and the Finnish People's Democratic League formed a coalition government with the Agrarian Party. Organisations of the extreme right

Wrestling at a TUL festival, 1954.

Girls from the sports club of Vaasan Kiisid.

Mass demonstration at a TUL festival, 1946.

were banned—including the defence associations whose members often moved into sport clubs instead. Many of the figures who had led TUL during the war were dismissed. TUL and SVUL began to work together on a basis of equality, although SVUL remained the sole body affiliated with international sport federations (Hentilä, 1984; *TUL Annual Reports*, 1945-1948).

During the postwar years, the sport movement grew to become a real youth's mass movement. In 1945, 1946, and 1947, TUL took part in meetings of the worker sport organisations of western countries and attempted to resolve the issue of whether LSI should be reestablished. TUL's original view was that the LSI should not be reconstituted unless all central worker sport organisations were involved. Otherwise, the Finnish body held that a flexible international unity of ideals would suffice (Hentilä, 1984).

In 1947, the USSR decided to apply for membership to international federations for each sport, and the worker sport movement's best strategy seemed self-evident; it could hardly do otherwise than cooperate with conservative organisations and take part in the Olympic movement. Each worker sport body was also to concentrate on making the conservative bodies more democratic (Hentilä, 1984; *TUL Annual Reports, 1948; Minutes of TUL Congress,* 1948). In 1948, TUL passed a resolution to the effect that competition between worker and conservative sport bodies meant that particular attention had to be paid to training top-level sporting performance. This, however, was not to be done at the expense of the organisation's ideals: education was to be stressed as well. The Finnish team at the 1948 Olympic Games consequently included TUL athletes, and the Helsinki Games of 1952 were facilitated by cooperation between the two central bodies.

Until 1948, TUL believed with the strong-left government that the establishment of a single democratic national sport organisation for Finland was feasible. SVUL, on the other hand, opposed the notion, holding that unity would come too close to being the popular front. The relative strengths of political parties changed in 1948, and the broadbased government was replaced by a minority social-democratic government. Inside TUL itself, this swing of the political pendulum meant that the social democrats now took a firmer hold on the federation's leadership. Despite the fact that SVUL had remustered its forces and brought international cooperation to a standstill, the social democrats urged the formation of a single, national sport body, arguing that SVUL could be overthrown from within.

The Cold War period, 1948-1962, was for TUL a continual struggle for its independent existence; most of its members and the communists were anxious to retain autonomy. At the end of the battle, 10 years later in 1959, the SDP had to admit defeat and founded a sports body

of its own. The new Worker Sports Central Federation had close connections with SVUL (Hentilä, 1984; *TUL Annual Reports*, 1948-1962; *Työläisurheilijan*, 1978).

During the struggle, SVUL put pressure on TUL by making it impossible for TUL athletes to compete internationally. TUL responded by establishing bilateral contacts with most of the socialist countries. These contacts safeguarded the organisation's independence.

Since 1962, TUL maintained its international-competition contacts by joining the national associations of each sport as a "competing member." Unity in worker sport was reestablished in 1979 when the social-democratic sport organisation returned to TUL (Hentilä, 1987).

Conclusion

The history of TUL, therefore, demonstrates that the labour sport movement constitutes an indivisible whole. It cannot be divested of its political nature, and it must also be competitive in a society where competition dominates the whole sphere of recreation. TUL continues to be a noncommercial organisation, resting on a foundation of sport for the ordinary people. Now, the situation has drastically changed. TUL is in the process of evolving a new, central, national sporting body in Finland. TUL will stay a member organisation of the central sporting body, but its competitive activities will be taken care of by the special sport associations, and TUL will be responsible for youth and fitness activities. Will TUL survive without competitive sport? The new situation demands a new orientation—or a return to the first utopias of worker sport based on the work of Viktor Damm. Where will the new bulk of membership come from when the traditional industrial working class has almost totally disappeared and the cradles of worker sport in the countryside, the worker houses, are empty? TUL's story of the worker sport movement as a *great story* in postmodern terms is over. Will it find its new strength and vitality in many *small stories,* in finding new people who have been longing for an alternative model?

I would ask different research questions today from those at the time when this research project was originally conceived in the early 1980s. Now we have to look for people, their dreams, daily life on the sporting fields and in the gymnastic halls, sweat, laughter, and joy. This is a story of survival in political life, of complicated political situations. But the whole story of TUL, just as much as of any other worker sport, is not to be reduced to mere political history. More research will find the real subject of TUL: boys and girls, women and men, their views on life, their vigour and courage, and their meaning of being part of a great human movement and dream (Laine, 1993).

References

Häyrinen, R. & Laine, L. *Suomi urheilun suurvaltana* (Finland as a Great Power in Sport) (Vammala, 1989).

Hentilä, S. *Suomen työläisurheilun historia* (History of Finnish Worker Sport), Vol. 1 (1919-1944) (Helsinki, 1982). Vol. 2 (1944-1959) (Helsinki, 1984). Vol. 3 (1959-1979) (Helsinki, 1987).

Hentilä, S. "Die Finnische Arbeitersportbewegung und ihre Beziehungen zu Deutschland bis 1933," in: A. Luh & E. Beckers (eds.), *Umbruch und Kontinuität im Sport. Reflexionen im Umfeld der Sportgeschichte* (Bochum, 1991), pp. 367-374.

Kosonen, P., et al. *Suomalainen kapitalismi* (Finnish Capitalism) (Helsinki, 1979).

Lahti, P. *Suomen työläisurheilun historia* (History of Finnish Worker Sport) (Unpubl. manuscript, Helsinki, 1948).

Laine, L. *Vapaaehtoisten järjestöjen kehitys ruumiinkultuurin alueella Suomessa v. 1856-1917* (The Development of Voluntary Organisations in Finnish Sport 1856-1917) Liikuntatieteellisen Seuran julkaisu, No. 93 A.B (Lappeenranta, 1984).

Laine, L. "The Formation of the Political and Ideological Roles of Finnish Gymnastics and Sports Organizations in the 1920s and 1930s," in: M.A. Olsen (ed.), *Sport and Politics 1918-1939/40* (Oslo, 1986), pp. 149-156.

Laine, L. "The Role of Sport in Replacing the Patriarchal Society by a Modern Democracy: Sports, Society and Social Relationship in Finland at the End of the 19th Century and in the Beginning of the 20th Century," *ICOSH Seminar 1986 Report: Civilization in Sport History* (Kobe, 1987), pp. 170-196.

Laine, L. "Käsi kädessä siskot veikot? Naiset ja työläisurheiluliike" (Hand in Hand Sisters and Brothers? Women and the Workers Sport Movement), in: L. Laine & P. Markkola (eds.), *Tuntematon työläisnainen* (The Unknown Worker Woman) (Tampere, 1989), pp. 186-209.

Laine, L. (ed.). *On the Fringes of Sport* (St. Augustin, 1993).

Laine (Pääkkönen), L. *Helsingin Jyry. 75 vuotta työläisurheilua* (The Helsinki *Jyry* Club. 75 Years of Worker Sport) (Helsinki, 1978).

Minutes of TUL Congress, 1948 (Helsinki, 1949).

Strunz, W. *Zur Soziologie und Sozialgeschiehte des Finnischen Arbeitersports. 1919-1959* (Münster, 1983).

TUL Annual Reports. 1940-1948 (Helsinki); 1945-1948 (Helsinki); 1948-1962 (Helsinki).

TUL Council Minutes, 1939. TUL Archives (Finnish Sports Archives, Helsinki).

TUL-lehti (TUL Journal) 1939-1944. (Helsinki).

TUL: n jäsenille—Liittomme suhde muihin urheilujärjestöihin (To TUL Members—Our Federation's Ties With Other Sports Bodies), Circular (Helsinki, 1937).

Työläisurheilijan Yhteiskuntaoppi (Social Studies for Worker Athletes) (Helsinki, 1978).

Chapter 5

Austria: "New Times Are With Us"

Reinhard Krammer

AUSTRIA

In 1930, the alpine republic of Austria covered 83,843 km^2 with a population of 6.72 million.

The Habsburg Empire never completely recovered from the damage it suffered after the Italian and German unification. Nevertheless, and particularly under Prime Minister Count Taaffe (1879-1893), there were a few successful steps taken to modernise the state economically and politically. The public debt was reduced, and agriculture and the country's young industry developed well under high, protective customs duties. At the same time, social-reform legislation was initiated. A relaxation of the electoral census finally led to the development of new parties that soon grew into mass organisations, as was the case with the Social Democratic Party (SPÖ) founded in 1889.

The 28 June 1914 assassination in Sarajevo of the heir to the throne, and the declaration of war on Serbia that ensued 1 month later—precipitating World War I—began the final chapter in the life of the Habsburg Empire. Despite the fact that the various fronts could be held in the face of initial setbacks, increasing supply problems and the nationality conflicts that were quickly turning into struggles for independence made the collapse inevitable. The allied armistice conditions were accepted by the last imperial government on 3 November 1918.

Defeat caused the Habsburg multinational state to disintegrate into nationally homogeneous divisions. In the centre, subsequent to the abdication of the emperor on 12 November, the Republic of German-Austria was proclaimed. The government was led by a social democrat, Renner, as head of a broad coalition of SPÖ and Christian Socialists (CSP), whose leading roles were clearly confirmed in the elections of February 1919. The new government was confronted with immense problems, not the least of which was the fight against the revolutionary aspirations of the communist left. That the revolutionary workers could be put on the defensive by the People's Guard and by progressive labour legislation only aided the new government's success. Once the communist threat had been neutralised, any nonsocialist interest in further cooperation with the SPÖ disappeared.

The subsequent governments, all showing a purely bourgeois outlook, sought to improve the dismal state of the nation's finances. The preconditions for this were created in 1922 when four European powers guaranteed a large international loan on condition of a continuing renunciation of unification with the German *Reich* and a 4-year control of state finances by the League of Nations. Stabilisation of the economy was not accompanied by a diminution of tensions in national politics; instead, the conflicts between the SPÖ—which after 1926 explicitly favoured the development of a socialist Austria—and the CSP—which tended more and more towards the antidemocratic concept of a cooperative state—were aggravated. The latter took recourse in the *Heimwehren* (home defence forces), organisations with strong links to Italian fascism, in order to encourage the SPÖ and its party militia to acts of terror and violence that could then, as in 1927, be brutally suppressed by instruments of the state.

Austrian democracy was finally destroyed in the wake of the Great Depression. In March 1933, Chancellor Dollfuss rid himself of the parliament to establish an authoritarian regime through emergency orders. This regime had no place for workers' organisations nor for the home-grown National Socialists who constituted undesired competition for the *Heimwehren*. After the bloody suppression of the so-called February "disturbances" in 1934, both SPÖ and trade unions were banned. The attempted coup by the Austrian Nazis in the following July led to a more energetic persecution of their leaders. Increasing German pressure not only put an end to the persecution of the National Socialists, but it also provided the explanation for the lack of resistance with which the government accepted the liquidation of the Austrian state and its absorption into the German *Reich* in March 1938.

The lost national sovereignty was returned to the country in 1955, when the victors of World War II declared an end to their occupation regime on the condition of Austria's perpetual neutrality.

Worker sport in Austria developed in close accord with a socialist cultural movement that was of considerable importance to the Austrian labour movement. It was based on the notion of "Austro-Marxism" that remained unique to the world (*Mit uns zieht die Neue Zeit*, 1981). Within the Austro-Marxist cultural concept, worker sport played a role that theoretically seemed unimportant, yet practically turned out to be overriding.

The inception of the worker sport movement did not appear to differ greatly from that in Germany, especially as the gymnastics or *Turner* organisations under the Danube monarchy were part of the *Deutsche Turnerschaft* and followed it both organisationally and ideologically. When the German-Austria *Turner* region affiliated with the *Deutsche Turnerschaft,* it was specified that the attribute "German" meant that within the multilingual state, Austro-Hungary, only the German language was to prevail. This was in accordance with the political thinking of the Austrian *Turner*, who themselves were German nationalists. The national problem in Austria was far more acute than in Germany. So the German fascist direction of the Austrian *Turner* fraternity, which fought everything "un-German" and "non-Aryan," was far stronger than within Germany. The *Deutsche Turnverein*, founded in Vienna in 1885, did not admit Jews, and it elected the leader of the *Alldeutsche Partei*, Georg Ritter von Schönerer, as an honorary member. The first *Männer Turnverein* banned all non-German participation in the anniversary meetings of 1886 and later amended its statutes so that only "Germans of Aryan descent" could be allowed to join the club (Mehl, 1923, p. 45).

Such tendencies, along with an increasingly aggressive attitude toward social democrats, made it more impossible for the growing number of workers within the *Turner* clubs to take part in *Turner* activities (Ardelt, 1969). This enhanced the need to set up worker *Turnen* free from the bourgeois and reactionary atmosphere of the *Turner* clubs.

Initially, the Austrian labour movement provided only very limited organisational facilities for members interested in gymnastics. By contrast to the labour movement in some parts of Europe, the social-democratic movement in Austria came into existence relatively late (1888-1889). Ever under the influence of its German model, the Austrian movement tended to be dominated by the stance of Victor Adler, the party founder and ideological leader, and by the specific conditions of the Habsburg dynasty. Social democracy in Austro-Hungary was dominated from the outset by attempts to resolve the state's national problem. Development of reform plans in respect to this central Austrian issue led to the intellectual emancipation of Austrian social democracy from the philosophy of the fraternal German Party. Here lie the roots of the ideological tendency of Austrian socialism that may be described as Austro-Marxism and that is specific to the Austrian labour movement.

Ever since the inception of the socialist labour movement in the 1860s, the cultural betterment of the Austrian worker was at the centre of all activities. On the one hand, the educational and cultural worker clubs provided a rare possibility for coalition, insofar as the government kept a close watch on every worker club, banning it at the slightest opportunity if it engaged in anything that smacked of illegal political activity. On the other hand, it was part of the overall ideology that matching the bourgeois educational and cultural lead was a prerequisite for the ultimate emancipation of the working class. This desire for emancipation was the

---

Code of the *Deutscher Turnerbund* (1919)

(1) The aim of the *Deutscher Turnerbund* and its clubs is the creation and strengthening of the spiritual and physical ability and the consciousness of the Germanness in the German people. The basis for such a *völkisch* racially based education is in the three wisdoms of *Turnvater* Friedrich Ludwig Jahn, i.e. *purity of the race, purity of the people,* and *liberty of the spirit.* Each member shall pursue these ends on the sports field and in his private life. . . .

(6) In all competition rules of the organisation the following has to be included: The testing of the knowledge about the racial foundations of our people has to be included in all events. The events to be part of the gymnastic competitions are not to be announced in advance so that there will be no undue specialisation. Military gymnastics are always to be included. . . . Members are permitted to take part in events of other organisations only under the condition that the events are exclusively performed by members of the Germanic race and that the three Aryan wisdoms of Jahn are not impeded. There will be no competitions for prices. Believers in internationalistic creeds have no moral right to become members of the *Deutscher Turnerbund.*

Quoted in E. Mehl, *Grundriß des Deutschen Turnens*, 1923, p. 12.

theoretical foundation of Austrian social democracy. From the labour movement's standpoint, cultural work meant from the outset raising the level of education and improving general schooling and specialist training on the job. Only mounting pressure from the grass roots of the party brought a widened discussion of what exactly was meant by "culture." It was through this that worker sport gained a great deal in importance, although it had to maintain itself originally against the attacks of both the party and the trade unions.

Originally, the *Turners* had found a place within the worker cultural clubs that permitted gymnastics on improvised apparatus in canteens and pubs on a regular basis. These *Turner* groups joined together in 1894 as the Eighth Region of the German Worker *Turner* Association (ATB). In 1909, however, they left the German association and became independent as the Austrian Worker *Turner* Association (*Österreichischer Arbeiterturnerbund*).

The party was sceptical about this development and at times openly rejected it. That gymnastics (*Turnen*) still bore the stigma of reactionary German nationalism may well have contributed to the party's coolness. On the other hand, social-democratic cultural politicians tended to regard as fallacious in principle anything that brought worker culture close to popular culture. The cultural tradition of the sub-bourgeois classes was either ignored or spurned, because any form of popular culture emanating from industrial capitalism was regarded as undesirable. The politicians were more inclined to strive for social democracy to inherit the European bourgeois cultural tradition; they saw Austrian social democracy and the Austrian working class as legitimate heirs to such a worthy tradition.

Sport and physical culture were regarded *a priori* as not being part of such a cultural tradition and were relegated to a subordinate role (Krammer, 1981). Sport seemed to the party to be as frivolous as a visit to a twilight variety show or the reading of pornographic literature; it would lead the workers up into the hills of fantasy and hedonism rather than into the urban crucible of actions against the government. So, when in 1895 some young workers and students, including Karl Renner (later both chancellor and president), aspired to found a worker rambling club, there was considerable resentment and opposition from the party executive before the club finally came into being. In actual fact, the club, *Die Naturfreunde* (Friends of Nature), became extremely popular, with branches set up prior to World War I in Munich, Zurich, Berne, Lucerne, Berlin, Paris, London, and New York.

At the 1898 party conference, the social democrats defined their position in regard to worker sport; they asserted that sport clubs were suitable only for people "who are not yet ready for serious work" (*Verhandlungen*, 1898, p. 121). In the same year, the Worker Cycling Federation was established, and by 1914 it had 423 clubs with 24,000 members (Gastgeb, 1952). The party's mistrust of worker sport had two sources: Sport was not considered part of the lofty culture to which the Austrian labour movement should aspire, and athletes had not succeeded in working out an ideal alternative to the bourgeois *Turner* and sports activities that would be more than a mere rejection of the status quo. The imitation of normal sport club practice provoked resentment that athletes were merely apolitical. So, the foundation of worker sport clubs was generally seen as unnecessary and even harmful in that it distracted attention from the overall work of the party and the trade unions. The opportunities of the *Turner* sport movement to integrate and educate young workers were on the whole rejected by the principal leaders of the party and unions.

During World War I, a development occurred in the Austrian labour movement that differed radically from anything in fraternal parties elsewhere. The "tolerant" attitude of the party leadership toward the government's war policy led to a crisis of trust among its supporters at the grass-roots level. An open breach between the executive and the grass roots was only avoided by Prime Minister Stürgkh ignoring parliament and ruling by emergency measures; the social-democratic leadership did not have to vote in favour of a war budget in parliament, thereby discrediting itself in the eyes of the grass roots.

When a left radicalisation of the party threatened, the strong power of integration in Austrian social democracy prevented a move to the left by the threat of a final split. Furthermore, the January 1918 strikes displayed the fundamental role of social-democratic policy in damping down worker actions for fear of an acute revolutionary crisis.

After the military defeat in the war came the political disintegration of the Danube monarchy. This did not bring, however, social disintegration. "It was not the revolutionary events that altered the form of the state, but rather the course of events when the victory of the capitalist West was apparent" (Neck, 1983, p. 227). The fate of the Soviet governments in Budapest and Munich demonstrated that the moderate stance of social democrats in Austria was evidently correct even in the eyes of the workers. When the social democrats took on government responsibility in coalition with the Christian Socialist Party until 1920, they were still able to maintain the political and trade union unity of the Austrian labour movement.

Although the Communist Party of Austria came into existence in November 1918, the first outside Soviet Russia, its participation in internal politics remained extremely modest; it made virtually no impression in the elections (Steiner, 1983). The social democrats showed the way, including for worker sport, maintaining that class reform in Austria needed to continue the long, strenuous

Flag swinging was one of the attractions for workers at the second Worker Olympics in Vienna, 1931.

Nusterer, winner of the men's tennis match at the second Worker Olympics in Vienna, 1931.

Poster advertising the first district sports competition in Linz, 1921.

My Apprenticeship in the Zieglergasse by Deputy Mayor Karl Honay [Vienna]

45 years ago [in 1907] I was permitted for the first time to enter the gymnastics room in the *Printers House* as a young member of the Association of Young Austrian Workers, Local Ottakring II. We had founded a gymnastic section in our local. At that time, a *workingmen's club* did not exist in Ottakring yet and the Christian-Social majority in the village council refused the use of the gymnastic halls of the local schools to us *red* youth. Therefore, we, the sporting apprentices had to depend upon the facilities of the local printers in the *Zieglergasse*. Gymnastics was every Sunday from 5 to 7 p.m. This was the only free time we had back then in the *good old days*. It is difficult to imagine to what extent the working youth was exploited. The ten hour day was the law, but in the small shops we had to work 12 or we would not have been hired. I spent my four years as an apprentice with such a small *master* in Rudolfsheim. The working hours were from 7 to 7 Monday through Friday. Saturday it lasted until 6, but then we apprentices had to sweep the floor and clean the place until 8 p.m. At midday, there was a short break for lunch. Twice a week there were the theory classes that went with the apprenticeship from 7 through 9 p.m. At Sunday, there was more theory at the trade school from 8-12 noon.

So the only time we had for gymnastics was Sunday evening. Why did we have physical activities at all under such conditions? This is due to the influence of comrade Zölch who talked to us about the one-sided use of the muscles in our job and convinced us that gymnastics were important for the harmonious build-up of the body. He pointed out in particular the *Turner fever* (muscle soreness) which would result from the first exercises in the first sessions being the best proof how many of our muscles were not being used in spite of our very physical work.

I still remember how bad I felt with all the soreness of muscles after the first training evenings. But this did not stop me from attending all the *Turner* evenings. It was really beautiful. After the training we sang all the old songs of the worker *Turners*, experienced the spirit of splendid comradeship and became friends of men of our own class. My poor life as an apprentice received a new sense with this new life. . . .

P. Nittnaus & M. Zink (eds.), *Sport ist unser Leben. 100 Jahre Arbeitersport in Österreich* (Vienna: Mohl, 1992, p. 24).

tradition of struggle for securing a majority of the people's minds and ballot boxes. The major arguments used by the leadership (Otto Bauer, Karl Renner, and Karl Seitz) against immediate socialist revolution were the expectation of strong opposition from the Christian Socialist Party that dominated the Austrian provinces and the likelihood of economic collapse as a consequence of massive boycotts by foreign capitalist states. "So in Austria events that bordered on civil war, like these at the inception of the Weimar Republic, were avoided. There was no Noske in Austria, nor was there a need for one" (Neck, 1983, p. 232).

A constructive element of this strategy was the unique development of a labour movement culture in the country. Initially, this was a socialist culture focused on "Red Vienna" that was under social-democratic administration and that was used as a countermeasure to bourgeois society. All initiatives were based on the conception of a "new person" who would develop through cultural education, such as propagated by Max Adler (Adler, 1924).

Within the broad spectrum of alternative activities, there was communal construction of apartment housing,

school reform, proletarian dress, and new socialist forms of child upbringing. The socialist clubs provided an alternative sphere of life that permitted the worker to be totally separated from the bourgeois world, that is, from the class enemy. The socialist club system enabled the worker to be among workers from birth to death.

The Vienna example did have some effect upon the Austrian provinces; the different social structure and the conservative parliamentary majorities provided, however, only limited results. Worker sport now had a new task. Originally pushed by the rank and file against the intentions of the party, the Austro-Marxist culture theorists now wanted to use it as a socialist form of class struggle. Bourgeois sport should be counteracted by a socialist sport movement, and worker sport was supposed to play an important role in the creation of the "new man."

Just as worker culture in general, so worker sport became determined by the ambivalent position of the Austrian Social Democracy: The celebration of the Republic by socialist clubs, the oath of allegiance to the republican state—the strongest and most reliable support came from the socialist clubs against the fascist movement—

connected with the hope that the Republic had nothing but a passing-through stage to the socialist society of the future. "The loss of utopia and the loss of reality were the two poles between which the worker cultural movement shifted" (Langewiesche, 1979, p. 48).

The Austro-Marxist schemes of verbal radicalism were typical of the new approach, and they were frightening to the bourgeoisie. "We have to plan and organise our work step to establish a socialist society in the long term. . . . Political revolution will be the result of powerful, but carefully determined work over the years" (Bauer, 1919, p. 5).

The conditions for worker sport in the Republic changed, inasmuch as a social reform sponsored by a social democrat, Ferdinand Hanusch, considerably improved the working and living conditions of workers and made mass participation in sport and physical culture possible.

On 19 May 1919, the authorities ratified the statutes of the Federation of Worker and Soldier Sports Clubs of Austria (*Verband der Arbeiter- und Soldaten-Sportvereinigung Österreichs*), an umbrella organisation that contained swimmers, football players, Friends of Nature, cyclists, and some army sport groups. As a consequence of the close alignment with social-democratic organisations, difficulties soon emerged. With the breakdown of the government coalition in 1920 and the break between socialists and the bourgeois parties, proletarian exclusivity and the rupture of relations with all bourgeois organisations were the political requirement of the moment. Within the worker sport federation, only the *Turner* had any sympathy for this situation, but worker soccer clubs in particular resisted fiercely; they did not think it necessary to forsake the bourgeois football federation, and they continued to play against bourgeois opponents in front of large crowds. When they argued that isolation from bourgeois clubs "would lose them thousands of members" (*Protokoll,* 1 February 1923, p. 6), they had the support of the cyclists and the Friends of Nature rambling clubs. So the gymnasts had to draw conclusions for themselves: "If we continue relations with a society that bears the Swastika on the one hand, and work hand-in-hand with socialist comrades on the other, we shall find ourselves in an unacceptable situation." The worker gymnasts, therefore, abandoned the Worker and Soldier Sports Clubs federation and were welcomed as a members of the Socialist Worker Sports International (the Lucerne Worker Sports International).

The conflict between the apolitical and political segments of the worker sport movement soon began to change in quality. When the bourgeois right had consolidated itself, certain expectations were made of worker sport. For example, from 1920, home defence leagues came into existence; these were paramilitary groups, explicitly antisocialist and politically close to the Christian Socialist Party, though some were obviously in favour of national socialism. The need for a physically strong worker who was prepared to fight and who came from the worker sport movement was central to the thinking of party leadership. In opposition to reactionary military organisations, such as *Heimwehr* (Home Defence) and *Frontkämpferverband* (Front Fighter Union), the Republican *Schutzbund* (Defence League) was formed to withstand the serious threat to the democratic Republic. Henceforth, worker sport and, by tradition, the *Turner* who seemed predestined for this role, were in constant danger of being reduced to a subordinate role by the *Schutzbund*. In reality, this meant "revolutionary discipline" and military drill rather than socialist creativity in an alternative cultural movement.

For the Social Democratic Party this utilisation of worker sport in a military defensive organisation was far more attractive than any countercultural perspective. Naturally, therefore, the party strongly favoured worker gymnasts and a union between them and the Defence League. In fact, the former Armed Forces Minister, Julius Deutsch, was concurrently head of the Republican Defence League and president of the worker *Turners*. From 1926, he was also president of the Austrian Worker Sports Association (ASKÖ) and, from 1927, president of the Lucerne Worker Sports International. As Deutsch put it, "Gymnastics makes workers stronger and readier to fight, to lead the liberation struggle which is their historical mission, and to ensure its success" (ÖATZ, 1924, p. 1).

After lengthy demands and appeals from the party, ASKÖ was reorganised and unified on 26 October 1924; Engelbert Zölch of the worker gymnasts (and therefore member of the militant wing) was elected president. Because ASKÖ had no points of contact with bourgeois sport, the soccer players did not join; they felt that matches against bourgeois clubs were more important. Shortly thereafter, ASKÖ joined the Socialist Worker Sports International (SWSI) in which Julius Deutsch was soon to play a crucial role.

By contrast with almost all other member-states of SWSI, ASKÖ was able to maintain internal coherence. Because they lacked the sort of political backing that a strong Communist Party might have provided, communist-oriented worker athletes tended to integrate with ASKÖ. This resulted in a more tolerant attitude by social-democratic officials towards them than existed elsewhere (Krammer, 1981, pp. 105-115).

The range of sports being practised was extended so that, in reality, reservations about bourgeois competitive sport were dropped. Apart from the traditional gymnastics, cycling, and rambling, ASKÖ now pursued swimming, combat sports (though boxing was banned for a long time), soccer, tennis, ice skating, shooting, chess,

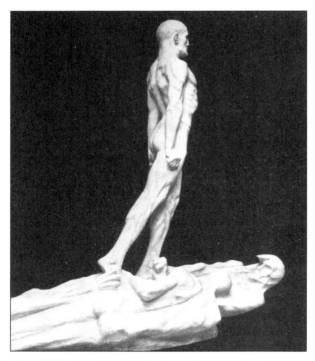

"The Will Is of Importance"—This image was placed at the top of the newspaper *First Austrian Sports Competition for Workers*, Vienna, July 1926, no. 3.

The Worker Athlete Union was founded in 1922 with six clubs and 132 members.

400-metre hurdling. Schubert (Austria) outstripped the Finnish athlete for more than 8 metres, but was disqualified at the final hurdle after plunging into it.

judo, flying, fishing, handball, fencing, and ice hockey. Other winter sports, with the exception of those outdoor pursuits that came within the Friends of Nature domain, remained the preserve of bourgeois sport. Moreover, the spreading of worker sport into the countryside, in particular into the Alpine region, was very limited owing to the political conservatism of those areas. Village councils tended to favour clubs of German-national or Christian-German origin. ASKÖ fiercely opposed this political position and found itself up against the *Deutscher Turnerbund*, an overt foe of social democrats and the church:

> We lead a struggle against all the enemies of our country, that is against Marxists and Bolsheviks, against Free Thinkers and Freemasons, against Jews and also against international conspiracy that would make the German people a servant of Rome. (*Zur Abwehr,* 1929, p. 9)

From the outset, the *Deutscher Turnerbund* engaged in military gymnastics, shooting, fencing, horse riding, and other military exercises to ensure that young gymnasts would receive the military training prohibited by the St. Germain Treaty. In spite of the state distancing itself from party politics, its spiritual proximity to national socialism was quite explicit:

> There is a storm bearing down on Germany. With precise logic our destiny will be fulfilled. . . . The time is fast coming when, through the insistent demands of youth, we know that victory will be ours.

In 1932, the ASKÖ had 275,000 members in 2,735 local clubs organised in 16 different sport associations, such as Friends of Nature, District 17 and 18 of the German ATSB, Austrian Amateur Soccer Federation, Worker Cycling and Motor Cycling Association, Worker Swimming Association, Federation of Austrian Strength Clubs, Austrian Team Handball Federation, Austrian Worker Marksmen and Hunters, Austrian Worker Aeroplane Association, Association of Worker Tennis and Ice Sport Clubs, Worker Chess Association, Federation of Worker Angling and Fishing Clubs, Federation of Socialist Youth Organisations, Apprentice Section of the Free Trade Union, and the Republican Defence League.

Beckmann's Sport Lexicon (Vienna: Beckmann, 1933, p. 156).

We are stepping along the path into the future with our valiant Storm Troopers. . . . The *Deutscher Turnerbund*, the great preparer of those troops, the great preparer of the folk awaking, has been ploughing the rocky furrow of the Fatherland for the past forty years; and now the fruits are being reaped. (*Salzburger Turnjugend—Jahrbuch 1932,* p. 5)

The anticlerical tendency of the *Deutscher Turnerbund* had already led, in the years before World War I, to the establishment of a Christian German *Turnerbund* that was pro-Catholic and militantly antisocialist: "The Social Democrats use blatant lies and will resort to any action against all that is holy before God and Nature" (*Verbandsturnzeitung der Christlich-deutschen Turnerschaft,* 1929, p. 99). And further, they use their *Turner* in the service of the struggle against "elements that are afraid of the light and the red flood" (*Verbandsturnzeitung der Christlich-deutschen Turnerschaft,* 1927, pp. 234-235).

In the years following World War I, Austrian worker sport possessed the largest gym hall in all Austria, one of the largest in the world. This was because of the ingenuity of the Viennese vice-mayor Josef Puchler, who saved the installations of the Vienna military airfield from demolition. For his help to the worker sport movement, he was elected president of the regional worker sport association. The conversion of the airpilots' mess hall into a gym took only 6 months: it was 56 m long and 18 m wide, with a large glass dome in the middle over all gymnastics apparatus. It became the Austrian worker *Turner* and sports school. Considering that travel was difficult and expensive, and that the number of instructors needed for the worker sport movement was rapidly increasing, this provided an alternative to the bourgeois preparation of instructors, and it was much cheaper than the comparable school in Leipzig. In May 1923, the first course was started.

The hall and the nearby barracks were supposed to be destroyed under the stipulations of the St. Germain Treaty by the Allied Forces, but Puchler succeeded in convincing the Allies that both were needed for housing and nonmilitary worker gymnastics.

P. Nittnaus & M. Zink (eds.), *Sport ist unser Leben. 100 Jahre Arbeitersport in Österreich* (Vienna: Mohl, 1992, p. 42).

In February 1934, many worker athletes, on the one hand, and Christian-German and German-National *Turner*, on the other, were to fight each other at the barricades.

As in other countries, worker sport in Austria emphasised counterculture and attempted to provide a socialist alternative within the cultural conception of Austro-Marxism and to work against the traditions of bourgeois sport. A qualitatively different sports practice grew out of the rejection of the principal criteria of bourgeois sport. Apolitical and neutral sport, which in reality was "utterly on capitalism's payroll," was opposed by explicitly political sport in the service of the emancipation of the working class. "Bourgeois sport is without exception geared to individual top performance. Records, records, records! That is that magic word that defines everything in bourgeois sport" (ÖATZ, 1928, p. 62). As in bourgeois society generally, it was felt that in bourgeois sport, everyone was performing for himself or herself alone; as a result, sport helped infuse the common people with the notion of a profit-oriented society. So social democrats rejected both athletic one-sidedness that emanated from the urge to break records and the tendency to display, and spectator sport that hampered people from pursuing sport themselves:

For people who go in for sport professionally, their bodies become merchandise; they are bought and

sold and cast aside when they are useless. Anyone can sit in the stands and watch these men in the sports arena without moving a muscle, just for the thrill of it. (ÖATZ, 1936, p. 58)

The only answer for worker athletes was to strengthen the workers' self-confidence rather than use a safety valve for working-class discontent.

Worker athletes want mass sport combined with political agitation. Not games and sports for the sake of entertainment, but physical activity in the knowledge that a worker has to be educated. (Gastgeb, 1933, p. 38)

The implementation of these aspirations in worker sport was not at all easy, particularly with the reduction in competition, as ordered by the party, and fewer victory ceremonies and prizes, which can run counter to the grass roots' interests and understanding of sport. Possibly the most important impact that Austrian worker sport had on worker culture in the First Republic consisted in its participation in and joint organisation of proletarian cultural festivals. Festivals and meetings with athletic clubs were among the most successful of all socialist actions, largely because they were organised from below and very seldom were artificial (something that could scarcely be said of meetings of the social democrats).

The conjunction of sport, festival, and political education succeeded for the first time on a large scale in the Worker Gymnastics and Sports Festivals held in Vienna in 1926. Athletic displays and competition alternated with mass marches, massed choirs, lectures and speeches, fireworks, and even a beach party. This successful synthesis of sport, culture, and political education was the basis for the success of the Worker Olympics in Vienna in 1931.

Austrian worker culture in the First Republic was generally rich in festivals and meetings that emotionally moved workers, especially youth, and brought them into the socialist movement spiritually. In competition with the Roman Catholic Church, the labour movement brought into being a whole range of festivals, some of which were introduced as a clear alternative to religious ritual and tradition. For example, young workers went to the youth ceremony as an alternative to their first holy communion, to the spring parade rather than the Corpus Christi procession, and to the winter solstice festival in place of Christmas (Cardorff, 1983).

These broad initiatives by the Austrian worker cultural movement were in sharp contrast to the attitude of many party officials and, particularly, the party press, which was obviously ignorant of these endeavours. This sometimes caused considerable ire among athletes, as when the *Arbeiter-Turn-Zeitung* (Worker Newspaper) criticised (and often failed to differentiate) sport in a

---

Statutes of the Christian German *Turnerschaft* of Austria

"The Christian German *Turnerschaft* of Austria is aiming at the general practice of German *Turnen*, the furthering of German consciousness and patriotric Christian belief as a means of strengthening the moral inclination and furthering the military readiness of the German people. The Christian German *Turnerschaft* of Austria works on the basis of solid Christian belief, of the faithfulness in the (catholic) belief of our forefathers, of the love for the fatherland and the German people. Therefore, membership in a club of the Christian German *Turnerschaft* of Austria requires the open confession to Christianity and our German fatherland."

Joseph Recla, *Die Christliche Turnbewegung* (Niedernhausen, 1982, p. 28).

patriotic mood of major bourgeois sports meetings, or when worker sport representatives were refused attendance at general party assemblies, or when no mention was made of worker sport, as in the Linz Party Programme of 1926 (Krammer, 1981).

On the whole, the party expectation of worker sport as a means to enhance the physical ability to fight and to join the paramilitary Defence League was generally not reconcilable with the counterculture conception. This was particularly apparent when the Defence League severely took to task worker gymnastics because they evidently lacked strict military discipline. The League believed that the paramilitary order and precision of movement of the reactionary German folk *Turner* clubs were what was needed in the worker gymnastics clubs (*Der Schutzbund*, 1924, p. 7). This relegated worker physical fitness to a common military denominator. "We must combat all reactionary forces that hamper our march to socialism. For this we need primarily discipline, iron discipline and selfless subordination to the great duty of ours" (Czerny, 1925, p. 29).

Gymnasts, cyclists, and combat-sport proponents were the most frequently encountered athletes in the Defence League parades; in fact, the gymnasts often had their own formations. Each military gymnast had to sign a declaration by which he promised to defend revolutionary gains and follow the orders of the workers' leaders at all times (*Bericht 1926-1928*, pp. 15-17). With the introduction of appointed leaders and the abolition of all discussion, this was the path that was followed. In spite of the increased discipline and the militarisation of large sections of the worker sport movement, the vitality of the athletes could not be subdued. This became impressively evident in July 1931 when the Worker Olympics in Vienna became a remarkable demonstration of proletarian solidarity.

The very granting of the Worker Olympics to Vienna was a political act. Austria's internal political situation had worsened towards the end of the 1920s as the *Heimwehr* had departed from "Western democratic parliamentarism and political parties" and initiated a fascist state in May 1930. The barriers between the two political groups had risen steadily and were now insurmountable (Jedlicka, 1963). So it was the object of the Worker Olympics to show the political adversary the strength and determination of Austrian workers.

> Everywhere in Europe democracy is being threatened by the most brutal and aggressive form of fascism, and young people need to feel more and more the power of socialism now that bourgeois parties have resorted to treason. The young strong fighting man and woman, whose physical strength is as great as their moral fortitude, will not yield without a fight

> "Like all the bigger clubs of the Austrian Worker Bicycle Association (ARBÖ) our club in Meidling (near Vienna) had a winter sport section. As we were not good enough to participate in the Worker Winter Olympics as athletes, we decided to take part as spectators. Five men and one woman took off on bicycle to Mürzzuschlag.
>
> Friday morning 9 a.m. we met at the city border. Everything went well till Traiskirchen when it started to snow. After some falls—which were harmless as the snow was by now one foot deep—we arrived at Schottwien at 4 p.m. The sun had disappeared already behind the mountains. It became very cold and a real snow storm started. The Semmering Mountains could no longer be done on bicycle. Thinking of ourselves as experienced winter sports people, we estimated that the southern slopes had less snow, so we pushed our bicycles to the top—3 hours of hard work. We were very disappointed when we saw even more snow on the other side of the pass. We decided immediately to continue pushing and so we arrived very tired at 10:30 p.m. in Spital on the other side. Fortunately one of the inns was still open, so that we could get a room for the night. On the next morning the snow was already 2 ft 9 in. so we continued to Mürzzuschlag by train."

Der Arbeiter-Radfahrer, March 1931, quoted in P. Nittnaus & M. Zink (eds.), *Sport ist unser Leben. 100 Jahre Arbeitersport in Österreich* (Vienna: Mohl, 1992, p. 61).

in the face of attacks on democracy. All social democrats are delighted that the next Olympics are to take place in Vienna where our Austrian comrades, who are valiantly fighting fascist reaction, have shown that they can be victorious. They need the solidarity of the international proletariat. (*Festschrift zur 2. Arbeiter-Olympiade Wien 1931*, p. 5)

This defiant gesture brought its rewards: as many as 77,166 participants, including some 37,000 Austrian worker athletes and 200,000 spectators, came to the new Vienna Stadium that had been built especially for the Olympics (Gastgeb, 1952, p. 69).

The Worker Olympics provided the opportunity to demonstrate all the strengths of proletarian culture: a festival of the proletariat and its final, future liberation, dramatically symbolised by the destruction of a giant tower representing capital's fortress.

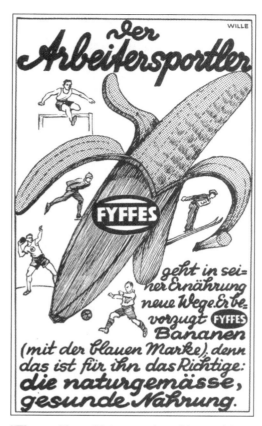

"The working athlete goes about his nourishment in new ways. He prefers FYFFES bananas (with the blue label) because that is right for him: natural, healthy nourishment."

Poster advertising a sports competition for workers in Vienna, 1926.

Compendium of general routines composed by Hans Freytag and Johann Renczes for men and women at the worker competition in Vienna, 1926.

The euphoria generated by the sports festival contained the danger of the festival's strength being identified with real political strength. Whereas those parts of the bourgeoisie that openly agitated for a fascist state order had become patently obvious, and the first Nazis had been elected to Austrian parliaments, these mass festivities could make the Austrian as well as the European working class believe that it was still powerful, if not superior in strength. In actual fact, it was not long after the Worker Olympics, on 13 February 1934, that the final defeat of Austrian social democracy took place. ASKÖ and all its federations and clubs were dissolved and, in June 1934, the home defence league "*Führer,*" Ernst Rüdiger von Starhemberg, was appointed supreme sports "*Führer*"; in 1935, the joint organisation of the Austrian Gymnastics and Sports Front came into being.

Poster advertising the second Worker Olympics in Vienna, 1931.

The Second Worker Olympics in Vienna, 19–26 July 1931

Participating Countries

Austria
Belgium
Czechoslovakia
Denmark
Estonia
Finland
France
Germany
Great Britain
Holland
Hungary
Lettland
Norway
Palestine
Poland
Switzerland
United States

Beckmann's Sport Lexicon (Vienna: Beckmann, 1933, p. 160).

Minutes of the First Postwar ASKÖ Conference, 27 October 1945

Comrade Winterer reports on behalf of the national leadership of the ASKÖ that our build-up activity is hindered by the division in the four zones of occupation. There are also some obstacles from a political point of view. So far, the only sports federation which exists is ours, i.e. workers, as we have been unaffected by the prohibition of Nazism after the defeat. The bourgeois organisations are all dissolved and not yet refounded as they were labelled Nazi. The Communist Party does not have any old sport structures left. Workers sport is solidly based. The comrades should continue to build-up the new organisation without rest and should try to reach particularly the youth so that the very comrades might retreat eventually. There is still continuous struggling against the old Nazis in many organisations. Particularly in the industries they have to be removed. The Communist Party is attempting to found a new sports organisation but we will not participate.

P. Nittnaus & M. Zink (eds.), Sport ist unser Leben. 100 Jahre Arbeitersport in Österreich (Vienna: Mohl, 1992, p. 93).

SPÖ: Sport Programmme for Austria (1982)

"The necessity of men to compare oneself with others and to perform has to be accepted. Elite sport is a way of personal fulfilment and individual self-realisation. It has an important function to encourage others to do sports. It has to be assured, however, more than before, that excesses are to be avoided in physical and psychological respects. They appear the most often when sport is not used for recreation, health or pleasure but for extreme personal or national prestige. Sport which reduces people to trade objects and are thus destroying the honor of man, are also to be defeated.

It is not to be accepted when children and youth are seduced or forced to do an excessive amount of sport which will cause physiological or psychological harm. Any form of manipulation (doping) is to be condemned. It is a duty of the social democracy to protect men from the misuse of sport.

Professional sports have an adequate place in our society. The social security of professional athletes has to be safeguarded to the same extent as those of any other worker.

In all spheres of sport the over-estimation and exclusive regard for victory and records has to be counteracted. This attitude is not only unjust, it also leads to the resigning and easy compensation by passive sports consumption by many and thus degrades the majority of people to spectators."

P. Nittnaus & M. Zink (eds.), *Sport ist unser Leben. 100 Jahre Arbeitersport in Österreich* (Vienna: Mohl, 1992, p. 126).

Generally speaking, worker athletes did not join these fascist organisations (Leichter, 1968, p. 118); in fact, many of them were involved in clandestine activities.

When in July 1934 the third Czechoslovak Worker Olympiade took place in Prague, many hundreds of worker athletes from Austria took part, displaying in the parade through Prague the portraits of labour leaders who had been murdered in Austria the previous February (*Arbeiterzeitung*, issue 8, 1934). A Central Committee for Worker Sport constituted itself to replace ASKÖ, and Julius Deutsch, who had fled to Czechoslovakia, remained president of SWSI. In spite of persecution by the Austrian authorities, worker athletes frequently distributed leaflets and illegal brochures, even under conditions of Austrian fascism. A worker sport official, Hans Kratky, took part in the revolutionary socialist conference in Brünn (later Bron) in late 1934 and lectured on the situation of the worker sport movement in Austria. In consequence of setting up an illegal sport organisation, when he returned home he was arrested with Franz Jonas—later Mayor of Vienna and President of the Austrian Republic—and Bruno Kreisky, later Austrian Chancellor, who was put on trial with other social democrats (Kykal, n.d.). Kratky was not imprisoned because his guilt could not be proved, and there continued to be actions by Austrian worker athletes right up to 1936.

After the conclusion of World War II, on 27 October 1945, representatives of the former ASKÖ federations came together in a national conference and restarted work full of the old trust and idealism (*ASKÖ 1945-1946*, p. 3). Under the new circumstances, the revival of the counterculture programme was no longer debated. In the same way, the Austrian Socialist Party no longer considered a class-specific policy and a proletarian culture. At the beginning of 1946, ASKÖ decided to cooperate with all Austrian sport federations and have sport competitions with them (Gastgeb, 1952, p. 96).

Continuity in the Austrian worker sport movement remained on the outside. Just as ASKÖ reconstituted itself, so its former clubs and organisations reappeared in new guise. Now, however, the social democrats used worker sport to achieve integration into existing society. Step by step, sport was depoliticised, and the principal criteria of a socialist physical culture fell into oblivion. With all the focus of attention on sport for all, ASKÖ now had far greater toleration and flexibility when it came to access conditions of bourgeois competitive sport.

Symptomatic of these developments was the change in name: ASKÖ dropped the "A" for "*Arbeiter* (Worker)" and replaced it by another "A" for the more neutral-sounding "*Arbeitsgemeinschaft*" (Working Group). Despite all the shifts, ASKÖ remains today the strongest organisation of the Austrian labour movement. It now has 4,000 clubs with a total of over 1 million members (*Österreichisches Sportjahrbuch 1981/82*, p. 78). The qualitative expectations of the socialists are quite different today from what they were during the First Republic:

We socialists see sport as an important area of life and a valuable form of human self-fulfilment. In our highly technical world of labour, the maintenance and improvement of health are of considerable significance. Essential elements in promoting a full personality include community enterprises as well as attempts to achieve a high performance without ulterior motive, as long as the individual observes the rules of fitness and toleration. (*Party Programme of the Austrian Socialist Party,* 1978, p. 577)

References

Adler, M. *Neue Menschen. Gedanken über sozialistische Erziehung* (Berlin, 1924).

Arbeiterkultur in Österreich 1918-1945. ITH-Tagungsbericht, vol. 16 (Vienna).

Arbeiterzeitung. Organ der österreichischen Sozialdemokratie 21 (1934).

Ardelt, R.G. *Inhalte und Strukturen des Deutschnationalen Gedankengutes in Österreich (1918-1930),* vol. 2 (Doctoral dissertation, Salzburg, 1969).

Der ASKÖ 1945-1946. ASKO-Tätigkeitsbericht über die Jahre 1945 und 1946. Erstattet dem ordentlichen Bundestag des ASKÖ am 19 und 20. April 1947 in Wien (Vienna, 1947).

Bauer, O. *Der Weg zum Sozialismus* (Vienna, 1919).

Bericht 1926-1928. 17. Kreis des Arbeiter-Turn- und Sportbundes (Vienna, 1928).

Cardorff, P. *Was gibt's denn da zu feiern? Linke Festlichkeit von den Anfängen der Arbeiterbewegung bis heute* (Vienna, 1983).

Carsten, F.L. *Faschismus in Österreich. Von Schönerer zu Hitler* (Munich, 1977).

Czerny, E. *Das Wehrturnen* (Vienna, 1925).

Festschrift anläßlich des 40-jährigen Bestandes des Arbeiterbildungsvereines Wien (Vienna, 1907).

Festschrift zur 2. Arbeiter-Olympiade Wien 1931 (Vienna, no date).

Freispruch Kratky (Strafsache Sozialistenprozeß 1935/36). Dokumen tationsarchiv des österreichischen Widerstandes No. 8050/6.

Gastgeb, H. "Panem et circenses," *Der Kampf. Sozialdemokratische Monatsschrift,* 1 (1933), pp. 36-38.

Gastgeb, H. *Vom Wirtshaus zum Stadion. 60 Jahre Arbeitersport in Österreich* (Vienna, 1952).

Jedlicka, L. "Zur Vorgeschichte des Korneuburger Eides, 18. Mai 1930," *Österreich in Geschichte und Literatur,* 7 (1963), pp. 146-153.

Krammer, R. *Arbeitersport in Österreich. Ein Beitrag zur Geschichte der Arbeiterkultur in Österreich bis 1938* (Vienna, 1981).

Krammer, R. "Die Turn- und Sportbewegung," in: E. Weinzierl & K. Skalnik, *Österreich 1918-1938. Geschichte der Ersten Republik* (Graz/Vienna/Cologne, 1983), pp. 731-743.

Kykal, I. *Der Sozialistenprozeß 1936* (Doctoral dissertation, Vienna, no date).

Langewiesche, D. "Arbeiterkultur in Österreich: Aspekte, Tendenzen und Thesen," in: G.A. Ritter (ed.), *Arbeiterkultur* (Königstein, 1979), pp. 40-57.

Leichter, O. *Zwischen zwei Diktaturen. Österreichs Revolutionäre Sozialisten 1934-1938* (Vienna, 1968).

Mehl, E. *Grundriß des deutschen Turnens* (Vienna, 1923).

Mit uns zieht die Neue Zeit. Arbeiterkultur in Österreich 1918-1934 (Vienna, 1981).

Mommsen, H. *Die Sozialdemokratie und die Nationalitätenfrage im habsburgischen Vielvölkerstaat. I. Das Ringen um die Supranationale Integration der zisleithanische Arbeiterbewegung (1867-1902)* (Vienna, 1963).

Neck, R. "Sozialdemokratie," in: E. Weinzierl & K. Skalnik, *Österreich 1918-1938* (Vienna, 1983), pp. 225-248.

Österreichische Arbeiter-Turn- und Sportzeitung (ÖATZ). Verbandsorgan des 17. und 18. Kreises des Arbeiter-Turn- und Sportbundes, 1 (1924), 6 (1928), 8 (1930).

Österreichisches Sportjahrbuch 1983/84 (published by Österreichischer Sportorganisation, 1984).

"Parteiprogramm der SPÖ 1978," in: F. Kaufmann, *Sozialdemokratie in Österreich. Idee und Geschichte einer Partei. Von 1889 bis zur Gegenwart* (Vienna/Munich, 1978), pp. 537-586.

Protokolleiner außerordentlichen VAS—Vorstandssitzung am 1.2.1923 (Typescript, ASKÖ-Bundessekretariat).

Renner, K. *An der Wende zweier Zeiten. Lebenserinnerungen* (Vienna, 1946).

Salzburger Ternerjugend—Jahrbuch 1932 (Salzburg, 1932).

Der Schutzbund. Monatsschrift des Republikanischen Schutzbundes. 6 (1924), 11 (1925).

Steiner, H. "Die Kommunistische Partei," in: E. Weinzierl & K. Skalnik, *Österreich 1918-1938* (Vienna, 1983), pp. 317-329.

Verbandsturnzeitung der Christlich-deutschen Turnerschaft. 5 (1929), 11 (1927).

Verhandlungen des Parteitages der deutschen Sozialdemokratie Österreichs 1898 (Vienna, 1898).

Zur Abwehr der klerikalen Angriffe gegen den Deutschen Turnerbund (Vienna, 1929).

Chapter 6

The British Workers' Sports Federation: 1923–1935

Stephen Jones

GREAT BRITAIN

In 1931, this island kingdom in the northwest of Europe had a population of 46.18 million spread over an area of 242,606 km².

Great Britain had advanced during the course of the 19th century to be the world's leading industrial, financial, and political power. Yet, toward the end of Queen Victoria's reign (1837-1901), often referred to as the Golden Age, this leading position was in danger. Britain lagged behind the United States and Germany in the production of industrial goods, and it was not able to compete in the new chemical and electrical industries. The role of the Royal Navy as ruler of the seven seas was also nearing its end. Because of the German challenge, the navy needed to concentrate its forces in the North Atlantic, and Great Britain entered into an alliance with Japan (1902) to safeguard British interests in the Pacific region.

World War I and its victorious outcome only checked the decline. True, the military and economic potential of a dangerous competitor had been considerably reduced, and the country's own resources had, at least theoretically, been expanded through the acquisition of new colonial territories, but against this stood both the rise of the United States to its position as the leading industrial and financial power and the growing reticence of the dominions to throw in their lot with Britain for any cause. Of even greater significance was the country's economic exhaustion as a result of the war effort. This greatly hampered the necessary modernisation of numerous industries between the wars, the fight against constantly high rates of unemployment, the institution of important social reforms, and the defence of British interests, first in the Far East and then on its own doorstep.

The war altered Britain's position in the world and the distribution of power in national politics. Animosity among its leaders changed the position of the Liberal Party in one decade from the sole ruling party to the brink of parliamentary insignificance. The liberals' fall was accompanied by a grandiose rise of the Labour Party, peaking in the elections of 1923. After the ruling Tories (conservatives) found little sympathy among the electorate for their planned relinquishing of the British free-trade policy, the electoral vote placed the Labour Party in a position to form the first labour government. Unfortunately, labour was dependent on the parliamentary support of the battered Liberal Party, which made the realisation of plans for social reform impossible. The rapid break with the liberals was, however, the result of the search for closer ties with the Soviet Union. Thus, new elections brought the Tories back into government at the end of 1924.

In 1926, the Tories were confronted with a national strike that had been called by the Trade Union Congress out of solidarity with the miners who were fighting massive wage cuts. Government promises caused the strike movement to crumble. The fact that these promises were not kept, the simultaneous limitation of the right to strike, and a lack of ideas in the government ranks for dealing with unemployment gave labour enough votes in the election of 1929 to again form a minority government as strongest party. The government was able to gain credit for its foreign policy through the settlement of German reparation payments and for disarmament initiatives, but it made little headway, as of 1924, on home affairs. This time it was not the liberals' fault but, rather, the consequences of the Great Depression. It was the inner-party strife over Prime Minister MacDonald's suggested cuts in unemployment insurance and other social services that caused the second labour government to resign in 1931.

The labour administration was followed by a national government headed by MacDonald until 1935, but controlled from the beginning by the Tories. Despite the pound leaving the gold standard, the dropping of free-trade policies, and increased public spending, there were no quick successes. Only the armament programmes that went hand-in-hand with the ill-famed policy of appeasement—nevertheless, only half-heartedly attacked by the Labour Party—were able to bring about a noticeable decline in unemployment after 1936.

During the interwar years, sport was a major working-class leisure activity; games like soccer and cricket were often grouped together as the "Englishman's religion." The labour movement could, therefore, hardly ignore the importance of sport and the influence it had on everyday life. Socialists of the late-Victorian and Edwardian eras were quick to recognise this; some regarded popular sport with antipathy, while others were anxious to provide and popularise general recreational activities. Either way, these negative and positive approaches highlight the fact that socialists were concerned about sport. On one level, there was a critical appraisal of sport under capitalism, and on the other, the proliferation of socialist agencies catering for sport, like the Clarion Cycling Club (CCC). So, by the 1920s, a specifically socialist sporting tradition already existed.

After World War I, the worker sport movement was adopted by both the political and industrial wings of organised labour. From the early 1920s, trade unions and local labour organisations were beginning to encourage the growth of worker sport. The sports meetings held by the Amalgamated Society of Carpenters, Cabinet-Makers, and Joiners in the immediate prewar period were heralded as models for future developments (*Daily Herald*, 27 May 1919). Sporting columns began to appear in trade union journals and party publications, and there were many contributions arguing the need for trade union sport. In the *London Citizen* (June 1921), for example, "Sporticus" advocated the formation of labour and co-operative sport clubs; he envisioned the day when the British cooperative commonwealth would play a test match against the Australian cooperative commonwealth, and a labour sport club would win the FA Cup. In fact, several such clubs were formed, with names like the Guildford Cooperative Societies Ladies Football Team, the Kings Lynn Labour Sports Club, the North London Workers Union Team, and the Southampton Transport Workers Social and Athletic Club, and many had sections

The Clarion Movement

In 1891, Robert Blatchford founded a socialist paper, the *Clarion*. The movement that also bears this title included Cinderella Clubs to provide meals and entertainment for poor children, Clarion Scouts and Clarion Vans to disseminate the socialist message throughout the country, and a wide array of societies to cater to cycling, rambling, and camping. The Clarion Cycling Club (CCC) was particularly strong.

The socialist character of the CCC was clear from the

A Clarion Van on May Day, taking families in Lancashire to the countryside.

inception of the first club in February 1894 at the Birmingham Labour Church. The following year, the National Clarion Cycling Club was established, and, with 80 affiliated clubs by the end of the year, its objective was "To propagate Socialism and Good Fellowship." Membership slowly increased to reach 230 clubs with over 6,000 members in 1909 and 8,000 members in 1913.

The sporting activities of the CCC were wide ranging. At its annual meet at Buxton in 1912, there were "smoking concerts and conferences, lantern displays, a visit to Poole's cavern, football, swimming, cycling, dances, socials, whist drives and meetings." A National Clarion Swimming Club came into being in 1905, and, by 1913, it had been joined by football, rambling, cricket, and field hockey clubs, even a Motorcycle Union. Cycling, however, reigned supreme because it was a *noncompetitive socialist sport*.

A family outing as part of the
Durham Miner's Gala, 1930s.

A cartoon from radical *Clarion*
newspaper.

Rambling was a possibility for
outdoor recreation.

The Cooperative Movement

The first cooperative society was set up in 1844 in Rochdale; soon every town had a "co-op" store. In 1862, the retail cooperative societies set up the Cooperative Wholesale Society (CWS), which manufactured and distributed goods to its members; its profits were ploughed back or distributed to member societies.

The cooperative movement membership rose from 4.1 million in 1919 to 8.5 million in 1939. The total environment of cooperation spawned opportunities for critical debate, education, drama, filmmaking, and other cultural interests. As for sport, by the 1930s many societies had their own sport clubs and teams, some with grand amenities. All sports were catered to, with particular support for women's sport—largely because of the strong influence of the highly popular Cooperative Women's Guild, a salutary attempt at voluntary self-help by committed working-class women.

In 1929, the CWS granted £10,000 for the purchase of sports facilities, and grounds were established in many towns. By 1932, the London Cooperative Society Employees Sports Club, for example, had 6,900 members, a fine ground at Chingford, and accommodation for many sports. That same year, the British Cooperative Employees' Sports Association came into being.

The Labour Party

The formation of the British Labour Party in 1900 gave expression to the sense of a working-class socialist movement; it quickly replaced the liberals as one of the two major political parties (along with the Conservative Party) and first formed a (minority) government in 1924 (and later 1929-1931). By 1912, more than one half of the trade union membership was affiliated with the Labour Party, and the cooperative movement had strong links with it.

After the British Workers' Sports Federation fell under communist control, the official labour movement promoted sport organisations of its own. During the 1920s, the London Party, under the leadership of future Minister Herbert Morrison, built a reputation for its cultural outlets—largely on the example of the German Social Democratic Party. Morrison sought to shape a form of counterculture: "There will be an Art of the People, produced by the people, for we will not be content with the commercialised stuff of modern capitalist society."

At the beginning of 1930, the Labour Party agreed to form a sport organisation, later to be known as the National Workers' Sports Association (NWSA); its major aim was to "encourage, promote and control Amateur Sport and Recreation among Working Class Organisations" by federating sports bodies "organised under the auspices of the Trade Union Congress and the Labour Party."

for soccer, boxing, cricket, socials and entertainment, children's treats, drama, and music (*Daily Herald*, 27 March 1922). If a club was fortunate enough, it might also possess its own sports ground—the Leicester Cooperative Society had cricket pitches, tennis courts, bowling greens, and soccer pitches, together with the necessary changing rooms (*The New Dawn*, 8 December 1923). Aside from this, the Clarion Cycling Club still provided opportunities for cycling and general sporting activities; the annual Easter meet continued with a whist drive, an international soccer match between the Clarion and a French team, a walk around the walls of Chester, political discussion, a dramatic entertainment and smoking concert, a grand dance, swimming, and, of course, a cycle ride (*The Clarion*,1 April 1921).

The British Workers' Federation for Sport came into being in April 1923 from the initiative of Clarion cyclists, Labour Party members, and trade union officials, with the object, as the *Daily Herald* (5 April 1923) put it,

of promoting labour sport internationally "to further the cause of peace between nations." The driving force behind the federation, which was soon to take its formal name of the British Workers' Sports Federation (BWSF) was a desire for international unity. This is hardly surprising, as the leading figure in the federation was Tom Groom, a dedicated internationalist. As chairman of the CCC, he attended the first international worker sport conference in Ghent in 1913, and the founding conference of the social-democratic Lucerne Worker Sports International (LSI) in 1920—with which the BWSF was affiliated—where he disseminated the related ideas of internationalism and sport among his socialist comrades; he details this drive in his book, *The Fifty Year Story of the Club* (1944). With slogans like "Footballs Instead of Cannon Balls" and "Peace Through Sport," the BWSF immediately established contacts with the LSI in the hope, as Tom Groom wrote in *The Labour Magazine* (May 1923), "that the future peace of the world may be secured in the democratic arenas of international sporting Olympiads." Even though the belief that international sport gatherings would promote international fraternity and replace the spirit of militarism with the spirit of sport was somewhat utopian, it did provide the federation with a kind of political legitimacy. This is not to say that there were no other objectives. Socialists of all descriptions had a passion for sport, and they were highly critical of the social system that denied adequate sporting facilities, playing grounds, and open spaces, and encouraged an aristocratic outlook towards games like cricket. Yet, it was the pacifist and internationalist ideas engendered by the nonchauvinist left before, during, and after World War I that gave the BWSF its ideological coherence.

In spite of the federation's precarious organisational structure, it did have some initial successes. The Scottish group had several sections embracing soccer, cycling, swimming, track and field, gymnastics, and boxing, with a membership of 1,000 (*Forward*, 10 March 1923). In London, contacts were also made with trade unions—the engineers, railwaymen, builders, clerks, and transport workers—as well as trade councils, the Independent Labour Party, and Labour Party branches. As far as sport was concerned, the BWSF participated in labour galas and sport days that, judging from one programme, were often colourful occasions: sprints, tug-of-war, children's races, three-legged races, one-mile walks, egg and spoon races, and a ladies thread-the-needle race (Manchester Archives Department, 1924). Even so, the federation was neither particularly dynamic nor a popular sporting organisation. Leading members like Tom Groom and George Bennett complained that little help had come from the Labour Party and its newspaper, the *Daily Herald* (*The Clarion*, 8 June 1923).

Toward the end of 1924, however, the situation began to improve. The London group sponsored a soccer tour of Germany and, most important of all, the trade union movement began to offer assistance. Representations were made with Fred Bramley, then General Secretary of the Trade Union Congress (TUC), and it was decided that worker sport would be best served by a policy of formal cooperation with the trade unions rather than by isolated growth through individual sport clubs. At the annual conference of the trade councils, a resolution was passed stressing the need for labour-sponsored sport and was followed by further developments on both a local and a national level. As Jack Cohen commented in *The Young Worker* (3 April 1926), "The agitation for the formation of a Worker Sports Organisation has been growing more and more popular." All sections of the official

The Trade Union Congress

The Trade Union Congress (TUC), formed in 1868, originally defined itself as a forum for debate and a voice for the trade union cause. Following the formation of the Labour Party in 1900, the TUC worked in close collaboration with "its" political party.

The growing importance of sport in everyday life meant that the trade unions could not ignore it altogether; the fact that the TUC, along with the Labour Party, was antagonistic to the communist-inspired BWSF necessarily led to the establishment of the NWSA under the guardianship of the official labour and TUC leadership. Following the successful Festival of Labour at the Crystal Palace, the TUC was instrumental in setting up the London Labour Party Sports Association that inaugurated a football competition for the Ramsay MacDonald Cup, an athletics meeting at Herne Hill, and a "Soccer for Sixpence" campaign: "it is scandalous that football clubs should spend their large surpluses in securing 'fashionable' players under the transfer system instead of improving their accommodation or reducing their prices."

Nonetheless, the TUC always perceived sport as of marginal importance when set alongside wages, unemployment, the rise of fascism, and other substantive issues.

labour movement were prepared to consider the question of worker sport, and in 1927 the TUC officially recognised the federation. Moreover, sporting activities were extended; tours were made of various European countries, culminating in the participation of Clarion cyclists in the second Worker Olympiad at Prague in July 1927.

Indeed, if the activities of the Clarion, the Woodcraft Folk, and the numerous semi-independent and autonomous socialist sporting bodies were also included in an assessment of labour sport, it would appear that the BWSF and its associated groups were providing a plentiful supply of recreational and sporting activities. However, outward appearances do not always reflect what lies beneath. It is true that improvements were occurring, yet by contrast with the European worker sport movement, the BWSF was a mere fledgling. The description made by the *People's Year Book* in 1927, though

Labour MP Arthur Henderson speaking at the 1933 Winnats Pass meeting of over 10,000 ramblers just before the leaders were imprisoned.

The *Worker Sportsman* was the journal of the communist-inspired British Workers' Sports Federation.

Boxing was especially popular in working-class districts.

perhaps unkind, was not far off the mark: "The British Workers' Sports Federation is a weak and puny body, hardly worthy of the name of a Federation." It was only when a more militant, dynamic, and communist movement began to exert some pressure that the federation started to make some kind of sporting and political impact.

British Communists and Worker Sport

The British communist movement began to see sport as a legitimate political issue in the early 1920s. It is likely that Marxists participated in some of the sports organised by the local socialist societies, the ILP, the Scouts, the Clarion cyclists, and the Socialist Sunday Schools. But it was only with the unification of British Marxism in 1920—in the formation of the Communist Party—that a coherent approach to sport becomes observable. It is true that some communists thought that the authorities saw sport as "the best antidote to Bolshevism," and they regarded it as "a dope for the working masses," but the communist leadership quickly realised that it could not ignore the workers' love of sport. In 1922, the Party Commission on Organisation stressed in its Report to the Annual Party Conference (7 October 1922) the political significance of sport that was reinforced by trends in international communism. The Red Sport International, founded in Moscow in 1921, was based on the idea that it was open to all proletarians who recognise the class struggle. This included British communists. Similarly, the Young Communist International drafted policies on sport that expressed the class struggle (*The International of Youth*, September 1922). A synthesis of guidelines from Moscow and indigenous developments signalled the commencement of a British movement for the organisation of communist sport.

At first it seemed as though the communists were about to establish their own sport organisation, as the Young Communist League (YCL) initiated a campaign for revolutionary sport. The aims of the worker sport movement were publicised, a call was made for "real" working class sport to aid the workers in their fight against capitalism, and a number of "Red" sport clubs were formed by local branches of the YCL. This aroused the interest of the national press, and the right-wing *Daily Mail* (10 February 1923) wrote of a communist plot, while *The Times* (12 January 1923) drew attention to "Communist Sports Propaganda." These developments, however, were checked by the creation of the British Workers' Federa-

The Communist Party of Great Britain [1920–1991]

Throughout the seven decades of its effective existence, the Communist Party of Great Britain (CPGB) was never of more than marginal significance in British political life. Restricting comparisons only to western Europe and leaving out the mass CPs of Italy, France, and the Iberian states, as well as the special case of Germany, it always remained of less account in numbers of influence than its counterparts in even Scandinavia or the low countries. Yet, for a minor party, its longevity was astonishing, far exceeding that of any comparable political organisation, and the tenacity of its hold upon the particular niche it chose to occupy continued up to the years of its terminal decline.

The party's formation was not only the culmination of developments occurring in Britain over more than a decade but also an episode in an international process that had begun years before the Bolshevik Revolution of 1917. Deepening interstate tensions throughout the first decade of the 20th century, issuing in the outbreak of general European war in 1914, are best viewed as one aspect of a general crisis of the late 19th-century global order dominated economically, politically, and culturally by the industrial states of Europe and the United States. Industrial militancy and class confrontation exploded throughout the developed economies. In Germany, the ostensibly revolutionary social democrats became the largest party in the Reichstag. In the United States, the American Socialist Party achieved the pinnacle of its influence and vote. Russia in 1905 and 1917, China in 1911, and Mexico in 1911, to name only the most significant, were swept by revolution. It was in these global circumstances that communist parties came into being, based on the teachings of Karl Marx and Friedrich Engels.

tion for Sport. It soon became apparent that both the CP and the YCL wished to shape the course of the Federation's development. Although there was no formal policy of infiltration, it is clear that the criterion for success was the extent of influence achieved in the BWSF.

The Young Communist League

In line with the organisation of the Communist Party of Great Britain in 1920 and the establishment of youth wings in all communist-type parties, the Young Communist League (YCL) came into being shortly after the party's foundation. Further, as in the international movement, the YCL was subordinate in all issues to the parent party. Again, like the parent party, the YCL was linked with all fraternal communist youth organisations in an International—the Young Communist International, which drafted policies on all matters concerning young people, including sport, espousing the message of class struggle.

In Britain, during the 1920s and 1930s, the YCL launched a sustained campaign against the ideas and activities of the Boy Scouts who were lampooned as obedient wage-slaves, militarists, and unthinking servants of the empire.

The First National Congress of the BWSF

The Congress was held in Birmingham in April 1928. It was here that the political differences between the social democrats and the communists came to a head with the election of a new and communist-inspired leadership: George Sinfield replaced Tom Groom as national secretary; even more importantly, the main task of working-class athletes as enshrined in a new constitution was the "unrelenting struggle against the existing capitalist domination of sport and the introduction of a socialistic content into sport and physical recreation."

Thus, after 5 years of relatively slow and uneven progress, a communist-styled sport organisation had finally come into being. In many ways, the split in the worker sport movement was inevitable. The division merely reflected opposing political ideologies, one Marxist, the other labour-socialist or social-democratic. It is certainly true that the Labour Party and TUC were intransigent to anything remotely communist, but the sectarian stance of the Marxist left also made compromise virtually impossible. The split was welcomed by revolutionaries, for they interpreted worker sport as being sabotaged by conspiracy and reaction, by what they called "mondism in sport"—a form of class collaboration or sell-out on the recreational front.

After all, the federation was considered as "an outcome of the class struggle" that had to be joined, helped, and supported, as the *Workers' Weekly* put it (28 April 1923), in order to "give it an impetus towards acceptance of the basis of the Red International of Sports." The Walthamstow Communist Party branch was admitted into the ranks, and the federation cooperated with the YCL, as the *BWSF Minutes* of 17 May 1923 show. Yet, despite policy statements to the contrary, the communist movement was lukewarm in its enthusiasm for worker sport and, as already mentioned, the BWSF remained a small, London-based organisation.

Even so, in 1926 the YCL once again opened up the question of worker sport. Recreational activities were organised during the 1926 general strike and the miners' lock-out, a number of positive contributions were made to the YCL journal, the *Weekly Young Worker*, and out of this came a further drive to build up the sport movement (5 June 1926). The ubiquitous nature of capitalist sport was opposed, that is, the system by which the minds of young workers were "carefully doped with imperialist and anti-working class teachings," and the YCL canvassed for sport "entirely controlled by the workers, without any capitalist influence" (*Workers' Life*, 22 July 1927). By 1927, it appears from the Marxist *Sunday Worker* (17 July 1927) that there was some success in this direction. Capitalist-controlled organisations were opposed, two

soccer leagues were set up in London, a cricket league was instituted, and contact was established between the metropolis and the provinces. Moreover, the National Committee of the BWSF now included two communists, Walter Tapsell and George Sinfield, and it was on their initiative that the federation was won over to the communist cause.

The political complexion of the London group was revealed with the organisation of a soccer tour to the Soviet Union in August and September 1927. The tour gave ordinary workers—railwaymen, woodworkers, and furniture workers—as *Young Worker* (27 August 1927) wrote, "the opportunity to see the Workers' State for themselves"; they did, however, lose all their matches by a big margin, including one by 0-11.

Street cricket, probably in London's East End in the 1920s.

An outdoor dart competition on Tyneside, 1938.

The London group, supported by the CP leadership, was now convinced of the need for a militant sport movement and resolved to end the social-democratic leadership of the federation. George Sinfield wrote a pamphlet in late 1927, entitled "The Workers' Sports Movement," that described the experiences of the BWSF team in the Soviet Union and also put forward the case for communist sport that would "struggle against all types of capitalist sport organisations." Tom Groom and his colleagues repudiated such statements and opposed the action of the London group in going to the Soviet Union, particularly its action of giving its share of gate receipts to the Russian Air Force. The communist position was vigorously defended in the communist press, which seemingly encouraged further growth—over 100 meetings were addressed by members of the London group and a number of communist sport bodies were formed in various parts of the country (*Sunday Worker*, 5 February 1928).

Following the change of leadership made at the First National Congress of the BWSF at Birmingham in 1928, the old leaders found the militancy of the federation incompatible with their politics. The General Council of the TUC could not approve the new constitution and soon withdrew its recognition; the Labour Party Executive was unsympathetic to the fact that "Communist influence dominated the British Workers' Sports Federation"; and the CCC, in complaining about the link with the RSI, also severed its connections (*Labour Party Executive Committee Minutes*, 23 May 1928; Manchester Archives Department, 016/ii/19; *TUC General Council Minutes*, 23 May 1928). Eventually, the social-democratic forces regrouped, and in 1930 formed an opposition body, the National Workers' Sports Association (NWSA). The process of disunity was complete by the end of the 1920s, when the Communist Party initiated its "Class-Against-Class" programme that intensified the fight against the Labour Party sport movement and the Clarion cyclists.

The Communist Philosophy of Sport

The discussion up to now has shown how a communist-inspired sport movement was created in the political conjuncture of the late 1920s. To fully understand the communist approach to sport, however, we should know something about the BWSF ideology. The most important principle of the federation, as revealed in so many policy statements, was a rigorous critique of capitalist sport in all its forms. To put it simply, it saw capitalist sport as a superstructural tool to aid the exploitation of the workers. Whenever the opportunity arose, leading members sought to expose and oppose the capitalist control of sport, and to this end the propaganda of the federation was aimed at three particular aspects: professional, amateur, and factory-controlled sport.

The early issues of the communist *Daily Worker* are full of derogatory articles and reports on the nature of professional sport. They attempted to illustrate the commercialism, the corruption, and the profit-making objectives of all types of sporting activity. In the first month of the paper's existence, opposition to commercialism was clearly shown by the disappearance of the horse racing results and tips from the sports pages. In the face of a barrage of criticism, the positive aspects of professional sport were never seriously posed. There was little detailed evaluation of professionalism and its relation to working class culture; analysis, at least in the first months of the *Daily Worker*, tended to be no more than rhetoric.

Voluntary or amateur sport also came under fire. Amateur games were seen as intrinsically linked to professionalism. It was alleged that amateurs took part in professional sport for which they received illegal payments, and that this was all part of a scheme, as the *Daily Worker* of 3 January 1930 put it, "for doping the workers into submission to worsening conditions." In the opinion of the leadership, even though subscriptions were still being paid to the Amateur Athletic Association, the class nature of voluntary sport was a matter for serious political consideration and attention. Consequently, there was also an antipathy shown towards the "bourgeois" youth movements that were viewed as militaristic and even fascist in character. The Manchester section of the BWSF was, therefore, following established policy when it informed a well-attended camp that groups as diverse in membership and outlook as the Boy Scouts, the Cadets, the Rambling Federation, and the Cyclists Touring Club were preparing working boys and girls for a war against the USSR (*BWSF Camp Souvenir*, 1932).

The federation waged even more intense propaganda against the third category of capitalist sport—factory-controlled sport. Industrial welfare clubs, which were proliferating at this time, were seen as an integral part of managerial strategy or, as *The Fan* (22 November 1930) put it, "a soothing syrup to mitigate the growing discontent that the continual worsening of conditions is producing." Propaganda sought to illustrate how the "boss"-subsidised sport clubs "duped" the workers and created an environment in which it was easier to impose rationalisation, speed-ups, and wage cuts. The BWSF tried to show how employers used sport to manipulate the workforce and provide them with a ready-made vested

Marxism

Marxism is the body of social and political thought informed by the writings of Karl Marx (1818-1883), forming the basis of the programmes of all communist parties. Much of Marx's writing, especially *Das Kapital*, was concerned with the economic dynamics of capitalist societies, seeing the state as an instrument of class rule supporting private capital and suppressing the masses. This situation would eventually lead to revolution, whereby the working class would seize the state and establish a dictatorship by the proletariat; class differences would disappear in a new socialist society. This classless society would eventually lead to the withering away of the state, producing a communist society.

It is generally recognised that Marx's writings regarding the transformation to socialism and the nature of socialism lacked detail. In consequence, Marxism subsequently adopted a wide range of interpretations, such as Marxism-Leninism and neo-Marxism.

interest in the running of the firm. Not only this, factory sport clubs were regarded as undermining militancy that, supposedly, further stimulated the development of a labour aristocracy to act as scabs and spies for the employer (*Daily Worker*, 14 February 1930). The recreational policy of firms like Pilkington Brothers was disclosed in such a way as to represent the capitalist nature of welfarism.

It is clear that the federation's ideological framework was incorporated within a communist analysis of society. Indeed, since the BWSF was a cultural adjunct of the Communist Party, it was intimately involved in the life of the British communist movement. One obvious example of this is that the revolutionary tenets of the federation were disseminated almost exclusively in the communist press. Activists used Marxism, if only crudely, as a way to explain the material basis of sport: Michael Condon, who had once played professional soccer for Leyton Orient, can be found quoting Lenin in the *Daily Worker* in order to illustrate the revolutionary potential of physical culture (Condon, 1930).

There is some evidence to suggest that the Communist Party and YCL manipulated the federation, in Martin

Bobker's words (personal interview), as "a transmission belt" for communist ideas and policy to the apolitical masses, involving them in both sport and politics. During elections, the federation helped communist candidates because it was thought that the aims of the worker sport movement could only be attained, as the *Daily Worker* (2 June 1930) wrote, "under the Revolutionary leadership of the Communist Party." Besides giving financial assistance to communist candidates in general and local elections, BWSF branches took part in industrial and other disputes. For example, the Leeds Red Wheelers and the local party branch rallied 400 workers to resist the actions of the bailiffs in trying to evict a working-class family (*Sport and Games*, January 1932). By supporting the Communist Party, it was argued that the federation aims were promoted and, given such mutual interests, it was hardly unexpected when the party sought some kind of institutional control with the introduction of a BWSF commission.

The federation did more than promote joint activities with the political and industrial wings of the communist movement; there were also links with the worker theatre and cinema organisations. Both Tom Thomas and Vic

Women and Sport

The 1920s witnessed a growth of female participation in track and field (the Women's AAA was founded in 1922), cycling, swimming, tennis, and physical fitness. The middle-class Women's League of Health and Beauty started in the late 1920s, and, by 1939, it had 166,000 members.

Worker sport was trapped in a society where working-class women continued to be unfairly treated at work and in the home, with unequal pay, hard domestic drudgery, and large families. It was,

North Kensington (London) Labour Party women's group just off for a rambling trip, 1923.

therefore, very difficult for women to "escape" into sport. The BWSF did develop women's sections, particularly in netball (50 teams competed in the 1931 cup competition), field hockey, gymnastics, rambling, and swimming. Although the BWSF may have placed "women and men on an equal footing," as Gladys Keable of the Red Star netball section explained: "There are too many in our movement who regard women as a bit of a nuisance, pushing themselves forward when the men want to get their important revolutionary changes."

Farrant argued that there were financial and intellectual reasons to relate sport to cultural pastimes, and many cooperative ventures were present at socials, dances, political meetings, and sports events (*Red Stage,* January 1932). The federation also cooperated with the National Unemployed Workers' Movement and the Workers' Defence Force, which had Michael Condon on its National Committee; it also had links with the Society for Cultural Relations with the USSR, the Friends of Soviet Russia, the League Against Imperialism, the International Class War Prisoners' Aid, the Teachers' Labour League, and the Young Pioneers.

The communist critique of capitalist society was, therefore, strengthened by an evaluation of sport that provided some kind of coherent answer to multifarious working-class grievances on sport. Notwithstanding the fact that many sections of an otherwise sympathetic potential membership were alienated by the obvious communist tutelage, the Marxist approach to sport led to various theoretical misconceptions and practical difficulties. There

was an evident tendency towards dogmatism in argument and sectarianism in position.

The consequences of a doctrinaire, inflexible analysis of sport undoubtedly meant a certain degree of isolation. One member of the Manchester YCL expressed alarm at "the puritanical act of dismembering the sports page [of the *Daily Worker*] by eliminating the racing articles." He claimed in the paper (3 February 1930) that those who had taken such a step did not understand the workers, and he likened the decision to the act of "a Bible-thumper trying to stop a gang of navvies from swearing and drinking." This was a valid point, yet many communists still failed to grasp that working-class attachments to sport often transcended political allegiance. The leadership did not seem to realise that the working class was organically linked with certain capitalist sports, especially soccer; although the federation was right to reveal the unsavoury aspects of commercial patronage and control, the "people's game" had evolved from the real experience of workers themselves; their ranks had supplied the

Soccer

Soccer (a corruption of the words As*soc*iation Football) had its origins in folk football that, in the 17th century, gathered round it large numbers of active participants and varied greatly in rules, organisation, and regularity from locality to locality. By the 20th century, football had been systematised and pacified (notwithstanding the hooligan-spectator element). It had become a spectator sport, organised on a national basis, and was an integral part of consumer culture. By 1920, there were 6,800 registered and paid footballers. The Football Association had been set up in 1863, and the game, run from a national headquarters in London, was exported through the energies of British businessmen, educators, army personnel, and empire-builders. At home, however, the sport was taken over by the proletariat that impressed its own culture upon football:

The final of the Association Football Cup between Manchester City and Portsmouth, 1934.

> Working-class people stamped sports like association football and rugby league with their own character and transformed them in some ways into a means of expression for values opposed to the bourgeois athleticist tradition: vociferous partisanship, a premium on victory, a suspicion of and often a disdain for constituted authority, a lack of veneration for official rules, mutual solidarity as the basis of team-work, a preference for tangible monetary rewards for effort and a hedonistic "vulgar" festive element, were all brought to sports.

overwhelming majority of players and the bulk of spectators. It was wrong to regard soccer and other sports as subsumed under bourgeois dominance. Indeed, there is no reason why a supporter of or a player on a capitalist soccer team should not also be a militant trade unionist or, for that matter, a member of the Communist Party. The idea that professional sport would go bankrupt in the face of advanced opinion and that the role of the spectator was a "mug's game" probably did not go down well in working-class circles. The purist ideology of the BWSF did not take fully into account the prejudices, sympathies, and motivations of those workers interested in sport.

Clearly, the political atmosphere of "Class Against Class" and the feeling that the revolution was just around the corner did not encourage a balanced perspective. It merely engendered a suspicion of reformism and a

reluctance to consider non-Marxist developments, however advanced. The NWSA, even though it included many socialists and trade unionists, was characterised as a comic outfit of "social fascists" and "renegades," or as *Labour Monthly* (April 1931) wrote, "a hothouse plant pruned and cultivated by job-hunters of the TUC." On one occasion, the leading Labour Party activist Ernest Bevin, who was addressing a conference of Clarion cyclists, was heckled and eventually driven from the platform by a group of communist supporters (author's interview with Bernard Rothman). It was this type of action that widened the divisions in the worker sport movement and reduced the federation's sphere of influence.

This general picture of sectarianism, however, needs to be qualified. The dogmatism of some leaders was by no means shared by all (not by George Sinfield, for example), and this was eventually recognised as the need for compromise grew. From early 1931, the militancy of the federation was moderated. It was realised, as the *Daily Worker* (12 February 1931) conceded, that "to generalise on the relationship between politics and sport is fatal when approaching your young chum, who can probably tell you by heart the names of the last 20 winners of the FA Cup, the holders of the world's boxing titles and Hendren's average for the last cricket season." Depending on circumstances, cooperation began to replace confrontation as the major organising principle of the federation. Eventually, in 1933, as a response to the rise of fascism, the "United Front on the Field of Sport" became official federation policy; policies and activities were to include participation with all progressive forces of the antifascist front.

The Rise and Fall of the BWSF in the 1930s

When the communists first seized control of the federation, it was small; by 1930, it had grown into a national organisation with branches in all the major regions of the country: London, Manchester, Newcastle, South Wales, and Clydeside in Scotland. By 1932, it also had branches in Derby, the Rhonda, Gateshead, Doncaster, Edinburgh Fife, and Nottinghamshire (*Sport and Games*, January 1932). Even during the period of utmost isolation, the BWSF could claim 3,000 members; yet, when activities were broadened, membership increased. In 1931, it had 5,000 soccer players associated with the federation, and club affiliations were, as the *Daily Worker* (31 October 1930) wrote, "coming in at the rate of two a week." Later in the year, there were 90 clubs in the federation with a membership of 6,000 (*BWSF Minutes*, 7 June 1931). Its influence increased with United Front action, boosting membership even further. Thus, when the BWSF helped to organise the campaign for Sunday League soccer in 1933, as many as 585 teams were represented (Condon, 1933). It was the working-class membership that made the federation so different from the mainly middle-class character of other sport organisations in Britain.

As far as local sporting activities are concerned, a wide number of sports were provided, ranging from soccer and cricket to netball and jujitsu. In Newcastle and parts of Scotland, boxing was a major activity, highlighted by a number of well-organised exhibition matches; in Manchester, outdoor activities like camping and rambling found favour; in London, soccer was a major interest. The BWSF had its own soccer leagues in London, South Wales, Derby, and Glasgow, in which players were "instructed to play the ball and not the man" (*BWSF Minutes*, 14 March 1930). Most branches had rambling and cycling sections, a number of which were relatively autonomous—the Spartacus, Equity, Whitehall, and Red Wheelers cycling clubs; many had gymnasiums and premises of their own, and the Essex group even possessed a permanent camp by the sea. For many youngsters, such clubs were the focal point of their leisure time. A diary of events produced by the Hackney sports club in London illustrates the rich diversity of activity: something to do on every night of the week, including education and cultural development on Tuesdays, boxing and road running on Thursdays, and rambles on Sundays (*Daily Worker*, 27 January 1932). Furthermore, although the federation was not exactly free of sexism, it is to its credit that women's sections were encouraged, particularly in London, where Clara Deaner organised activities such as netball and gymnastics.

The federation also arranged special sport meetings. In April 1930, for example, two major BWSF soccer matches took place between representative sides from England and Wales—one attracted a crowd of 3,000, a greater attendance than at the Merthyr Town versus Fulham Third Division game in the Football League. The federation also organized a Red Sports Day with 1,000 spectators and competitors from 10 clubs (*Daily Worker*, 8 April 1930). Sport meets of this kind were a feature of BWSF activities designed to attract workers to a combination of countercultural events that included sports, plays, music, and a host of amusements. In this way, the federation certainly brought greater variety into people's lives.

Despite the effort and enthusiasm that went into sport, the primary objective remained political; sport was not regarded "as an end in itself, but as a means of fitting the workers with the necessary energy and stamina to face up to the class struggle of today, and the greater ones of the future" (*Daily Worker*, 13 November 1930). The political nature of BWSF sport was clearly reflected in international events. After 1926, British soccer players, boxers, swimmers, track and field athletes, and netball players competed against communist athletes in the Soviet Union, France, Switzerland, Norway, Germany, and Holland, while in the same period, sport delegations came to Britain from France and Germany. The overtly political basis of these sporting occasions is vividly expressed in the way the federation courted Soviet sport. From the first soccer tour of 1927, continuing through the Moscow *Spartakiads* of 1928, 1931, and 1932, BWSF delegations were apt to praise the sporting and economic achievements of the "Workers' Homeland": the great sport stadiums, the highly specialised instructors, and the abundance of technical equipment (*Sport and Games*, October-November 1931; *Sunday Worker*, 7 October 1928; *Young Worker*, 10 October 1927).

The political nature of relations between British and Soviet athletes led J.R. Clynes, the Labour Home Secretary, to refuse entry visas to a team of Soviet soccer players in April 1930. It was the overt politics of the BWSF, ranging from formal support of Soviet sport to the use of the hammer and sickle as a motif and the presentation of red banners to successful teams, that distinguished it from traditional sport organisations.

The political role of the BWSF extended to militancy in sport itself. The revolutionary posturing of the communist movement did not preclude the campaign for piecemeal reform. Although it was thought that under a communist system, the quality of working-class sport would inevitably improve, in the meantime it was important to fight within capitalism for improvements. Throughout its short history, the federation campaigned for all kinds of short-term objectives, especially access to the countryside, organised Sunday sport, and better playing facilities for working people.

The best known militant stand of worker athletes in the 1930s was the Mass Trespass, when hundreds of northern ramblers trespassed on the area around Kinder Scout in Derbyshire (part of the country estate of the Chief Scout, Lord Baden Powell). What is less known is that the trespass was a political act designed under the BWSF auspices. From its inception, the federation had promoted the rights of the open-air movement, including the demands and grievances of ramblers. This support was put on an organisational basis in 1931 when the Manchester branch formed a Ramblers' Rights Movement to fight for the "opening to hikers of all parts of the countryside, including private property" (*Daily Mail*, 3 July 1931). Even at this stage, the "establishment" press, in the guise of the *Daily Mail*, was apprehensive about the determination of communists to "tramp our footpaths, careless of rural charm, musing only on the iniquities of the capitalist system."

The truth of the matter was that a group of workers just wanted to roam the countryside free from the fears of prosecution and the encroachments of the grouse shooter. The details of the trespass have been well chronicled (see, especially, Bernard Rothman, *The 1932 Kinder Trespass*, 1982). It is interesting to note, however, that the fight for ramblers' rights was a logical extension of the political commitment of the BWSF. This incident, above all others, captures the way in which the philosophy of the federation was translated into practice. Indeed, this extra-parliamentary way of achieving things—attacked, incidentally, by all the official rambling

associations—reflected the politics of the communist movement and led to the imprisonment of a number of activists. It is hard to assess the political impact of the Mass Trespass, but, along with similar actions, it awakened public awareness and gave further momentum to several parliamentary initiatives.

In other campaigns launched by the BWSF, success was more immediate. The London group campaigned for the rights of workers to play sport on Sundays and for improvements in the provision of recreational amenities. Michael Condon exposed the society that expected working-class youth to play games in the street "with one eye on the possible arrival of a policeman." In illustrating the lack of facilities, he also pointed out the high cost of the London County Council soccer pitches, the falling area of open spaces, and the restrictions on Sunday sport, "the only day . . . when workers are free to play their games." The picture he painted was a dismal one, with London boroughs such as Islington and Walthamstow especially susceptible to capitalist economies in recreation (Condon, 1931). The lessons to be drawn from such an analysis pointed to some kind of political action, and this came with the BWSF-backed campaign for Sunday soccer and finally ended in the lifting of the ban in May 1931, despite opposition from the Salvation Army, the Sunday School Union, and other religious groups. This success gave the London leadership valuable political experience of the ways in which to mobilise athletes around a militant programme, experience that was later used in the struggle against the London County Council for organised Sunday soccer.

Between 1931 and 1934, the political campaigns of the federation had resulted in some positive gains, while sporting activities continued on both domestic and international fronts. However, the regular features in the *Daily Worker* gradually diminished as the 1930s wore on, until, from early 1935, mention of the federation in the paper's columns was rare. By the end of 1935, it appears that the federation was no longer influential. In some areas, the local branches were replaced by YCL sport sections, in others they simply faded away, took on a nonpolitical character, or were supplanted by the National Workers' Sports Association. As a distinctive Marxist, cultural organisation, the BWSF fell a victim to the United Front—it was at odds with the aim "to establish close and friendly relations with the . . . non-fascist sports organisations," as M. Woolf put it in a report to the Sixth World Congress of the Young Communist International in 1935. Even so, the demise of the BWSF was more deep-rooted and can be traced to a number of organisational and political problems.

Organisation had always been a major problem in the sense that it was hard to coordinate sport and political activities on a nationwide scale. Because the leaders of

The Kinder Trespass [1932]

On 24 April 1932, perhaps the most famous incident in the history of the movement for access to the countryside occurred:

> After a "mass rally" in the village at which they were exhorted to demand open access, low fares, non-militarism in rambling groups, cheap catering and the removal of restrictions on open-air singing, they marched to the top [of Kinder], to be met by temporary wardens. The pushing and shoving that followed saw only a few open fights; then they left. As they returned to Hayfield singing revolutionary songs, five of the "ring leaders" [plus one other] were arrested and charged with violence and causing grievous bodily harm to one of the keepers.
>
> Although one defendant was discharged, the other five received prison sentences ranging from 2 to 6 months.

Keepers using their sticks on some of the trespassers during the Mass Trespass on Kinder Scout, 1932.

I'm a rambler, I'm a rambler from
   Manchester way,
I get all my pleasure the hard,
   moorland way.
I may be a wage slave on Monday,
But I am a free man on Sunday. . . .

He said "All this land is my
   master's."
At that I stood shaking my head,
No man has the right to own
   mountains
Any more than the deep ocean bed.

(The Manchester Rambler)

> **B. W. S. F.**
> **RAMBLER'S RALLY.**
>
> The Rally will take place on Sunday April 24th. at 2 o-clock on Hayfield Recreation Ground. From the Rec we proceed on a MASS TRESPASS onto Kinder Scout. This is being organised by the British Workers Sports Federation, who fight for Ramblers:-
> "Against the finest stretches of Moorlands being closed to us.
> "For Cheap fares. For cheap catering facilities.
> "Against any war preparations in rambling organisations.
> "Against petty restrictions such as singing etc.
> Now: young workers of Eccles, to all, whether you've been rambling before or not, we extend a hearty welcome.
> If you've not been rambling before, start now, you don't know what you've missed. Roll up at Eccles at 8-15. on Sunday Morning. and come with us for the best day out that you have ever had.
> FARE 1/6 Return.   TEA 8d extra.   Eccles Cross 8-15 a.m.

Invitation to people in Eccles to take part in the Mass Trespass organised by the British Workers' Federation.

the federation were workers themselves, organisation was hindered by a dearth of time and finance. The arrangement of forthcoming events usually took place after working hours, and it was commonplace for the committee to adjourn meetings very late at night. Then there was the problem of cash. The federation was self-financing through dances, socials, and other like events, although funds raised tended to be insufficient for the purchase of equipment, the hiring of premises, or the publication of a sports paper; the journals of the federation all collapsed after a short period, first the London group's *Worker Sportsman* in 1929, then *Sport and Games* in 1932, and, finally, *The Worker Sportsman*, also in 1932. Michael Condon was quickly led to confess that the facilities of many BWSF clubs were "contemptible," and the situation only marginally improved (*Sunday Worker*, 9 December 1928). Organisation on a national scale was nearly impossible under such circumstances, so activity tended to be local in character.

A genuine explanation of decline must also take account of the political nature of the federation. Aside from the various theoretical misconceptions and the distortions of "Class Against Class" previously mentioned, the controls exerted by the Communist Party did not encourage growth. Although the political position moderated with time, it always remained a sympathetic adjunct of the party. Because of this open relationship, it let itself be open to criticism from both the left and the right: from the left because radicals wanted the federation to become more of a Marxist organisation, with fewer ties to Soviet sport, and from the right because right-wingers wished to see an apolitical sport organisation. The federation never really had the will to pronounce a clear, coherent position of its own, free from the expedience of practical politics and the policy dictates of a political party. In short, it failed to be autonomous, to gain an independence that would have made it possible to propagate a wide-ranging socialist theory of working-class culture.

The amalgam of organisational and political problems reduced the potential for mass national growth, especially as the federation was up against a capitalist culture that was the very antithesis of what it itself stood for. It could not hope to compete with the many establishment clubs if it could not even put its own organisation and politics on a sound basis. There was the absurd contradiction of some branches cooperating with church groups, while others were reluctant even to approach the local trade union. In such circumstances, it was extremely difficult to create and sustain a viable Marxist sport body.

Undoubtedly, the BWSF made a number of errors, yet to characterise it in this way alone would be unfair. Some of the problems it faced, especially in regard to finance, were inevitable and intractable with all the organisational and political will in the world. Its achievements in sport and political campaigning are substantial. The federation organised all manner of sport that provided many workers with an active recreational outlet they might otherwise have had to do without. True, ordinary workers had provided some sporting activities for themselves long before the Communist Party arrived on the scene, and a proliferation of proletarian sport clubs did exist in the interwar period. But the BWSF explicitly showed what was possible without middle-class patronage. In a sense, it offered an alternative to the capitalist modes of spare-time activity. In political terms, the federation was a pioneer in the struggle to improve the quality of worker leisure. Campaigns initiated in the localities, to the extent

that they were successful, brought permanent benefits to all types of men and women who wanted to play a sport or enjoy recreation. It is creditable that a politically motivated organisation, by no means perfect, was able to shape a movement that challenged the hegemony of British sport tradition and questioned the dominant structures of sport. The BWSF constituted a major chapter in the history both of sport and of the labour movement.

References

BWSF Camp Souvenir (Manchester, n.d. [1932?]).

BWSF Minutes. 17 May 1923; 14 March 1930; 6 June 1931.

The Clarion. 1 April 1921; 8 June 1923.

Communist Party of Great Britain Report to the Annual Party Conference (London, 7 October 1922).

Condon, M. "Lenin knew the value of good health," *Daily Worker*, 11 February 1930, p. 11.

Condon, M. *The fight for the workers' playing fields* (London, n.d. [1931?]); see also *Daily Worker*, 16 January 1931, p. 6.

Condon, M. *The case for organised Sunday football* (London, 1933), pp. 1-2.

Daily Herald. 27 May 1919; 27 March 1922; 5 April 1923.

Daily Mail. 10 February 1923; 3 July 1931.

Daily Worker. 3 January 1930; 3 February 1930; 14 February 1930; 8 April 1930; 2 June 1930; 31 October 1930; 13 November 1930; 12 February 1931; 27 January 1932.

The Fan. 22 November 1930, p. 4.

Forward. 10 March 1923, p. 3.

Groom, T. *The fifty year story of the club: National Clarion Cycling Club 1894-1944* (Jubilee souvenir, Halifax, 1944).

Hansard. (Commons) 5th Ser., Vol. 238, Cols. 349-350, 1 May 1930.

The International of Youth. September 1922, p. 26.

The Labour Magazine. May 1923, p. 9.

Labour Monthly. April 1931; February 1958, p. 95.

Labour Party Executive Committee Minutes. 23 May 1928.

The London Citizen. (Tottenham Edition) June 1921, p. 2.

Manchester Archives Department. 061/I/31 Programme, BWSF (London Group), First Annual Sports and Gala 3 May 1924.

Minutes of the National Committee of the CCC. 6 May 1928.

The New Dawn. 8 December 1923, p. 19.

The People's Year Book. 1927, p. 272.

Red Stage. January 1932, p. 7.

Rothman, B. *The 1932 Kinder Trespass: A personal view* (Timperley, 1982).

Sinfield, G. *The Workers' Sports Movement* (London, n.d. [1927?]).

Sport and Games. October-November 1931; January 1932.

Sunday Worker. 17 July 1927; 5 February 1928; 17 June 1928; 7 October 1928; 9 December 1928.

Times. 12 January 1923.

TUC General Council Minutes. 23 May 1928.

The Weekly Young Worker. 5 June 1926.

Woolf, M. *Report of Comrade M. Woolf*, October 1935, "The Day Is Ours!" Sixth World Congress Young Communist International (1935), pp. 30-31. The tasks of the United Front of the Youth: Resolutions adopted at the Sixth Congress (1935), p. 11.

Workers' Life. 22 July 1927.

Workers' Weekly. 28 April 1923.

Young Worker. 3 April 1926; 27 August 1927; 10 October 1927; 5 May 1928.

Chapter 7

A Vital Period in Swedish Worker Sport: 1919–1936

Rolf Pålbrant

SWEDEN

In 1930, 6.14 million people lived in this Scandinavian kingdom that covered an area of 448,439 km².

The middle of the previous century set the foundation for Sweden's development into one of the world's most affluent, industrialised countries. The abolition of the old-fashioned guild system and the end of trade monopolies, import-export restrictions, and state involvement in the construction and management of the railway system provided the necessary framework for the development of free enterprise. Particularly, new techniques for iron processing and paper manufacture greatly accelerated the process of industrialisation in the last quarter of the century. This industrialisation was accompanied by the emergence of an increasingly confident liberal bourgeoisie and a large growth in the working class that organised itself into the Social Democratic Party (SAP) in 1889. Their common demands led to the electoral reform of 1909 that granted universal and equal male suffrage for elections to the second parliamentary chamber and, thus, provided the SAP with opportunities to shape events that went far beyond those responsible for the rudimentary laws concerning work standards. The reform also helped Sweden to distance itself from Marxist positions.

At the outbreak of World War I, Sweden declared its neutrality, but the war nonetheless demanded a large price from the country. The Allies instituted a drastic reduction in important trade with Germany that led to considerable supply shortages during the second half of the conflict. At the same time, trade with the Allies suffered from attacks by German submarines.

Despite the splitting off of the left-wing socialists, the period immediately after the war saw the SAP emerge as the strongest political party in the country. Party leader Hjalmer Branting was appointed prime minister in 1920, a development fostered by the introduction of voting rights for women in 1919 and by the government of the liberal Eden, the first administration with social democrat participation.

Further reforms, such as the introduction of unemployment insurance and the right to nationalisation and state control of private enterprise, were hampered both by the lack of a clear majority and by the bourgeoisie's unwillingness to cooperate; on the one hand, bourgeois forces grew ever more confident as a result of the failure of revolutionary movements outside Russia, and, on the other, the exceptional economic upturn in the postwar years.

As in other countries, the Great Depression created a new power balance in Swedish politics. In the face of rapidly growing unemployment, spectacular collapses of trusts that had previously been highly praised, and escalating labour conflicts in connection with the question of wage reductions—all of which had been met with helplessness on the part of the liberal and conservative cabinets alternately holding power since 1926—the SAP returned to government after huge electoral gains in the 1932 elections. With the parliamentary support of the Farmers' Party, enticed to cooperation by promises of agricultural subsidies, the SAP was able to overcome the crisis through state regulation of foreign trade and, in particular, a broad expansion of public investment much more quickly than governments in most other industrialised states.

The implementation of the second part of the government programme, the institution of a comprehensive welfare state to care for the needy individual, had to wait until after World War II. In the face of growing international tensions, the SAP realised that, without fundamental military strength, paper declarations of neutrality were no protection from attack by potential German aggressors. The temporary priority accorded to military investment proved beneficial; unlike its neighbours, the country was spared the fate of German occupation.

Historical Overview

The relationship between sport and the labour movement in Sweden has been complex and contradictory. Even though radical workers have always taken a dim view of the pleasures of the upper classes—and they include sport as one of those pleasures—some leading social democrats, including party leader Hjalmer Branting, have looked upon healthy sport as an element in society that is important to workers as long as it is democratic. Immediately after World War I, the left wing of the worker sport movement, which had broken with the Social Democratic Party (SAP) in 1917, began to engage in worker sport. New attempts to organise sport had originated in the left leadership and its youth organisation, which saw international models—a "red sport"—as an alternative to the bourgeois federations that they considered hostile to workers. But generally, the membership was reluctant to become involved in sport in the 1919-1920 period. The image of sport remained bourgeois, so a true worker would not join, in spite of the extensive advertisement campaigns in the Party press.

When the left formed the Communist Party (SKP) and a section of the Comintern in 1921, it tended to follow the instructions of international communism. At the 1921 congress of the SKP youth movement, therefore, a new strategy was established that followed the Comintern policy of working within cells and prevailing on the established sport movement from the inside. In 1921, the party leaders came to the conclusion that sport policy should move with the times; it established the first worker sport movement (AIF) in Stockholm in 1921, and its members included Oskar Samuelson, Nils Lindbergh, Johan Nord, and Henning Ehn.

The AIF programme, based on the class struggle and class divisions within society, aimed to promote a physical culture for the working class. Yet, for strategic reasons, the programme was not revolutionary. In the months to come, prominent party officials, such as Oskar Samuelson, launched a campaign among members to form an independent worker sport federation and worker sport clubs. But results were disappointing, and, despite further attempts, only very few clubs, such as *Härnösand* and *Hällefors*, were formed.

There were economic and political reasons for this relative failure. The workers were fighting a rearguard action in the face of bourgeois economic policies. In response to labour resistance, the employers instituted lockouts and wage cuts that caused a split in the SKP in 1921 and 1924. Long-lasting resistance by some party members caused the relative unpopularity of the new SKP-sponsored sport clubs.

Further initiatives for worker sport came from the enthusiastic action of a number of party members and the strategic line of the Comintern and its sport organisation, Red Sport International (RSI), formed in 1921.

From 1926 to 1927, the Comintern and the RSI repeatedly advocated for Swedish communists to establish a worker sport federation. Such efforts were particularly intense preceding the *Spartakiad* to be held in Moscow in 1928. In the summer of 1927, the SKP judged the circumstances favourable to inaugurate its national worker sport federations, and, through intensive agitation, many worker sport clubs were founded. According to estimates, there were 50 clubs with a total of 6,000 members. On 16 October 1927, the Worker Sports Federation (*Arbetaridrotts föreningarnas Samorganisation* [AFS]), representing 37 clubs, came into existence. The statutes were identical to those written in 1922 for the Stockholm worker ports club, and the AFS elected to remain a member of the bourgeois Swedish Sports Federation (RF). The inaugural meeting also called for closer cooperation with the RSI.

The second congress of the AFS, on 2 December 1927, decided to break with the RF and become a member of the RSI. However, because of some members' resistance, a complete break did not occur until the end of 1929, a result of the conclusion of the power struggle between left and right groups within SKP and AFS leadership. Many of these problems were less serious after the party split in October 1929. At the annual congress of the AFS, preceded by an intensive propaganda campaign, the revolutionary group within AFS gained control of worker sport in Sweden. The contention between followers of the Comintern and the Communist Party, later changed to the Socialist Party (SP), came to an end in November

"Comrades, worker sportsmen and women in town and country, young workers, male and female! On December 2, 1928, the 2nd Annual Conference of the Union of worker sports clubs took place in Stockholm. After thorough analysis of the situation it was decided to form a worker sport association and to join the Red Sport International.

On behalf of the Executive Committee of this organization we welcome the decision of our Swedish comrades and promise to help the Swedish worker sports in all its problems and make it a valuable member of the fighting Swedish working class."

Information-Bulletin, RSI, 1929, No. I.

Position Paper of the RSI Annual Congress, 1929

Leaders right—Masses left

7. It is obvious that on the one hand the social-democratic leadership is openly moving into the bourgeois camp and on the other the masses of the workers are moving to the left. This is not surprising but the result of the same fact: The increased class antagonism and class struggle.

8. Indicators of the movement towards the left in the workers sport organisations are also

    a) the forming of independent workers sports organisations in Sweden, England, Canada, the United States and other countries;

    b) the fight of the workers sports *Kartels* in Germany and other countries against the united front of the reactionary forces;

    c) the open struggle of the SWSI rank and file against their own leaders after having been betrayed by them, e.g. in England and Alsace-Lorraine;

    d) the self-liberation of the members from the influence of the reformists (general elections in the Swiss SATUS and election of a left majority in the National Assembly of Sport in Finland);

    e) in spite of the prohibition of competitions against teams of the RSI and the USSR, members of the SWSI maintained their sporting relations (France, Switzerland, Estonia, England etc.). . . .

1930 when the SP established its own worker sport federation (AIU) in Stockholm.

The years following the split were the most politically active period in the history of worker sport. The AFS encouraged a policy of political class struggle, as interpreted by the SKP. At the level of sports, this meant the general physical and mental training of the working class and solidarity with international worker sport. The ban on competition with athletes from bourgeois sport clubs, participation in party politics, and pursuance of the Comintern's and RSI's United Front tactics led to worker sport's increasing isolation. In 1934, however, the Comintern agreed to the new Popular Front policy through which the worker sport federations attempted to emerge from their isolated position. The 1934 Paris rallies and the Göteborg Games in 1935, all associated with antifascist declarations and slogans, demonstrated these attempts to achieve a Popular Front.

The worker sport movement, however, did not succeed in establishing a united front for all workers, irrespective of political affiliation. This is apparent in membership numbers that, despite an increase between 1930 and 1933, did not exceed 8,000. This relative stagnation led to self-criticism, evident in the congress minutes of the worker sport movement. A last attempt by worker sport federations to gain a broader basis through the boycott campaign against the 1936 Berlin Olympics failed.

In the spring of 1936, RSI instructed its sections, following the Comintern Popular Front policy, to affiliate with bourgeois federations, thereby making contact with workers active in sports generally, and to establish an antifascist sports front. Discussion within the leadership of the worker sport movement in Sweden produced an agreement on this new policy, inasmuch as the political crisis in Europe made it imperative. The official decision by worker sport clubs to rejoin the RF was reached at the fifth congress in May 1936. This decision reestablished the worker sport movement and its statutes, and, by 1940, the movement was fully integrated within the bourgeois RF.

The Swedish Sport Movement: Development of the Swedish Sports Federation

The Swedish sport movement began to develop seriously around the turn of the century as industrialisation and urbanisation grew. Modern, elite sport in Sweden had its roots in the development of British-organised sport in the last decades of the 19th century. In contrast with other countries, the Swedish sport movement came into existence relatively late. Sport clubs were the basis of organised sport, and the initial clubs reflected the class structure of Swedish society.

In the 1890s, two federations were established: one for gymnastics, headed by General Viktor Balck—the so-called "father of Swedish sport"—and one for sports generally, headed by the industrialist Sigfrid Edström in Göteborg. After a bitter struggle for unity, the Swedish Sports Federation (RF) was founded in 1903. Edström played a significant role in this federation and was certainly the strongest personality in the RF during the first

Sweden and the Olympic Games—1936

"The government party, The Social Democrats, and the leaders of the trade union movement were in a dilemma before the Olympics 1936. On the whole, the principle of the Swedish Sports Federation that sports should be kept free from politics had been accepted. The problem was that many party members and members of the trade unions (about 150,000 out of the 700,000 members of the Swedish Confederation of Trade Unions) were against participation in the Olympic Games. In April 1936, the leaders of the Confederation of Trade Unions decided not to boycott the Olympics in Berlin and also that the federations should not take measures against participating members. The government party was of the same opinion after the question had been dealt with by the party congress in April 1936. The question of Sweden's participation was left to the sports organizations themselves to decide. The political Right was of the same opinion. These decisions were probably dictated by foreign— as well as trade political reasons. . . .

Finally even the government estimated that the majority of the people were for participation in the Games. This decision implied an acceptance of the thesis of the sports movement and the political Right that sports and politics should and could be kept apart in spite of the general brutality of the Nazi regime and its expected propaganda gains in connection with the Games."

Lars-Olof Welander

Table 7.1 Membership of the Swedish Sport Movement: 1910–1980

Year	Members
1910	55,000
1920	120,000
1930	180,000
1940	410,000
1950	740,000
1960	1,200,000
1970	2,000,000
1980	2,500,000

of the membership. With the introduction of the 8-hour day after World War I, there were greater opportunities both for the public's leisure time and for an extension of sport's social basis. Industrialists tended to look favourably on the promotion of sport because they thought that physical recreation enhanced labour productivity and intensity; furthermore, they believed that sport helped to establish a class consensus that could distract workers from political and class struggle and trade union activities.

The evolution of mass sport is apparent in Table 7.1. The sporting success of Swedish athletes in international competition has been considerable. Athletes have won 155 Olympic gold medals between 1896 and 1980, and such famous sportsmen as Björn Borg and Ingemar Stenmark have gained worldwide reputations. The extent of the mass sport movement is evident in the fact that there are 2.5 million members in 38,000 clubs—all in a country with a population of only 8.2 million. Much of this may be attributed to parental encouragement and the work of the many volunteer sports coaches and administrators. On the other hand, it has to be said that sport in Sweden is also big business today, with as much as 15 billion krona invested annually. So, the trends are today negative as well as positive; commercial and elitist interests stand opposed to fitness activities and sport for all.

The Swedish Worker Sport Movement

The most influential members of the Swedish worker sport movement have been Evert Leijon, Viktor Wallin, and Folke Tiderman. Leijon was the first advocate of the movement; he was also secretary of the AIF, a member

decades of its existence. Local clubs were quick to align themselves beneath the umbrella of the new federation that set up separate regional organisations and federations for individual sports.

Once the RF began its activities, its development progressed extremely quickly (Table 7.1). In fact, probably no other country had such a strongly centralised sport organisation from the very outset.

The RF leadership consisted primarily of army officers, businessmen, and civil servants. Sources on membership are rather vague, but it would appear that few, if any, women were among the RF members. It is claimed, however, that, in 1910, workers made up three quarters

Sweden

"It seems as if Sweden was one of the earliest countries in the modern era in which the government was paying directly for sport and the preparation of athletes. As early as 1877 the government provided the funding of the trip of a team of gymnasts to Belgium. *Swedish Gymnastics* of father and son Ling was so synonymous with Sweden that the government did not only pay for the funding of the Central Institute of Gymnastics (*Gymnastiska centralinstitutet*) in Stockholm but also for the sending of teams of voluntary gymnastics clubs to further the interest in Swedish gymnastics abroad and to be able to send representative teams. The government payed 50% of the bill of a strong gymnastics team to the 1900 Paris Olympics which finished 8th (one place behind Australasia). In 1903 the Swedish Sports Federation (RF) was founded which demanded from parliament funding as an institution to assure a rational organization of sport including international competition. Between 1902 and 1906 this request was turned down three times. The success of Swedish athletes in the 1906 Olympics and the secession of Norway from the Swedish Kingdom in 1905 assured the funding of the Swedish trip to the 1908 Olympics. Here Sweden finished a respectable third behind the UK and the U.S.

In preparation of the 1912 Stockholm Games, the Swedish government gave permission to the RF to use some of the money from a national sports lottery (decided already in 1908) to pay for the new Olympic stadium. Sweden finished a surprising first at these Games and showed by this what a good preparation on the basis of a solid funding and a united national effort could do. They also showed that questions of *amateurism* were a matter of definition and not of principle. Already in 1906 the RF had decided: 'Military men on active duty are amateurs.' This paved the way for athletes to serve in the military to be permitted full-time training. . . .

IOC member Viktor Balck, who was the dominating Swedish sports leader at the time and succeeded in interesting the highest Swedish social strata for sports, was in favour of the British *natural method,* while Sigfrid Edström, later president of the IAAF (International Amateur Athletics Federation, which was founded in Stockholm 1912) and as of 1946 president of the IOC, stood for an American type of training. Both agreed on a strong ideological national rhetoric which combined the thinking of sport with that of Social Darwinism.

For the Olympic Games of 1912 they went about their preparation very systematically. It resulted in Sweden finishing first, ahead of the U.S. and Great Britain. This caused a revolution in the thinking in many countries. Federations and governments considered investing into the selection and preparation of Olympic athletes to achieve medals as symbols of national success, courage and vigor—just as the Swedes had done. The presence of the Swedish royal family in the Olympic Stadium gave this national comparison even more credibility. Moreover, the Royal House took an amazingly active part in the Swedish sports movement in general and the 1912 Olympics in particular. Just like in Germany, the success of the young sports movement over the old gymnastic movements was fastened by the royal support.

In 1913, when the lottery for the stadium and the preparation of the Games was over, the Swedish state finally stepped in and paid for the Swedish sports movement in general on an annual basis, including the preparation of the athletes for the 1916 Olympic Games."

Arnd Krüger: "Providing a Magnificent Advertisement for Our Young Country: The Origins of Sport as a Means of National Representation. 1912-1914," in: *Proceedings 10th ASSH Conference* (Canberra: NIS, 1993).

of the executive of the Communist Youth League, editor of the sports daily newspaper *Idrottsfolket* (Popular Sport) and a journalist on the newspaper *Ny Dag* (New Day). He also wrote most of the bulletins and letters to AIF members. Wallin and, later, Tiderman were presidents of the AIF between 1930 and 1936.

Since the 1930s, no separate worker sport movement has existed, and those worker sport clubs that still exist exclude mention of political sport or class sport from their statutes.

During the 1920s, the ideology of the worker sport movement was largely restricted to propaganda. The international ideals of "red sport" were posed as an alternative to the bourgeois RF. Following the lead of the Moscow-based RSI, AIF leaders criticised bourgeois sport for its concentration on individualism and competition. Proletarian sport, they argued, should by definition be collective. Whereas bourgeois sport focused attention on elite performers and stars, the aim of proletarian sport was the cultural enhancement of the working

"For Red Sport Unity. The Workers Sports Federation invites all proletarian athletes to prepare for the World *Spartakiad* in Moscow, August 1934."

A typical noncompetitive worker sport tableau.

Part of the mass demonstration against the Ådalen murders in May 1931. The Workers Sports Federation standard is among those flying.

Helgensen, winner of the high jump with 185 metres at the Moscow *Spartakiad*, 1928.

people and the harmonious development of the entire body. The record-mania and nationalism of bourgeois sport stood out in contrast to the aims of proletarian sport.

Sport was to be part of the creation of a socialist culture. Because it was considered impossible to create a general physical culture within capitalist society, worker sport was intended to pave the way for a classless society, to unite working people to fight in the class struggle. It was quite clear to leaders of worker sport that at the other end of the political spectrum, bourgeois sport prepared people for combating the working class.

As long as no opportunity existed for establishing their own worker federation, working-class sport clubs remained within the framework of the RF that advocated nonpolitical sport. That did not prevent members of AIF clubs from frequently attacking, in SKP and its youth periodicals, the allegedly antiworker nature of the RF. They pointed to the bourgeois character of the Swedish state and the need to create a socialist state in which sport would take on a new meaning.

Owing to the widening social divisions as a consequence of the depression in the late 1920s, sport politics and ideological analysis were increasingly influenced by communist ideas. It was felt blatantly obvious that the bourgeois forces in the class struggle were trying to integrate working-class youth into the bourgeois sport movement. Furthermore, it was alleged, the sport movement was evidently becoming openly militarised and fascist. Although it pretended to be neutral, the bourgeois sport movement was filled with a spirit of nationalism, at the same time as bourgeois society was shedding its democratic traditions and enforcing its own imperialist interests. In this developing confrontation, bourgeois sport evidently aligned itself with reactionary forces while worker sport aligned itself with the antifascist forces. Because youths were being prepared through sport for the military service of the bourgeoisie, the only effective action could be the establishment of a real worker sport federation. The Communist Party, therefore, decided to call on its members and supporters to withdraw from bourgeois sport federations.

The paramount ideological orientation of the Swedish worker sport movement was to follow the ideological and strategic changes instructed by the Comintern. The movement to the left by the Comintern in 1928, which led to a third political group splitting from the SKP, meant stepping up the campaign against the leadership of the social democrats that had to be isolated from the mass of workers through the United Front.

One important precondition for the development of the worker sport movement was the attitude of the social democrats. It is noteworthy that social democrat leaders, including President Hjalmer Branting, had regarded healthy sport as a means of democratisation in the early 1920s. They did attack occasional tendencies toward commercialism and elite sport, but they were generally in favour of sports. The major argument put forward by party leader Per Albin Hansson, later to become the Swedish prime minister, and other social democrat leaders was that sport had a salient democratic and social function. In order to ensure democratic development of the RF, therefore, the social democrats felt it necessary for their members to get themselves elected to the leadership of local sport clubs, federations, and associations.

When the first worker sport federation (AFS) was established in 1927, leading social democrats disassociated themselves from it on the grounds that it was part of a communist propaganda offensive that would only create a split in the RF. This attitude has to be seen in the context of the political polarisation between the social democrats and the communists. In 1931, the social democrat executive declared that the membership in its party or its youth organisation was incompatible with the membership of the AFS. A social democrat, Minister Arthur Ehrberg, later declared in parliament that the class-political division of the sport movement had been imported into the country from abroad and was to be deplored.

The favourable attitude of the social democrats toward competitive sport also had some positive consequences in that the sport movement, which had never enjoyed substantial financial support, now received direct government funding. Between 1936 and 1939, this funding amounted to as much as 15 million krona. The close collaboration of the social-democratic government and RF circles certainly illustrated the cooperation policy pursued by the social democrats.

Some social democrats, notably Rikard Lindström, attempted to win over the party to an affiliation with the Socialist Worker Sports International (SWSI), but this was rejected largely because of social-democratic opposition to the popular community ideas; they preferred understanding and cooperation with the bourgeois sport organisations to class exclusiveness. This policy was particularly pursued by Prime Minister Per Albin Hansson, who preferred evolution to revolution, thrusting Marxism into the political background. In contrast with the traditions of other European labour and social-democratic parties, the Swedish social democrats had little concern for Marxism as an ideology.

Despite rejection by the social democrats, the leadership of the worker sport movement had high hopes for backing from the trade unions. Such hopes were not entirely without foundation, because communist influence within the trade unions was certainly greater than their 10 to 11 percent union membership. Because the worker sport movement lacked finances, its members tried to gain financial backing from the trade unions in 1928 and 1929. All they managed to obtain, however, was 200 krona from the 14 trade union sport clubs. Subsequently, they received no financial support either from the trade unions, the state, or the urban councils.

Formation of the AIF

The second AFS congress took place on 2 December 1927. Its decision to sanction the split from the RF was taken on organisational as well as political grounds. From the organisational point of view, the worker sport federation now had 6,000 members in 50 clubs. The decision to form an independent worker sport federation and to affiliate with Red Sport International was taken unanimously; only four members wished to postpone the decision for another year.

The ideological *raison d'être* of the new federation was spelled out at the general meeting:

1. The class nature and antiworker hostility of the bourgeois sport movement
2. The burgeoning political and economic struggle
3. The objective of the worker sport movement to educate the working class for running a class society in the long term
4. The international unity of proletarian athletes in the class struggle

AIF was, without a doubt, an offspring of the Communist Party. The communist leaders supported the formation of an independent worker sport federation and paid it 500 krona in October 1920. Communist relations with the RSI dated back to the early 1920s. At the 1924 Moscow RSI congress, Henning Ehn had been elected a member; he was then representing the "worker sports movement in Sweden and, simultaneously, the sports section of the Swedish Communist Party and the Communist Youth League. Comrade Ehn is a member of the Communist Party of Sweden." Other Swedish representatives were Nils Björkmann and Johan Nord who, in 1926 and 1927 respectively, took part in a meeting of the Swedish Communist Party and the RSI executive in Moscow.

It is evident from the minutes that the Comintern and the RSI put pressure on the Swedish communists to form a separate worker sport federation. A certain "EXR" (representative of the Comintern Executive Committee) or "Arthur" (identified as W. Mehring) had been in Sweden between 1922 an 1926 to carry out Comintern instructions in regard to worker sport. Fritz Reussner, secretary of the RSI, had recommended to the Swedish Communist Party and its youth organisation that the newly formed amalgam of worker sport clubs (AFS) should form an independent organisation prior to the Moscow *Spartakiad* in 1928.

What set the seal on the ideological orientation was the leftward shift of the Comintern in 1928 that envisaged, *inter alia,* stepping up the struggle against the social democrats; this led to a third split within the Swedish Communist Party and to struggles within the worker sport movement. For the time being, the establishment of the AIF was postponed. Evert Leijon and Herman Jonsson relied on the left of the party in the AFS leaders and launched an intensive propaganda campaign to establish a separate worker sport federation. They reiterated the class arguments that had been made throughout the 1920s.

The split in the Communist Party on 9 October 1929 also affected the future of worker sport in Sweden. At the AFS conference that took place at the end of the year, the power struggle between the left and the right in the AFS leadership was resolved by the revolutionaries gaining all the seats on the executive committee. Therefore, they declared that an independent worker sport federation (AIF) would now be a "section of RSI on the basis of revolutionary class struggle. This was to be inscribed in the federation's programme, emphasising that it ad-

---

"What was the analysis of the situation of the international workers sports movement?

(1) The bourgeoisie which is intensifying its fight against the working class is also acting against the revolutionary worker sport. At the same time the bourgeoisie is increasing its own activities on the field of sport.
(2) In its fight against the revolutionary worker sport movement the bourgeois is aided by the reformists of the SWSI. The leadership of the SWSI is intending to destroy the character of class struggle of worker sports and by this dissolving many member organizations.
(3) The leadership of the SWSI has placed its organization into the general imperialistic front against the revolutionary workers of the USSR.
(4) While this is taking place at the top, the masses of worker sportsmen and women are becoming more radical and move away from their leadership."

Report on the Plenary Session of the Executive Committee of the RSI, 30 May-3 June 1929 (Helsinki: Työväen Arkisto).

hered to revolutionary communism. The programme meant a radicalisation and strengthening of the communist orientation of the organisation. It further emphasised that the AIF would take part in the war against imperialism in defence of the USSR.

By advocating worker sport, the programme stressed the following ideological propositions: In class society, the bourgeois forces tended to step up efforts to integrate working-class youth into the bourgeois sport movement. This was where the blatant militarisation and fascist development of bourgeois sport was to begin. The bourgeois sport organisations were replete with nationalism, even though they pretended to be neutral; they were aligning themselves more and more with the forces of reaction, which was why worker athletes were to join the struggle on the other side to oppose the fascist forces. There was only one effective means to combat this nationalistic campaign of hate to inveigle youth support: create an independent worker sport movement. The Communist Party made it clear that it was in urgent need of the movement to bring together its members and supporters to extricate them from the bourgeois sport movement.

Popular Front Tactics of the AIF

It is not easy to distinguish the various ideological and strategic shifts within AIF. After 1930, the Communist Party attempted to strengthen its hold upon AIF. It is apparent in the minutes of the sport movement that the party was attempting to impose a political model of work upon the worker sport movement, whereas the bulk of worker athletes preferred sports to politics.

Politicisation reached its zenith in 1931 and 1932. The federation staged a number of demonstrations and political rallies against fascism and war. Thus, the Communist Youth League newspaper, *Sturmklockan* (Storm Bell), called for a protest rally on May Day 1930, so that "arm in arm the revolutionary worker athletes will march as physically-strong fighters against capitalism." The revolutionary policy of the Communist Party was thereby supported by direct political action, in one case, for example, by a protest against the shooting of five men during a 1931 uprising in Adalen. The number of new members gained by the AIF in Adalen, however, was disappointing.

Politically, the movement followed national and international communism. Accordingly, bourgeois sport organisations were branded as an arm of the Swedish imperialists preparing for war. The object of work in the field of sport was to form a red Popular Front under communist leadership. It was in this spirit that the third congress of AIF, in 1932, dealt with the federation's para-

> "As top events of their activities for the coming years both internationals planned major international sports events for 1931. But only the 2nd Workers' Olympics of the SWSI in Vienna took place. The RSI had planned to stage their counter-olympics, the *Spartakiad,* at the occasion of its tenth anniversary in Berlin. But the social-democratic police president of Berlin did not permit the manifestation, so that the RSI did not have the opportunity to propagate its movement in Germany and among its foreign membership. The sixth plenary session of the RSI did take place in Berlin at the time, but the members from the Soviet Union were not permitted to participate as they did not receive German visa. . . . The plenary session decided that the 1932 congress should take place in Moscow and that the first *World Spartakiad* should also be staged in Moscow in 1933."

H. Dierker, *Arbeitersport im Spannungsfeld der Zwanziger Jahre* (Essen: Klartext, 1990, p. 48).

mount objective: revolutionary struggle against imperialist war and the establishment of a Popular Front against capitalist arms policies. The congress, consequently, advocated defence of the Soviet Union as its prime task. The worker sport federation was termed "a defence organisation of the proletariat against fascism." In fact, the federation aspired to being an organisation of the entire working class, even though it pursued the Communist Party's "class against class" policy when fighting the Swedish socialist parties.

The Communist Party leadership repeated frequently that work within AIF was of political significance. It was an aim of AIF to demonstrate political unity with the SKP, and the political demands and slogans of the SKP and the Comintern were supposed to be guidelines for the AIF. Thus, the SKP required AIF members to show communist discipline, adhere to the principles of democratic centralism, and not go against the party's interests.

One communist demand was that members of AIF should not compete against athletes from the bourgeois sport federations, but that they should take part in the political actions of the Comintern and RSI. This policy, however, increasingly led to obvious isolation. The ban on competition against RF clubs was an effective barrier against further contact with proletarian athletes within RF. A change occurred in 1934 in connection with the Popular Front policy implemented by the Comintern. The major rally in Paris in 1934 and the Göteborg Games of

Unity From Below

"The struggle for the unity of the worker sport movement can only be led against the leadership of the reformist SWSI. This leads to the necessity to show the divisionist activities of the leadership of the SWSI and the construction of a united revolutionary worker sport from below.

What means unity from below?

This means that the emphasis of all of our actions will be placed at the basis of the organisation, to free the masses of the rank and file from the social-democracy. This means constant lively contacts to the basis of worker sports inside and outside the SWSI. The revolutionary comrades have to take the leadership of the more backward sports groups. Each class conscious worker sportsman has to start an exchange of letters with at least one nonrevolutionary worker in a different town of our county to propagate our position. Unity from below means we have to qualify our class conscious members as coaches to gain importance on the level of the technical instructors."

Gen. Kedroff, "The Divisionist Activities of the Social-Democrats and the Tactics of the RSI," *Central lecture of the 5th Plenary Session of the Executive Committee of the RSI, May 31 1929*, p. 44.

1935 featuring antifascist slogans were two such attempts to implement the new policy. In fact, the resolution given at the Paris rally on behalf of 40,000 Swedish workers and the Göteborg Games was certainly successful in terms of large-scale organisation and sport politics.

But the AIF did not succeed in realising its principal aim of establishing a Popular Front of all proletarian athletes irrespective of political affiliation. This is apparent from the membership figures. In spite of a certain increase in membership in the 1930-1933 period, subsequently, the movement stagnated and membership never exceeded 8,000.

At the AIF congress in 1934, Viktor Wallin and Evert Leijon proposed that henceforth worker athletes might be permitted in certain circumstances to take part in competitions against RF athletes and clubs. They pointed out the shifts in orientation and policy of RSI and the new Popular Front strategy. In their own, oft-repeated self-criticism, they lay the blame for the relative lack of success at the doors of economic crisis, the isolation of the

proletarian masses from the AIF, and their own sectarianism and opportunism.

The 1934 resolution pointed out that worker athletes were not obliged to deal with the bourgeois leadership of the RF and that it was the duty of AIF to attract proletarian members of the RF over to the AIF. So, it was a major objective for the future to educate AIF members in class and sport politics in order to enable them to attract other proletarian athletes into their ranks.

From 1934, political and ideological education actually increased; for example, they included theoretical tests in the "Ready for the Final Struggle" sports badge and formed a Popular Front of all athletes against militarism and fascism. The 1936 Berlin Olympics presented an opportunity for the AIF to achieve some of its aims. From 1933, the anti-Semitism in Germany had affected Jewish and worker athletes, thereby resulting in worldwide protest. In 1934, the RSI had called in Paris for a boycott of the summer 1936 Nazi Olympics. One consequence for Sweden was the bone of contention over granting financial backing to the Swedish Olympic team; in fact, the SKP, AIF, and radical trade unions called upon the social-democratic government to refuse to pay such funds and to withdraw from the Berlin Olympics.

In addition to its slogans for fighting fascism and the anti-Nazi Olympic rallies, the Stockholm AIF staged boycotts against the soccer match between Sweden and Germany in the summer of 1935, flying balloons over the stadium and dropping leaflets upon the spectators. Furthermore, an anti-Olympics conference was held in Stockholm; it attracted fairly extensive participation, including supporters from leading trade unions. The joint declaration by the Red Sport International demanded a boycott of the Nazi games; this, undoubtedly, helped the efforts of AIF to achieve concerted actions by all antifascist forces of worker athletes. It also supported United Front tactics to bring together all antifascist forces, and particularly social democrats, against fascism and militarism.

After the intrusion of German troops into the Rhineland and the judgement in Hamburg against the two sailors, Jansson and Mineur, in March 1936, the tide of public opinion against the Berlin Olympics was running strong, particularly within the trade unions. With the formation of the Jansson-Mineur Committee, headed by SKP leader Knut Olsson, one of several attempts was initiated to establish an antifascist front against the Nazi Olympics. In fact, the AIF did manage to undertake united action with radicals in the Stockholm sections of the social-democratic youth organisations and with other left-wing groups. Some members of the Swedish Olympic squad, for example, including six soccer players, refused to go to Germany for the Olympics. A number of worker athletes, mostly members of AIF, travelled in July 1936 to Barcelona, intending to take part in the Worker Olympics. As it turned out, the Barcelona games did not take place because of a fascist coup.

Despite considerable opposition to the Nazi Olympics, particularly from the trade union movement (20 percent had supported demands for a boycott) and despite cooperation between some social-democratic groups and communists, the AIF did not attain its major goal of establishing an antifascist sports front.

Because of this relative failure, a tactical shift took place within the AIF so as to put an end to the federation's isolation. The economic crisis was considered to be so dangerous that, if it was to be successfully combated, all forces had to come together to form an antifascist front. The fact remained, however, that the AIF had only 8,000 members while the RF had 300,000. When the question of the future of the AIF was debated at the fifth congress in May 1936, mention was made of the RSI encouragement to its affiliates to establish a Popular Front. Because it was highly unlikely that the 300,000 RF members would join the 8,000 AIF members, what the Popular Front meant in practice was the AIF sections would have to join the bourgeois sport federation in order to maintain contact with proletarian athletes who practised their sport within the RF. Otherwise, there was no question of establishing an antifascist sport front. The appropriate official resolution was accordingly passed. The tactical and organisational changes recommended by the RSI were that

1. AIF clubs would join the RF in order to form a Popular Front against fascism, and
2. the AIF would remain an independent federation, maintaining its contact with the SKP.

We have to ask why it was that the AIF did not succeed in establishing itself as a force to be reckoned with. The answers given at the 1936 congress were that its hoped-for support from the trade union movement was not forthcoming, that the social democrats had resisted rather than pledged support, that the AIF itself had suffered from sectarianism and inexperience in political tactics, and the radical workers generally had taken a negative attitude toward sport. The idealism and enthusiasm of the AIF leadership were insufficient to compete with the bourgeois sport movement in order to reinforce worker sport as an independent organisation. Attempts by the Communist Youth League to set up a caucus within the RF had come to nothing, and, as it turned out, the sporting aspects of club work were far more important to members than the political issues.

Despite these setbacks, the history of the worker sport movement in Sweden provides us with lessons for posterity in terms of idealism and political consciousness.

Notes

The only scholarly work on worker sport in Sweden is my own dissertation, *The Labour Movement and Sport in Sweden: 1919-1939.* All information contained in this chapter is taken from that dissertation. To my knowledge, the only other published work on the worker sport movement in Sweden is the jubilee publication of the Kiruna worker sport movement, *Fifty Years of Worker Sport: 1927-1977,* 2 vols. (Stockholm, 1979).

Chapter 8

Landmarks in the History of Norwegian Worker Sport

Gerd von der Lippe

NORWAY

This kingdom in northern Europe occupies 323,895 km² and had 2.81 million inhabitants in 1930.

For centuries Norway was closely linked with Denmark; then, as a consequence of the Napoleonic troubles, Norway united with its Swedish neighbour in 1814. Sweden, on the basis of its constitution in the same year, allowed Norway to retain extensive control over home affairs and financial policy. The Swedish king, however, was in supreme command of the military forces, and he held the decision-making power with regard to foreign policy.

Norwegian politics soon settled on two topics: complete independence and the institution of a government solely responsible to parliament (*Storting*). The latter was achieved in 1884 when the *Storting* forced the resignation of ministers loyal to the king, and the monarch had to assemble a cabinet that gained the confidence of the parliament. The wish for independence, which had been kept alive because of the country's need to pursue its own foreign policy, was not fulfilled until 1905 when the separation of the two countries was reached by mutual agreement; Norway forthwith recruited its own monarch from the Danish royal family.

By the end of the century, Norway's merchant fleet had advanced to its status as the third largest in the world, an expansion that provided decisive impulses for the country's process of industrialisation. This not only enhanced the political influence of the liberal bourgeoisie, but it also went hand-in-hand with the appearance of an organised workers' movement that led, in 1887, to the founding of the Labour Party (DNA). The demands of these two groups were responsible for the introduction of universal male suffrage in 1898. The process of industrialisation, accelerated by the economic prosperity of the years prior to World War I, brought more voters to the DNA. As a result, the party's greater influence was felt in a number of social reforms, such as a factory act with paragraphs protecting women and children, health insurance, and the 1915 law establishing the 10-hour work day.

Although Norway declared its neutrality at the outbreak of World War I, it was confronted with formidable war costs. No less than half of its merchant fleet fell to the war at sea waged by the Germans. At the same time, the Allied blockade policy served to cut off the country from its German export market. Because the results of these developments were predominantly felt by those with small incomes, increasingly radical tendencies within the workforce were hardly surprising. After 1919, this trend led to the DNA joining the Third International, or Comintern, and there was no way that nonsocialist parties sought coalition with it.

The upturn of the world economy in the mid-1920s scarcely touched Norway. Consequently, various bourgeois governments had been plagued by mass unemployment long before the Great Depression. Their inability to deal with the matter became obvious when a policy of extensive reductions in governmental expenditure pushed the unemployment figures to such heights that every third employed person had lost a job in 1933. This situation, together with demands for an expansionist financial policy and emergency relief measures, produced a sweeping victory for the DNA in the 1933 elections; the victory brought the party into government 2 years later. By 1940, the new government had managed both to institute a step-by-step reduction of unemployment and to improve conditions for large social groups by means of a massive state investment programme and an ambitious social policy.

Norway, as a neutral country, had little success in its attempt to survive World War II relatively undamaged. On 9 April 1940, German troops began the occupation of the country that ended, despite both the dogged resistance of Norwegian troops and the Allied forces sent to support them, with the country's surrender in mid-June. The king and his ministers fled to London, and the Germans set up a puppet government under the leader of the Norwegian Nazi Party, Vidkun Quisling. The legitimate government returned in May 1945, subsequent to the capitulation of the occupation forces and Germany's overall collapse.

Background to the Development of Worker Sport

When the Worker Sports Federation (WSF) was set up in Norway in 1924, Norway's most circulated newspaper, *Aftenposten,* wrote that nobody would remember it the following year (Lorenz, 1974, p. 35). The paper was wrong.

Until it achieved independence from Sweden in 1905, Norway had been a country mainly of farmers, fishermen, traders, and housewives; it had a relatively small group of industrial workers (Furre, 1971, p. 305). The years 1905-1916 witnessed the longest continuous economic growth in the country (until 1940). An industrial revolution took place during this prosperous period in which the industrial working class increased to 160,000 (1916), and the 8-hour work day was introduced for industry (1919).

There were a number of reasons why the WSF came into being (Edin, 1970; Furre, 1971; Kristoffersen, 1974; Larsen, 1979; Lorenz, 1974). Until 1924, very few sport clubs for workers existed within the Norwegian National Federation of Sport (NFS). The NFS was heir to Norway's first modern national sport federation, dating from 1861. Most of its members were from the middle class—only a handful came from the working class, of whom women made up a very insignificant number (von der Lippe, 1982, pp. 80-86). Organisationally, the NFS was connected with the Ministry of Defence, within which the NFS was directly subordinate to a military committee (Edin, 1970, pp. 55-58).

The division of the sports movement into worker and bourgeois organisations occurred during the economic depression as a result of a bitter struggle between worker organisations and employers.

After a brief postwar boom, the economic depression reached Norway in 1920. The Norwegian trade unions called a strike in 1921 to oppose up to 30 percent reductions in wages. As many as 120,000 workers actually came out on strike. In defence of their own interests, the bourgeoisie formed the *Nothilfe,* analogous to the German *Technische Nothilfe.* In the capital of Oslo, in Bergen, and in other cities, sport clubs were collectively enrolled into the *Nothilfe,* which was concerned with organising strike-breaking (Hofmo, 1933, p. 15).

In 1922, the Workers Sports Opposition was established within the NFS; one of its aims was to combat the strike-breakers within the sport organisation. This was far from popular among the NFS leaders, who argued that their organisation had been politically neutral in regard to the *Nothilfe* (Tyrihjell & Nordaul, 1961, p. 145).

After a short while without any serious efforts at compromise, the WSF emerged in 1924 as an alternative to the NFS. The initiative primarily came from the communists, particularly the communist youth. In contrast with Sweden and Denmark, the prevailing policy of the

"We have to discuss especially the errors of our Norwegian comrades. These errors are particularly opportunist. The comrades who have permitted these errors have gone so far that they have discussed—sufficiently prudent, however—the question of maintaining the membership of the AIF [WSF] in the RSI. . . . The AIF, which is a section of the RSI, has been strengthened recently and is currently having about 30,000 members. Concurrently, the membership of the bourgeois sport federation is decreasing. This rise in membership created considerable interest on the side of the bourgeoisie and also in the reformist SWSI. With promises of material subventions and the availability of free sporting grounds and of friendly cooperation, the bourgeois sports leaders attempted to create unity with the AIF. The leadership of the Norwegian section of the RSI rejected all such offers of cooperation of the class enemy.

This did not end the offensive of the enemies of the AIF. This time, the social fascists of the SWSI tried to divide the forces of the AIF and subdue a part under bourgeois leadership. . . . It is therefore the duty of all members of the AIF to show publicly the divisionist policy of the SWSI and work with all forces to maintain the unity of the AIF with the RSI. . . .

Comrade Brandstorp maintained in a newspaper article the opposite. He wrote, 'The connection of the AIF with the RSI is weakening and not strengthening the organization.' In a different newspaper article he wrote, 'While the AIF has 25,000 members, 75% of the bourgeois sports federation are workers. . . . The main reason for this is that our AIF is a member of the RSI and many workers do not want to join a communist organization.' . . . Comrade Olsen, the president of the AIF declared that the executive committee as much as the membership wanted to stay in the RSI and continue to fight side by side in the class war. . . . The plenary session accepted this declaration with satisfaction . . . and warned comrade Brandstorp . . . that with the next step against the RSI or the unity of the AIF . . . he would be expelled."

Note. In November of the same year Brandstorp was made editor-in-chief of the AIF journal and member of the executive board of the AIF.

I. Scholdak, *Minutes of the 4th Plenary Session of the RSI,* Charkow, 30 May-3 June 1929, p. 17ff.

Gunnar Wein using the then popular ski-jumping style at the Worker Championships in Oslo, 1940.

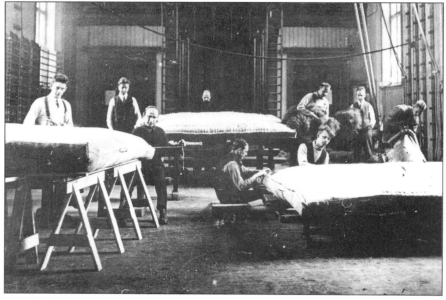

Wrestling mats made by wrestlers in the Worker Sports Club and used by 15 wrestlers excluded from national competition for singing the "Internationale."

Female members of the Oslo Sleipner Track and Field Club, early 1930s.

Diploma issued at the Oslo Worker Games in July 1925 for running the 180 metres in 24 seconds. Note that the race was called a "propaganda" competition.

Poster advertising the 1928 Winter *Spartakiad* in Oslo. The program featured boxing, wrestling, skiing, and ski jumping.

Poster advertising the 1936 Winter *Spartakiad* in Oslo. It mentions ski jumping in the Nydals Hills involving competitors from the Soviet Union, Finland, Sweden, and Norway, and a cross-country race for men and women.

labour organisations in Norway favoured the revolutionary (rather than reformist) policy in the early 1920s. In 1921, the WSF joined the Red Sport International (RSI) based in Moscow (Edin, 1970, p. 45; Kristoffersen, 1974, pp. 39-40; Pålbrant, 1977, p. 99).

In 1925, there were more than 2.5 million people in Norway, of whom one twenty-fifth were in organised sport. At that time, most women, children under 16, and much of the male working class were outside organised sport.

WSF Objectives

"The federation's aim is to unite worker sports clubs in Norway and to work for the development of physical and mental culture for the good of the working class" (Hofmo, 1937, p. 30). The political foundation was developed in several reports. It was strongly felt that the working class could fight the middle class only if their people were strong, tough, and healthy. "There is no sport without class struggle" (Aasebøe, 1927, p. 8). Otherwise, the values of bourgeois sport would prevail within the workers' organisation.

To Aasebøe, the NFS leaders were army officers, traders, and fascists. Hofmo (1937) develops this line farther: "through sport these leaders are trying to obtain a mental hold on the working class by making them interested in the class struggle" (p. 4).

In the everyday work of the WSF, it was primarily the *means* and not the sports themselves that distinguished it from the NFS; one spoke about a culture of physical activity for the working class. The WSF was not against results in themselves, but the leaders were opposed to the cultivation of elite athletes as stars. Such a policy would, in their view, undermine sport for the common people. As a consequence of this objective of sport for all workers, most of the WSF clubs developed a clear social profile.

Some of the worker sport clubs put on theatrical performances with a sporting theme in which ordinary club members took an active part. The clubs also arranged study groups, and, on 1 January 1933, the WSF affiliated with the Workers Education Association (Larsen, 1979, p. 35). It was to this end that Rolf Hofmo wrote his book *Sport and Politics.*

Sport and Politics Within the NFS

According to Paragraph 1 of its rules, the NFS was the national organisation for all sport clubs in Norway. It aimed to lead and to promote a healthy and rational way of life in Norway (Edin, 1970, p. 52). In 1934, the following sentence was added to the first paragraph: "The NFS is entirely apolitical" (*NLFI,* 1934).

What was the NFS's interpretation of the term "political"? In 1928, the organisation had sent the following instructions to its clubs and associations:

[U]ntil now organised sport in Norway was above and outside political parties and classes. This has been of great advantage to sport and is in line with the policy of the NFS and the National Assembly. In contrast, the WSF has a clear political objective which is even more important than the task of promoting sport. This abuse of promoting sport must not lead to a change within the NFS whose objectives and rules are sanctioned by the National Assembly. (*Socialdepartementet,* 1936, p. 24)

The definition of politics tended to "very narrow" and "traditional." The leadership argued that its organisation was neutral in regard to the work of the *Nothilfe,* and no formal decisions were made about the objectives of the strike-breaking organisation within the NFS bodies. Nonetheless, members of the WSF and the NFS confirmed that abuses had occurred (Edin, 1970, p. 52; Kristoffersen, 1974, p. 32). The NFS kept up its contacts with Nazi Germany, including participation in the Olympic Games of 1936, without ever recognising this participation as a political act. No matter what the actions possessing political implications initiated by the NFS, the leadership would continue to insist on their apolitical nature. This attitude is evidently in accordance with the tradition of bourgeois sport organisations in Norway (Kristoffersen, 1974, pp. 104-106).

The WSF had the greatest increase in percentage terms, whereas the overall membership increase for each organization was roughly the same (Table 8.1). In this period, many newcomers came into organised sport, in contrast to a decade earlier when the increase was very small (Edin, 1970, pp. 63-64) and the decade after 1945 when membership actually diminished (von der Lippe, 1982, pp. 21-22).

Table 8.1   WSF and NFS Membership Between 1925 and 1940

Year	WSF	NFS	Total
1925	6,608	104,200	110,808
1930	12,321	105,699	118,020
1935	55,120	128,339	183,459
1940	104,114	195,828	299,942

Data from Edin, 1970.

In light of the WSF's brief history, its growth in membership is impressive. Its fellow organisations in Denmark and Sweden never gained the influence in their respective countries as the WSF had in Norway. At most, the Danish organisation had 8,000 and the Swedish had 14,000 members ("Den Jydske Historikers Redaksjon," 1982, p. 181; Pålbrant, 1977, p. 141).

Communists and Social Democrats Within the WSF

In the early years, communists dominated the WSF leadership. There was, therefore, no need for them to intensify their struggle against the social democrats as long as the Labour Party showed no interest in the WSF. But in 1927, the political situation changed. The social democrats joined forces with the Labour Party, and the communists found themselves in a clear minority within the worker organisations. The Labour Party leadership took an interest in the WSF; it soon gained a majority on the board, and, in 1931, the communists left to form a new body—the Federation of Struggle for Red Sport Unity. We cannot be certain of how many members left the WSF. From present-day sources, it would seem that between 5,000 and 6,000 out of a total of 16,000 members is a realistic estimate. The WSF, however, did not formally join the Lucerne Worker Sports International—the reconstituted body of the Socialist Worker Sports International (SWSI). That would probably have annoyed many ordinary WSF members because the affiliation with Red Sport International (RSI) had brought many popular Soviet athletes to Norway. Henceforth, social democrats in the WSF strove to maintain informal contacts with both the RSI and the SWSI.

Key Decisions

Equality characterised the work of the WSF in many areas: its organisational structure, campaigns to bring in more female members, decisions to make a more fair classification for young people and adults, and involvement in company-organised sport.

The organisational structure was based on sport for all working people and equality. From the very start, the General Assembly was the supreme body, in which 150 to 200 representatives were elected from each community. It had, for example, no separate organisation for track and field responsible to an international federation,

as the NFS had. Consequently, the various sports were not economically independent. If soccer had more money one year, it was obliged to support other sports with little cash (Larsen, 1979, p. 106). The National Board had powers of decision in the interim period between general assemblies.

The aim of the WSF—sport for all working people—included women. The leadership did its best to attract more female members, but it was not until 1931 that the national leaders seemed to be at all vigorous in this campaign (von der Lippe, 1982, p. 90). At that time, a relatively large increase in female membership actually did take place. Nothing similar was attempted in the NFS. WSF female members were encouraged to take part in such activities as track and field, swimming, tennis, cross-country skiing, slalom, rowing, and speed skating. At that time, these were all the sports, with the exception of swimming and tennis, that were supposed to be male preserves (von der Lippe, 1982, p. 96).

In order to boost its female membership, the WSF tried to appoint women leaders; a Women's Central Committee was set up and linked to regional and local women's committees. In 1934, as many as 47 percent of the local clubs in Oslo had organised such committees (von der Lippe, 1982, p. 91).

Resolution concerning the relationship between the AIF and RSI

"1. The Norwegian Workers' Sports Federation (AIF) maintains its membership in the RSI.

2. The AIF has received declarations and manifestos from the RSI in recent years, which—if actually put into action—would have brought the majority of the membership of the AIF into conflict with their political views.

Considering that the basis of the work of the AIF is class solidarity, . . . the congress declares: The Congress will not approve of those declarations and manifestos from the RSI which will bring its membership into conflict with our other class organizations, notably the Norwegian Workers Party and the Norwegian Trade Union Congress."

Material from the *6th General Assembly of the Norwegian Workers' Sports Federation, AIF*, Oslo, Nov. 1-2, 1929. Report dated Dec. 18, 1929, p. 5f.

Resolution concerning women's sport

"The Congress agrees that in all meetings and competitions in *Turnen* and games, which are staged by organizations which have also female members, at least one competition for women has to be included."

Material from the *6th Congress of the Norwegian Workers' Sports Federation, AIF*, Oslo, Nov. 1-2, 1929. Report dated Dec. 18, 1929, p. 8.

In 1937, a form of sex quota was instituted in Oslo, whereby the women's committee had the right to attend the annual meetings of the various sports if any female member was registered in that particular sport. It is difficult to evaluate the results of this encouragement for women. By today's standards, the WSF women members did not attain equal rights formally inasmuch as male members were able to take part in more activities, events, and contests than women. Even now, there are no equal rights at a formal level in Norway's organised sports.

The General Assembly of 1935 decided to make "physical age" the basis for classification in competition for young people of both sexes (Larsen, 1979, p. 107). The basis for calculating this was a person's height, weight, and chronological age. Traditional classifications, of course, only took age into account, and big differences in physical development often made competitions unfair for the smaller youngsters.

Because schools were already measuring height and weight, it was relatively easy to put this policy into practice. In 1937, 40,000 pupils obtained their school badge for general proficiency in sport on the basis of this "physical age" (Larsen, 1979, p. 105). This was considered an excellent beginning.

From 1 January 1932, the following rules were established. There were three groups for both adult female and male members: A, B, and C (Larsen, 1979, p. 105). Group A was for the best athletes and Group C for beginners. To attend Group A, the women in track and field had to perform the following: 8.8 seconds in the 60-metre run, 70 seconds in the 400-metre run, and 8.60 metres in the shot put. Men in Group A had to run 100 metres in 11.7 seconds, 200 metres in 24.2 seconds, and throw 12 metres in the shot put. To qualify for promotion the results had to be produced twice a season. It was possible, for example, to take part in Group A in the 100 metres and in Group C in the shot put.

Henceforth, these rules were followed in all competitions, including the WSF national championships. Both sexes took part, and participation increased, especially in Group C.

From their inception in 1924, few clubs existed based on company-organised sport (Larsen, 1983, p. 16). The first competition in which only company-organised members participated did not occur until 1929 in Oslo, where 500 competitors from 150 firms were involved (*Arbeiderbladet,* 1929). The arrangement turned out to be quite successful. Two years later, the General Assembly decided that the WSF should include sport organised by firms for their employees (Larsen, 1983, p. 17). The reasons for this decision included the need to compete for those workers within the NFS and to attract new members, thereby boosting WSF influence.

The sports that were most popular included soccer, track and field, speed skating, skiing, swimming, walking, rowing, shooting, bandy, chess, bridge, lorry racing, and cycling. The central leadership did not favour lorry racing for safety reasons. Only members who did not take part in ordinary sport competitions were permitted to compete in this sport. It was precisely through lorry racing and soccer that the WSF gained many new members in the late 1930s.

The 1931 decision on company-organised sport marked a turning point because this WSF organisational structure influenced sports' present-day form. Furthermore, sport organised by companies for employees today constitutes one of the major groups of the National Confederation of Sport, which includes over 250,000 members (*NIF*, 1983, p. 51).

The Ban on Competition Between WSF and NFS Members

Between 1924 and 1926, a number of reconciliation meetings between the two opposing sport organisations were arranged (Edin, 1970), but no major compromise was reached.

The NFS board, in 1925, inscribed into its minutes the following note: "Members and clubs in NFS are forbidden from taking part in competitions arranged by sports organisations and clubs that are not affiliated to NFS" (Edin, 1970, pp. 60-62). The following year, the WSF similarly responded with its policy that "No WSF member is permitted to compete with bourgeois athletes [members of the NFS]" (Hofmo, 1937, p. 38).

The situation was discussed in the Norwegian National Assembly in 1926 and 1927, and the Defence Ministry appealed to the NFS to take a new initiative toward the WSF. It did so the following year, though in vain. The WSF leaders had made up their minds not to come to an agreement. Instead, the 1928 General Assembly requested

"The arguments of the AIF leadership is of particular interest: 'We cannot realize the decisions of the RSI concerning the First of August [1929], as they are directed against the Norwegian Party to which we belong.' What were the decisions of the plenary meeting of the RSI in Charkow concerning the 1st of August? The Plenum agreed that its members should actively participate in the August demonstrations under the motto: 'Fight against war! Against the preparation of war against the first workers' state, the USSR. In the field of sport against the blockade of the USSR instrumented by the social fascists in the SWSI, the bourgeois sports movement, and the fascists.'

It is not surprising that the revolutionary decisions of the RSI are against the principles of a social democratic party, but all of these decisions are the consequences of the votes in the Charkow plenary session of the RSI which were supported by the Norwegian leadership of the AIF."

Material from the *Minutes of the 6th General Assembly of the Norwegian Workers' Sports Federation, AIF*, Oslo, Nov. 1 - 2, 1929. Report dated Dec. 22, 1929, p. 6.

members of worker organisations, both within the administrative districts and the National Assembly, to support the WSF (Larsen, 1979, p. 71).

As a consequence of this, the bourgeois newspapers—the overwhelming majority of the press—did not report the workers' sport activities. Until fresh reconciliation meetings took place in 1935, the bourgeois tactics isolated the WSF. Owing to this isolation, the WSF received no grants from the state or the administrative districts until the Labour Party had won the majority of councils. In most places except Oslo, this situation lasted until the mid-1930s. In fact, from its inception in 1919, the National Assembly had resolved that the NFS was the sole administrator and distributor of state funds for sport in Norway (Edin, 1970, p. 7).

Most sport centres belonged to the NFS and the administrative districts. As a result of the split between the two opposing organisations, the NFS urged the administrative districts not to allow local sport centres to be rented by the WSF (von der Lippe, 1981, p. 70). For a long time, therefore, the WSF was excluded from these centres. Even the request for a small amount of money for starting a course in lifesaving was turned down by the bourgeois parties at the local-government level (von der Lippe, 1982, p. 92).

After the social democrats had gained a majority on the WSF board, however, the Norwegian Trade Union Congress granted a small annual grant to its sport organisation. And once the Labour Party had gained a majority in local government elections, the WSF was allowed to use the local sport centres. In 1935, when the Labour Party formed the government, and fresh reconciliation meetings commenced between the WSF and NFS, the WSF was finally granted state funds.

In spite of the lack of state cash and the isolation tactics of the bourgeoisie, the WSF actually increased its membership and developed extensively between 1924 and 1935.

Unity Against Nazi Germany and Fascism

One year after the worker sport movement in Germany had received its death-blow from the Hitler regime, the Norwegian Trade Union Congress decided that no union-organised worker would be permitted to compete with German athletes as long as the ban on German trade union and worker sport existed (AIF, 1939, p. 4).

From the WSF records of 1933-1935, we find the following under the heading "For Worker Sport Against Fascism": "Organised workers are forbidden from competing with German athletes who represent a state that has destroyed and outlawed German worker organisations." From then on, most WSF clubs discussed the theme of fascism. Even at the very first meeting when a sport club was to be formed, this issue was debated under the heading "Sport for the Workers. Sport for the Fascists" (Larsen, 1979, p. 61).

During May Day celebrations in 1934, several WSF clubs were given permission, by way of an exception, to compete against German athletes, but no sporting contact between WSF and Nazi Germany occurred after that—in contrast to that between NFS and Germany. NFS contacts took place at local and national levels, even when Hitler's top people made speeches before NFS competitors (von der Lippe, 1982, p. 93). This was in line with the attitude taken by NFS leaders: "We regard a break with German athletes affiliated to the same international organisation as us to be an unfriendly act against the German state" (Lie, 1945, p. 18).

As a result, the NFS sent athletes to the Berlin Olympics in 1936, while WSF athletes headed for Barcelona. The bourgeois press focused attention on NFS athletes and their opportunities to win Olympic medals, while the worker press launched a propaganda campaign against Nazi Germany and fascism. The content of the bourgeois and worker newspapers of the time depicts two totally

Resolution concerning the organizational cooperation between the AIF and the Norwegian Workers Party and the Trade Union Congress

"1. . . . The congress is accepting with satisfaction that the union of the working class of the year 1927 has also opened new possibilities for the AIF. . . . The massive amount of new members are the best proof that the union of the working class has its positive effects upon the AIF.

The AIF will, therefore, have to form a working group with the Norwegian Workers Party and the Norwegian Trade Union Congress. Our congress is, therefore, asking the two organizations to form a joint working group with us. The future leadership of the AIF will have to take the steps necessary for such a working group.

2. The actions of the bourgeois sport of the past years are the living proof that this federation is not politically neutral, but that it is a part of the organizational superstructure of the existing social order, which has as its primary function to maintain the current capitalist mode of production. All workers which are still members of bourgeois sports clubs should, therefore, join the AIF as soon as possible and realize its importance in the class struggle.

3. The congress is asking the Norwegian Workers Party and the Norwegian Trade Union Congress to force its members to leave the bourgeois sports organizations and to join the AIF.

4. The congress is asking the workers' representatives in the Norwegian Parliament and in all City Councils to support the AIF as legitimate representative of the interests of Norwegian workers in the field of sport."

Material from the *6th General Assembly of the Norwegian Workers' Sports Federation, AIF*, Oslo, Nov. 1-2, 1929. Report dated Dec. 18, 1929, p. 6f.

different worlds with utterly different values; there was almost no communication between them in regard to the Nazi threat.

One attempt at unity against fascism was another reconciliation trial between the two opposing sport organisations. From 1936 to 1939, WSF and NFS did communicate with one another, primarily through a committee set up at the initiative of the Social Affairs Ministry. With the Labour Party in office, it was impossible to organise sport in Norway under the Defence Ministry. As a result, the WSF received state grants, and the two sport rivals were bound to arrange competitions involving participants from both organisations (Edin, 1970, p. 92).

Toward a Single Norwegian Sport Organisation

Sources differ on the principal reasons for unification of the sport clubs. Most stress the work for unity against the threats of Nazi Germany and fascism, the fact that the Labour Party was in power, and the leadership of the two sport organisations.

In 1935, most of the leadership of the two general assemblies was probably opposed to reconciliation. Decisions on starting work on unification were taken at board-level and not discussed in the general assemblies or among ordinary members (Edin, 1970, p. 73). This was unusual on such a major issue.

The following leaders in favour of reconciliation are worthy of mention: Rolf Hofmo, Trygve Lie, Oscar Torp, and Karsten Granlie—all Labour Party members. Rolf Hofmo was, however, regarded largely as a WSF leader. After the war and until his death, he was the leader of the new national, government-appointed body working for sport and youth. Trygve Lie was the WSF chief in 1935, though he had earlier been an NFS member. In addition, he was a member of the 1935 labour government, and, after the war, he was a member of various movements formed by the Labour Party. Oscar Torp was the leader of the Labour Party at the time, a position he held from 1923 until 1945; he was also a member of various labour governments before and after World War II. Karsten Granlie is not as well known as the others, although he was one of the first social democrats to join WSF. Three of the reconciliation leaders of the WSF were top politicians within the Labour Party. On the other hand, none of the NFS negotiators held similar positions within bourgeois political parties.

At the WSF General Assembly in 1939, the principle of unity with NFS was decided (Kristoffersen, 1974, pp. 45-46). During the debate, Rolf Hofmo argued that he would withdraw if the meeting voted against him. In fact, the trial vote resulted in 92 votes for unity and 77 against, but, in the end, 121 voted in favour and "only" 48 voted against (Kristoffersen, 1974, p. 46).

To formulate regulations for the new organisation, a committee with representatives from both organisations was set up in the autumn of 1939. Communists in the

"The political leadership of the Labour Party—to a large part synonymous with the leadership of the AIF—tried to tread water without committing themselves too much. One of the reasons for this was probably that a take-over of government offices was no longer such a distant dream. The 'responsible' Socialists did not want to be placed in a ruling situation in which they would have their hand tied by resolutions from the Trade Union Congress or the AIF. Statements from two central politicians from the Labour Party revealed some limitations on their former 'class solidarity' stand, when it came to practical politics. The Foreign Minister in the new Labour Government from spring 1935, Halvdan Koht (historian by profession) later asserted that it had never been in his mind to support any boycott of Germany. In fact the only precondition he had made for entering his post was that the cabinet should commit itself to end all boycotts towards Germany 'for example in sport. . . . '"

Quoted from Matti Goksøyr, "Attendence or Absence? The Nazi Olympics of 1936 and Their Influence on a Little Country: Norway," in: A. Krüger & B. Murray (eds.) *The International Reaction to the 1936 Olympic Games* (Champaign, IL: UIP, 1996).

WSF and, particularly, the soccer leaders in the NFS were opposed to the committee. It certainly looked as if the committee was going to have a hard job on its hands. One meeting was interrupted by an air-raid warning on the evening of 8 April as the Germans began their occupation of Norway. This was not the time for sophisticated disagreement. A provisional board consisting of WSF and NFS leaders was established. In this way, Norwegian sport clubs succeeded in forming a "sporting front" against the Nazis. They did not, however, succeed in developing the ideological precepts and traditions of the worker sport movement in the new organisation (von der Lippe, 1981).

The National Confederation of Sport (NCS) was formally established in 1946, but its basis had been formed before the war when it had been made clear that the attitude of the new organisation toward politics was one of neutrality—an important legacy of the old bourgeois National Federation of Sport.

The European Track and Field Championships took place in Oslo in the summer of 1946. Although the USSR took part in international bourgeois competitions only after 1952, when it entered the Olympic Games at

Helsinki, Oslo was different. A strong Soviet team finished a credible second behind Sweden, which had been neutral in the war and had maintained a strong track-and-field tradition. The Soviet team could take part as in the enthusiasm of the alleys because of the victory over Hitler; differences were lulled for some time before the Iron Curtain came down later. But most of all they could participate in Norway, because the RSI tradition had been absorbed by the NCS.

Conclusion

The WSF (1924-1940) was an alternative sport federation to the bourgeois NFS with the objective of promoting physical activity for the working class. In its everyday work, it was primarily the means and not the sports themselves that distinguished it from the NFS.

During the period of isolation, up to 1935, the WSF developed its sport policies and made the following key decisions:

1. Equality was the keyword throughout the organisation: in the organisational structure, men's and women's sport, classification for the various participants, and company-organised sport.
2. No sporting contact existed between WSF and NFS members. The economic policy of the National Assembly was based on this situation, while the WSF received a small amount of money from the unions and nothing from the state.
3. The anti-Nazi and antifascism campaign for unity educated WSF members in regard to sport and politics; it made it easier for the rival sport organisations to unite into the National Confederation of Sport.

References

Aasebøe, C.O. *Idrett og klassekamp* (Oslo, 1927).
AIF. "Forholdet til staten og NLFI," *Utarbeidet til AIF's 9 ord. landsm.* (1939).
Arbeiderbladet. 3 July 1929.
"Den jyske historikers redaksjon," *No. 19-20 Sportshistorie* (Werks Offset, Århus, 1982).
Edin, I. *Politikk og idrett* (Universitetet i Bergen, 1970).
Furre, B. *Norsk historie 1905-1940* (Det norske Samlaget, 1971).
Hofmo, R. *Idrett og politikk* (Oslo, 1933).
Hofmo, R. *Folkeidrett-arbeideridrett-borgerlig idrett* (Oslo, 1937).
Kristoffersen, K. *Frihet, sunnheit, kapital* (Pax, 1974).
Larsen, P. *Med AIF-sjerna på brystet* (Tiden, 1979).
Larsen, P. *Hele folket i idrett* (Tiden, 1983).

Lie, K. *Slik kom idrettsfronten* (Eget forlag, 1945).

Lorenz, E. *Arbeiderbevegelsens historie II, 1930-1973* (Pax, 1974).

NIF. Norges idrettsforbund Årbok, 1983.

NLFI. Offisielt meddelelsesblad, No. 9, 1934.

Pålbrant, R. *Arbetarrorelsen och idrotten 1919-1939* (Uppsala universitet, 1977).

Socialdepartementet. Stortingsprop. No. 1, Tillegg No. 39, 1936.

Tyrihjell, O. & Nordaul, G. *Norsk idrett gjennom hundre år, 1861-1961* (Oslo, 1961).

von der Lippe, G. *AIF* (Unpublished dissertation, Telemark distriktshøgskole, 1981).

von der Lippe, G. *Kvinner og idrett* (Gyldendal, 1982).

Chapter 9

Worker Sport in the New World: The Canadian Story

Bruce Kidd

CANADA

This second largest country in the world (9,556,817 km^2) with the British monarch as head of state had a population of 10.35 million in 1931.

The origins of the country go back to the 1867 British North America Act that gave expression to the will, determined by economic necessity, to form a union of the modern provinces of Nova Scotia, New Brunswick, Ontario, and Quebec.

The first decades of the oldest British dominion were characterised by economic stagnation and antagonism between the population's English-speaking majority and the French-Canadians living predominantly in Quebec. In 1896, a new era was ushered in when the Liberal Party under Laurier took over the government. As a French-Canadian, the prime minister reduced the fears of Quebec. Economic prosperity was generated by the vast expansion of the transcontinental railway, by the unchecked growth of the mining industry after the gold finds on Klondike Creek (1897), and by the huge growth of immigration as a result of the Gold Rush.

Canadian efforts to supply the Allies with raw materials and food during World War I made the country an industrial nation, equipped with a workforce whose increased self-confidence found expression after the war in a broad strike movement that was brutally suppressed. With regard to foreign policy, Canada's huge contribution to the war—documented by its loss of 60,000 soldiers—was internationally recognised, and Canada was no longer a speechless colony when it came to external issues. There were hardly any objections to Canadian participation at the Conference of Versailles and, of even greater importance, it received full membership in the newly formed League of Nations. Apart from the assumption of diplomatic relations with the great powers and from the negotiation and signing of treaties, this factual independence did not lead to increased international activities. Canada's policies under liberal rule were strictly isolationist out of consideration for important liberal clients in Quebec. Obvious examples were the attempt to eliminate all obligations for assistance to victims of aggression from the league covenant, the leading role in the discussions concerning the Westminster Statute (1931) that legally fixed the conversion of the empire into a commonwealth of equal and completely independent nations, and the whole-hearted support for the British appeasement policy in the late 1930s.

As far as the economy was concerned, long before the outbreak of World War II Canada had to learn that it was impossible to isolate itself from international developments. Blessed with a short postwar boom, the country then showed itself to be largely unable to cope with the consequences of the Great Depression. Therefore, the refusal of the liberals—who pursued a rigorous policy of deflation—to give federal funds to the provinces to combat unemployment and its dire consequences brought a number of the poorer amongst them to the brink of bankruptcy. The customs preferences on commonwealth markets obtained by the conservative government at the Imperial Economic Conference in Ottawa (1932) showed little success, too, despite the simultaneous expansion of protectionist barriers. Thus, a noticeable improvement only came with the rising import needs of the expanding economy south of the 48th parallel. The most interesting result of the crisis was the foundation of the Cooperative Commonwealth Federation that, with its demands for nationalisation and state economic planning, gave the nation its first party with a socialist (reformist) outlook.

A new Canada was created by its participation in World War II. At times the most important ally of Great Britain, the country was often forced to efforts that made it into an important centre of finance and a leading industrial power—with a slowly developing social welfare system—that had more than just raw materials or food to offer. The isolationist dreams of the period between the wars had disappeared. From then on, attempts were made in the United Nations and the commonwealth to forge coalitions with middle and small powers against the decision-making monopoly of the great powers. Finally, the war brought the country closer to its so far happily ignored, powerful neighbour in the south, a step that was not universally applauded in view of the dangers of economic subjugation and involvement in anticommunist crusades.

Worker sport was not indigenous to North America. In both the United States and Canada the movement grew out of the attempt by radical immigrants and communists to transplant what they understood to be a European tradition of class-conscious life to North America. In the case of the United States, the Labour Sports Union created by the Communist Party of the United States was primarily made up of immigrant groups and confined to just a few cities; the Communist Party was perhaps more successful in its campaign against racial discrimination in major league baseball than in establishing worker sport groups (Naison, 1979; Riess, 1982). Nor did Canada offer a receptive climate to worker sport. Although the social historian can enumerate a long list of utopian socialists and industrial unionists who sought to create what Kealey and Palmer (1982) call "an alternative hegemony, a movement culture of alternatives, opposition and potential," none of these efforts lasted very long or achieved a mass following.

By the 1920s, when the Workers' Sports Association of Canada was formed, most workers and their families had been well integrated into bourgeois forms of popu-

---

Hegemony

The concept of hegemony was developed by Antonio Gramsci (1891-1937) while he languished in an Italian fascist prison. This concept helps to explain why socialist revolutions have not occurred in advanced western societies—as they should have according to Marxist theory—given the oppressive nature of capitalism.

Gramsci analysed the common sense of the people and how they were influenced. He differentiates between coercion and spontaneous consent, between dictatorship within the political society and hegemony within the civil society. Hegemony refers to the way in which the dominant group(s) of society, through intellectual and moral leadership, the use of language, and the rules of the game, win the consent of the subordinate group(s).

As common sense develops through participation, popular culture and sport become a field of resistance and incorporation, of what Gramsci called "a compromise equilibrium." The search for alternative forms and meanings within the worker sport movement and not just for alternative leadership is, therefore, of particular importance in the hegemonic sense.

---

lar culture and recreation. In sport, it had long been the practice for employers, church leaders, and urban reformers to recruit working-class athletes into their amateur and company- and church-sponsored leagues, to reduce class tension, and, as Gruneau (1982), Metcalfe (1978), and Mott (1983) have written, to "solve the urban crisis." Many of the star performers in the increasingly popular commercial sport spectacles were working-class men; workers were frequent consumers of these spectacles and of the ideologically powerful sport magazines and newspapers that were sold at the same time. Whereas in Europe, trade unions and socialist political parties provided leadership and resources to develop an oppositional worker culture, in North America these institutions left the terrain of leisure largely uncontested. By the beginning of the 20th century, the most powerful unions and labour centrals had rejected the strategy of class struggle for the pragmatic business unionism of Samuel Gompers (Babcock, 1974). In the political sphere, socialists have always been on the margins in the United States. They have enjoyed considerably more success in Canada, but the party that emerged as the symbol and standard-bearer of the left, the Cooperative Commonwealth Federation–New Democratic Party, has confined itself to electoral reform. A worker culture, let alone worker sport, has never been on the agenda.

Nevertheless, in the years between World War I and II, a small group of sport enthusiasts and political activists tried to cultivate a worker sport movement in this unpromising soil. They attempted to create a network of community clubs where the best European traditions would be adapted to Canadian conditions, and some of them sought to contest the bourgeois definition and domination of Canadian sport. But while they achieved a measure of success, the national federation they set up ultimately failed. It provides a telling reminder of the extent to which sport movements interact with and are structured by the economic, social, and political conditions of the time.

The Finns

Although the Workers' Sports Association of Canada was not established until 1928, several immigrant groups had practised a form of worker sport well before that date. The most prominent, as Lindstrom Best (1981) has shown, were the Finns, who came to Canada in the early years of the century, some to escape tsarist Russian oppression, most to obtain the free land promised by the government and railway recruiters. By World War I, 17 percent of all Finnish emigrants were living in Canada. After the Civil War in Finland, the flow resumed. While

"Who is blaming the workers' sports movement that it also contains athletes who are keen on records or fanatic on point scores—bourgeois and capitalists traits—has not understood which role the workers' movement has in this society and—in reality—can only have. The constant contradictions of bourgeois, petit-bourgeois and proletarian convictions are necessarily working within its ranks. Only through such contradictions can the true class based thinking of the proletarian class develop itself.

Such complaints against the workers' sports movement are unfounded, as they demand more from the proletarian movement than it can develop within a capitalistic class structure. They would only be justified if they could prove that the workers' sports movement furthers the capitalists traits of sports on purpose—such as the bourgeois sports movement is doing. Under such conditions, a worker sports movement would not only be superfluous but counter-revolutionary. Under such conditions the worker sports movement would only be a particular brand of the bourgeois sports movement, it would be the movement of holders of a certain job or profession as there are other clubs which limit its membership to certain factories or social ranks.

But the true nature of the worker sports movement consists in taking the sports interested masses away from the blind followership of the bourgeois sports—by counteracting the bourgeois conviction of sports with a proletarian one. The whole direction and tendency of the worker sports movement are opposed to the bourgeois sports movement. The worker sports movement is not already a true *proletarian* movement because it is performing already the true socialist sport, but because it is attempting to develop it. It is not pursuing the utopian notion of a little *socialist* island in the otherwise capitalist world, but the abolition of capitalism. Therefore, the worker sports movement is a socialist movement."

H. Wagner, *Sport und Arbeitersport* (Berlin: Büchergilde Gutenberg, 1931, pp. 159ff.).

most Finns were described as "farmers" on the immigration cards, even political refugees like Finland's first prime minister, social democrat Oskari Tokoi, very few ever settled on homesteads. The land they were given was often unsuitable for agriculture, or they lacked the capital to be successful; most ended up as wage labourers in the mines, railroads, and lumber camps of the resource hinterlands of northern Ontario and British Columbia. Here they quickly developed a reputation for labour radicalism. Most of them were socialists of some kind who had supported the Reds during the Russian Civil War. In the Finland they had left, trade unions and socialist political parties had been accepted well before World War I, so it was hardly surprising that they formed similar organisations to help them combat exploitative employers and a repressive state in Canada. Finnish forestry workers played a leading role in organising the Lumber Workers Industrial Union of Canada and the Finnish Socialist Organisation of Canada, later renamed the Finnish Organisation of Canada (FOC), and conducted endless support activities for trade unions and activists. Finns also shared a common cause with Canadian socialists, as the Finns were active in the Socialist Party of Canada, the Social Democratic Party of Canada, and the Communist Party of Canada (Laine, 1981).

Wherever they settled in numbers, Finns created a rich social and cultural life for themselves, usually in their community halls (*haali*). They ran educationals and camps for their children; published and discussed their own newspapers, novels, and political literature; wrote and performed their own plays; and listened and danced to their own orchestras and choral groups. They also formed sport clubs. By 1906, there were clubs in Toronto, Beaver Lake, Sudbury, Copper Cliff, Timmins, and Port Arthur. While they restricted their own membership to working-class athletes, they were quite prepared to compete against all. In 1920, one Toronto Yritys wrestler, Enok Lopponen, represented the Amateur Athletic Union of Canada (AAU of C) in the International Olympic Committee's games in Antwerp. After the founding of the Finnish Worker Sport Association (TUL) in Finland in 1919, which was avidly followed through the Finnish-language press, the Canadian clubs sought to create a sport federation that would both recognise and contest the domination of Canadian society by a capitalist minority and would conduct programmes and competitions for the working masses alone. In 1924, the clubs in the Sudbury area formed a Central Ontario Gymnastics and Sports Federation, and, 1 year later, the northern and northwestern Ontario clubs joined to form the Finnish Workers' Sports Association of Canada (FWSAC). It

Wrestling was particularly popular among Finnish clubs. The backdrop on the stage illustrates the haunting northern landscapes of Finland.

Running tracks were carved out of the rough ground of northern Ontario. This was Comet's field in the 1930s, which was located along the Mattagami River near Timmins.

Mass gym group performance at Camp Tarmola in Toronto, 1927.

Comrades!

In August of this year it will be the 15th anniversary of the beginning of the bloody imperialist war. In the defence of its own capitalism, millions of betrayed proletarians left their lives on the battle fields. Hundred thousands of the best workers' sportsmen were sacrificed for the imperialist interests of the capitalists. The spirit of this war of 1914 is still alive. The pain of the disabled, the sorrow of the orphans, and the daily worries of the millions who lost their property because of the war are still an active reminder of the war.

The capitalists called it the *war to end all wars*. . . but in millions of ways and by thousands of methods humanity is being prepared for the next imperialistic war. . . . The contradiction of interests of the various capitalistic countries are undissolvable and will surely lead into the next war. The capitalist beasts are only united in their hatred against the Soviet Union, the only republic with a proletarian dictatorship which will build up socialism—the trauma for all capitalists. . . .

Worker sportsmen!

You must know that the capitalists will only use you as cannon fodder and will throw you without mercy into the next war. By the price of your life, your blood, the capitalists of your home country will purchase the right for an even more thorough exploitation. The capitalists are given millions of dollars, marks, and francs to rule the sports and bring it into line for capitalist rationalisation and the preparation for the next war.

Worker sportsmen!

Look closer and you will see millions of beautiful proletarian boys and girls which are part of the bourgeois sports movement and do not know nor foresee that they are going to be slaughtered for the benefit of the capitalist imperialists' plans.

Worker sportsmen!

Do you know why the ministers of war are so interested in sports? Do you know why the bourgeois governments help to support sports and the establishment of committees for them? It is a shameful lie that they are just interested in the benefit of sports or our class conscious proletarian sports organisations would receive help as well—but as usual they are cruelly persecuted under capitalist rule. The whole interest of the bourgeoisie in the sports of the workers has as sole interest their striving for ever more profit and their unresistable wish to bring about the next war. . . .

Long live the united revolutionary class front of the proletariat!

Circular Letter of the Executive Committee of the RSI to All Member Organisations, June 1929 (Helsinki: Työväen Arkisto).

was closely associated, but never formally affiliated, with the FOC. The first secretary was Hannes Sula, a former Finnish champion in the 100 metres, who had been a fierce Red partisan during the Civil War. He was also editor of *Vapaus*, the FOC's daily newspaper.

The favoured Finnish activities were track and field, wrestling, and Nordic skiing. No matter how rocky or forested the terrain, they always managed to clear and level enough for a 300- or 400-metre track. In the mining districts, they practised skiing at night with the aid of their miner's lamps and raced on the weekends for sweaters and socks—"not that useless bourgeois stuff, cups and medals," one participant remembered. They did not compete in gymnastics, but each year the national executive would determine a new set of routines to be practised by individual clubs and then performed *en masse* (with barely a day's rehearsal) at the annual summer festival. They were always prepared to travel long distances to engage in these events, even if it meant hopping freight cars or bundling up in open trucks during the winter. One annual trek is noteworthy. During the 1930s, when many were unemployed, the clubs around Timmins and Sudbury would each stage a ski race. One week, the men from Sudbury would ski to Timmins—a distance of 240 kilometres—stop at lumber camps along the way, race, and return. Two weeks later, the Timmins men would do the same in the opposite direction. By comparison, the longest ski marathon in Canada today, the Canadian Ski Marathon from Lachine to Ottawa, is a mere 160 kilometres!

The Ukrainians

Radical Ukrainian immigrants also engaged in an early form of worker sport. Ukrainian immigration to Canada began in the 1890s and increased dramatically in the decade prior to World War I. After the war, it increased again and continued unabated until the Great Depression, when the Canadian government closed its doors to newcomers. Most Ukrainian immigrants had been peasants in the overpopulated western Ukraine, and they went straight to the western prairie provinces where they struggled with the soil, the railroads, the bugs, and the banks to eke out a living on their homesteads. Despite constant Anglo-Saxon chauvinism, those who settled on the land were generally resigned to their fate and were politically conservative. Later they would support the movement for an independent Ukraine and agitate against the Soviet Union. But a few ended up in the cities and the industrial projects in the resource hinterlands, where they worked as unskilled or semiskilled labourers and often spent long periods unemployed. These became the radicals who formed trade unions, joined in socialist political struggles, and created cultural organisations to provide resources and a social basis for this activity. The first of these, the Taras Shevchenlco Society, was formed in Winnipeg in 1904 with a membership of 400. The Soviet Union inspired many more such organisations, and, by 1924, there were enough to form a national federation, the Ukrainian Labour Farmer Temple Association (ULFTA). Unlike the Finns, who created separate clubs, the Ukrainians conducted physical activity within the framework of the ULFTA. They rarely engaged in competitive events or games; they preferred gymnastics, tumbling stunts, and feats of strength, all of which could be performed as part of a cultural concert. In addition to the Finns and Ukrainians, the left-wing Czech, Slovak, Hungarian, and Jewish communities also conducted some form of physical activity for their members and children.

Role of the Communist Party

It was the Communist Party of Canada's Young Communist League (YCL), taking its direction from Red Sport International (RSI) through the Young Communist International, that sought to pull these various strands together, as well as to form new clubs to build the worker movement among the Canadian population. In 1924, the YCL instructed every branch to form a Worker Sports Association (WSA). It hoped the WSAs would become one of the most powerful of the Communist Party's "mass organisations," designed to win both sympathetic and uncommitted Canadians to the communist cause. WSA members were not required to be communists; the organisation would be controlled by a "faction" of YCL members acting under party discipline (*Young Worker,* October 1924; February 1925).

Despite the lack of specific guidance from the YCL, the branches were quick to take up the challenge. In 1925, soccer teams were started in Montreal, Toronto, and Winnipeg (called the "Hammer and Sickle Club"); smaller centres such as Oshawa, Renfrew, Kirkland Lake, Lethbridge, and Drumheller reported field days, team games, boxing clubs, swimming parties, picnics, and hikes. In 1926, WSAs were set up in 17 centres. The Toronto WSA operated a seven-team softball league, with two teams of cigar makers, one of jewellers, one from the Earlscourt Labour Party, and three WSA teams. The Montreal WSA was soon fielding senior and junior teams in the city soccer and basketball leagues that attracted large followings. "You didn't have to be a Communist to go to Fletcher's Field [in the centre of Montreal's working-class district] on a Saturday afternoon and cheer for the WSA. It was a great morale builder for all the tailors and workers in the area," one participant remembered (interview with Dave Kashtan). During the 1930s, the Toronto and Montreal soccer teams played each other on an annual basis to crowds as large as 5,000. Games were followed by speeches, songs, a collection, and an invitation to the WSA dance in the evening.

Outside Montreal and Toronto, the staple of most clubs was gymnastics. The great bulk of WSA members remained immigrants for whom it was a popular activity. In Toronto, the Jewish Workers' Sports Club held competitions, but elsewhere gymnastics was practised for mass exercise and display. Summer and winter groups would perform long sequences of carefully coordinated exercise and a variety of tumbling and acrobatic stunts. The most frequently performed routine was the multiperson pyramid that the YCL encouraged to depict working-class solidarity in the class struggle. In Winnipeg, under the skilled leadership of the Kaczor brothers, Walter and Fred, the WSA developed gymnastics to such a performance art that many of its members subsequently made careers for themselves as circus and nightclub performers. The club held daily classes in gymnastics, strength fitness, boxing and wrestling, weekly dances, and choral concerts. Almost every week, its top

"During the 3rd congress of *Comintern* (the Communist International) in the summer of 1921 the role of the Communist Youth International (CYI) was newly defined: It stopped being an independent organisation and became voluntarily a branch of *Comintern*. By this it also changed its character. During and directly after the war it had been an anti-war organisation which in many countries fulfilled the role of a not yet existing *Communist Party*. With the formation of the CP and *Comintern* this role was no longer necessary. It could therefore go back and stress more the actual youth activities. Consequently, general educational courses, meetings, the cinema, and other forms (like sports) which would attract youth were to be stressed. By this it also raised the question how communist sport ought to be organized: Within the CYI, in a separate RSI or as communist opposition within the social democratic SWSI."

F. Nitsch, "Die Internationalen Arbeitersportbewegungen," in: A. Krüger & J. Riordan (eds.), *Der Internationale Arbeitersport* (Cologne: Pahl-Rugenstein, 1975, p. 186).

team travelled to small towns in Manitoba, northwestern Ontario, and North Dakota staging displays. Twice a year the club staged a choral and gymnastics festival in the Winnipeg Auditorium.

From the outset, the YCL tried to set up a national organisation. In 1927, the first attempt to line up the various WSAs failed when no club outside Toronto was able to send a representative to the founding convention. But a second attempt in 1928 was successful, and the Workers' Sports Association Confederation (WSAC) came into being. Twenty clubs joined directly, and the Canadian Labour Party, the FWSAC, and ULFTA joined as affiliates (*Young Worker*, May 1928). In 1929, the national committee began to stage regional and national events, keep national records, and appoint regional and national organisers to help newly developing clubs. That same year, it affiliated with the RSI (*Worker*, February 1928). By 1932, the WSAC claimed a total membership of 4,000 (*Worker*, October 1932) and, by 1933, 5,000 in about 100 clubs, 40 of which were Finnish (*Young Worker*, July 1933).

Although these numbers were small in comparison with the memberships of the powerful European movements, the organisation had gained a foothold in many communities that was no small accomplishment. But growth was slow and uneven. It proved extremely diffi-

cult to win workers away from the well-established amateur, church, and company clubs, many of which enjoyed superior facilities, emphasised the more popular Canadian games of ice hockey and baseball, and often induced top athletes with payments or soft jobs. In the 1930s, the WSAs had to contend with the economic and social dislocations of the Great Depression. Never abundant, funds became so scarce that organisers and athletes had to travel to out-of-town competitions and meetings by riding the rails ("the side-door Pullman," as the *Worker* called it). In the smaller resource centres where the membership was almost entirely made up of single men, a mass layoff might force the entire organisation to leave town in search of employment, causing the club to suspend operations until someone else came along to resume them. In the early 1930s, when the Communist Party was under fierce attack from the state, employers, and a range of established community organisations, the WSA suffered from police repression (Betcherman, 1982). The national secretary at the time, Dave Kashtan, spent most of his 2-year term in prison for, as he told this author, "seditious conspiracy." Police raided the Vancouver WSA office and seized schedules, membership lists, and equipment. On another occasion in Toronto, they stopped a WSA boxing tournament (*Young Worker*, May 1931).

In addition to their athletics, the WSAs supported a number of political campaigns. In 1928, as part of the RSI attempt to discredit "bourgeois sport," the Jewish WSA in Toronto demonstrated against a gymnastics competition held at the Canadian National Exhibition under the auspices of the AAU of C (*Young Worker*, September-October 1928). In the years of the IOC's Olympic Games, the WSAs staged counter-Olympic campaigns. In 1935-1936, they conducted a year-long agitation against the Berlin Olympics and enlisted the support of a number of prominent public officials, church leaders, union leaders, and intellectuals. In conjunction with the Canadian Jewish Congress, they sent a six-person team to the ill-fated Worker Olympics in Barcelona. The team included two Jewish boxers, Sammy Luftspring and "Baby" Yack, who had been widely expected to go to Berlin, and Eva Dawes, the 1932 Olympic silver medalist in the women's high jump, who had been suspended for life by the AAU of C for her participation in a WSAC sports tour of the Soviet Union in 1935 (Kidd, 1978).

WSAs also linked their activity to national and local YCL campaigns. In 1931, for example, the Vancouver WSA took advantage of the drawing power of its baseball league to solicit signatures and contributions in support of the national Communist Party leaders facing trial in Toronto (*Worker*, July 1931). In 1932, during a wrestling tournament, it persuaded YMCA members to join it on a march for the unemployed (*Worker*, March 1932).

Jewish Workers' Sports
Gymnastics Club in
Toronto, 1927.

Whether indoors or out,
gymnastic pyramids were
a favourite form of
training and perfor-
mance.

Finnish ski competition, early
1940s.

> "The growth of the class consciousness of the proletarian sports masses can also be seen by the formation of proletarian sports organizations in a number of countries, breaking away from the bourgeois sports movements, e.g., in Sweden, Canada, the United States, etc. In spite of their formation, they have still many difficulties to overcome. All of these organizations maintain a definite class line and they will all join—just like the Swedish *Kartel*— the RSI."

Gen. Kedroff, "The Divisionist Activities of the Social-Democrats and the Tactics of the RSI," *Central lecture of the 5th Plenary Session of the Executive Committee of the RSI, May 31 1929*, p. 30.

WSA gymnasts frequently performed at rallies and fundraisers. In 1934, after Communist Party leader Tim Buck was released from a 3-year prison term, the Toronto WSA provided him with a guard of honour of 100 gymnasts at several well-publicised welcome-home rallies around the city (*Toronto Daily Star,* 1934). The WSA's presence on a public platform was warmly appreciated by the political leadership. In Winnipeg, according to former party alderman Andrew Bileski, "as long as the WSA was on hand, the fascists never dared to interfere with our rallies" (personal interview).

But each of these undertakings was initiated outside local WSAs, a circumstance that became a constant source of friction between the political leadership at the centre and the organisers of day-to-day activities in the individual clubs. Following the RSI, the Canadian YCL wanted to use the movement as a recruiting ground for the revolution. Sport, it believed, developed in step with the very conditions of industrial capitalism that gave birth to the proletariat. As long as capitalism alienated the workers' physical labour, it theorised, they would be driven to some form of sport as recreation. If this need could be channelled into a revolutionary sport movement, it could fuel the overthrow of capitalism as well as shape the development of physical activity in the new society. The strategic task for the YCL, then, was to motivate the worker to take up sport—that was already being done by the basic conditions of capitalist production, as was evident by worker membership in the already existing sport clubs. Nor was it to wage a public campaign for improved recreational opportunities for workers, although some WSAs did this as well. The primary task was to draw workers away from bourgeois sport and the notion of "sport for sport's sake" into a movement where physical

activity would be planned to prepare cadres for the revolution (*Young Worker,* June, July 1925).

For their part, the YCL and the national WSAC leaders pursued this task aggressively by an unrelenting propaganda campaign against bourgeois sport. In the party press, at WSAC meetings, and at competitions and rallies, they polemicised against the churches, the YMCAs, the Boy Scouts, the AAU of C, and the other sponsors of sporting activity where working-class participants were to be found, arguing that these were class institutions that used sport to recruit workers to fight in the imperialist armies (the Boy Scouts were usually described as "future White Guards") and to scab on their militia brothers and sisters. In perhaps the most insightful analysis of the commercial sport press to be published in Canada prior to the critical scholarship of the last two decades, they regularly dissected the leading stories of the day to show how the allegedly neutral presentation and interpretation of sport served to validate the hierarchy and inequality inherent in capitalism. While they derided the idea that sport was innocent play that could be pursued, regardless of its auspices, for its own sake, they extolled the accomplishments of physical culture in the Soviet Union where athletes "vied with each other in raising production" (*Worker,* August 1933) and "took their full share as the physically most perfect specimens of the Russian working class in the construction of socialism" (*Worker,* October 1928). They planned elaborate strategies to undermine bourgeois sport, urging WSA members to infiltrate established clubs to turn the membership against its leadership (during the Comintern's "united-from-below" phase) or to establish factory leagues in unorganised plants as a preliminary to forming unions (*Worker,* March 1931).

But this campaign and the political work it required found few supporters among the WSA organisers struggling to make ends meet. "We must maintain a proper balance between propaganda and serious athletics," one secretary wrote to *Young Worker* (October 1926); "a successful team should give us all the propaganda we care for." Few local leaders and fewer members shared the YCL's belief in the primacy of WSA political work. They were sympathetic to socialist causes, and many would subsequently volunteer for the Spanish Civil War and, among the Finns, for Soviet Karelia. But their chief motivation in joining the WSAC was to participate in physical activity. They were not prepared to drop what they were doing for the unlikely projects the YCL wanted—trying to win members away from the YMCA or leafleting plant gates in an attempt to create factory leagues. Yet the YCL was insensitive to these views, and before too long began to include the WSAs in its attacks. The WSAs are "completely isolated from the general sports activities

The Limits of the Notion of Sport

"The soccer match Austria vs. England, the *match of the century,* as the bourgeois press named it, is still in vivid memory of those interested in sports that we can use it as starting point for our discussion from the point of view of a worker sportsman—without any prejudices. What is the position of us worker sportsmen towards such professional use of athletic skill? After all, this event was named *sport,* and it was brought to us in a perfect way via the radio waves. Many were listening and that included many of us worker sportsmen. Could we do this, considering that sports does play an important front-role in the class struggle?

There are, of course, some people who remain cold, but we should not take these to be the communist *also-athletes.* Those so-called *revolutionaries* report—on the contrary—about their collaboration in sports with the bourgeois athletes. For us, a clarification of the positions seems to be more important than a radical division.

Sport has become a name for a class of different things which should better be called acts of a circus or variety show. *Sports* contain boxing matches in which the gate receipt is more important than the presentation of natural physical talent. Six-day bicycle races, horse racing, motor racing, free-style wrestling in the circus tent—all *sports.* All those athletes who have dedicated their lives to sport—oh, what an irony of the use of language that such an odd mixture is called *sport.*

Sport, is this not the just name for games and physical exercise, a way to achieve a healthy body? Truely developed by millions of worker sportsmen and -women all over the world? Yes, this *is* sport! The professional exploitation of physical exercise is partially consciously, partially unconsciously favoured by the bourgeois sports movement. Just remember the ongoing struggle whether soccer should become fully *professional* or not.

The worker sportsman will always be interested in the attraction of such a professional specialisation—the interest one has towards a good variety show in the interest of entertainment. But sport, sport you do not do as a spectator in the stands, but on the sports ground, in the gym hall, in the swimming pool among comrades of equal position and equal interest—in the worker sports club."

H. Braueck, "Grenzen des Sportbegriffs," *Sportpolitische Rundschau,* vol. 6 (1933), 1, p. 2.

of the working-class youth," Dave Kashtan wrote in a long, preconvention article in 1931. "The issue of workers' sports versus bosses' sports has not been brought out clearly to expose the bourgeois sports organisations. . . . [Many clubs] bear the character of ordinary sports clubs while carrying the name of the WSA" (*Young Worker,* June 1931). This criticism was deeply resented by club members who considered themselves socialists and were proud of what the WSAs had achieved.

Canadianisation

These tensions were further exacerbated by the issue of Canadianisation. During this period, the Canadian communist movement was frequently bedevilled by the conflicting loyalties of class and ethnicity (Avery, 1980). After 1924, the mainly Anglo-Saxon leadership sought to "bolshevise" the party by dissolving the Jewish, Finnish, and Ukrainian sections that then existed, and,

after 1928, to involve party members in the mass organisations such as the FOC, ULFTA, and WSAC in much more explicit political work. But these efforts aroused much resentment among the largely immigrant membership. In sport, they had sought to minimise the problem of divided loyalties by instructing branches to set up clubs that would be autonomous from the other mass organisations (*Young Worker,* October 1924). Initially this had been successful; although most WSAs used the facilities and social networks of cultural organisations like ULFTA, they kept a distinct identity. ULFTA was initially an affiliate, but most Ukrainians joined the WSAs directly. The only significant exception was the radical Finns, whose clubs had been formed well before the WSAs came into being.

After the Sixth Congress of the Communist International, in keeping with the renewed emphasis on bolshevisation, the YCL decided to accelerate the campaign to establish new clubs in the factories. To execute this strategy, it felt it had to stress "mass Canadian sports."

The Finns, in particular, were urged to take up "Canadian" games and to throw their considerable organisational skills into recruiting native Canadian members. "We do not wish to be too critical of the Finnish Workers' Sports, which forms the vanguard of our movement," the *Young Worker* (May 1930) wrote in the midst of the campaign:

> but there is a strong need for augmenting these individual sports with popular group sports such as hockey, basketball, football and baseball, which will more readily interest the broad strata of workers in mines, factories and farms.

At the organisational level, the WSAC repeatedly sought to "liquidate" the FWSAC in the interests of building a "unified" national body (*Young Worker*, April 1931).

In 1932, in part through the persuasiveness of the new national secretary, Jim Turner, a charismatic Finnish communist, the FWSAC agreed to dissolve. Yet neither the

---

"The whole plenary session of the 5th executive meeting of the RSI was filled with discussions about changing the sport organisation into active participants of the proletarian class struggle. The participation of the workers' sports organisations in the economic battle of the proletariat [e.g., strikes]—which was discussed at length—are a big step forward in this direction. The ever increasing class struggle which will lead to ever more and bigger class fights is demanding the undissolvable union of all proletarian forces. The recent economic struggles are showing that all the enemies of the proletariat are uniting, from employers and the police to the reformist trade unions. The latter is taking the important role for the bourgeoisie to split the ranks of the proletariat. It is obvious that all revolutionary forces—including workers' sports—should unite and get stronger to counteract the united front of employers and reformists with the *Iron Front* of the true proletariat. . . .

The question of the participation of the workers' sports organisations in the economic struggles of the proletariat has been discussed in full length for the first time and should make the various national organisations more active in this regard than before."

Minutes of the Plenary Session of the RSI, May 30-June 3 1929, Charkow, USSR (Helsinki: Työväen Arkisto, p. 21f).

Finns nor the other immigrants who comprised the majority of WSA members were prepared to give up their favourite sports, and the campaign failed. In 1935, disillusioned with the national leadership, the Finns voted to reestablish their own national organisation. They now called it the Finnish Canadian Amateur Sports Federation (interview with Alex Hunnakko).

Some of these tensions were reduced after the Seventh Congress of the Communist International and the turn to United Front strategy. The YCL dropped its campaign against bourgeois sport and now encouraged clubs to make alliances with their old enemies to fight against fascism and to press public authorities for improved recreation. The party press began to give regular coverage to the once despised commercial sport spectacles: "our paper is not printed for the die-hard labour man, but the masses in general," the sports editor explained when a reader asked why it had begun to handicap commercial horse races (*Clarion*, 4 July 1936). The national organisation was renamed the Canadian Amateur Sports Federation (CASF), and local associations became Universal Athletic Clubs.

This change allowed individual clubs to operate with the approval of the YCL leadership, but, otherwise, the movement carried on very much the same. The Montreal group continued to challenge for the supremacy of the city leagues. In Toronto, the Canadian-born members played softball and soccer, while the Ukrainians and Czechs were more interested in gymnastics. Southern Ontario enjoyed a period of growth; Fred Kaczor, now national organiser, travelled from town to town organising new clubs and providing instruction. In mining and lumbering towns, the nature and level of activity varied from year to year, depending upon who was available. Although the Finns were no longer members, they continued to invite CASF athletes to their competitions and share their facilities. Winnipeg continued to be the flagship of the movement. It increased the membership, published a monthly newsletter, and became so well known as a training centre for recreation leaders that the Manitoba government hired its senior members to conduct the instructors' courses it offered under the federal-provincial Youth Training Act. One of them, George Nick, would become the provincial supervisor of all school physical education.

Most of this activity came to a halt in 1940, however, when the cabinet ordered the Royal Canadian Mounted Police to seize the amenities of the communist mass organisations (Kolasky, 1979). After Germany invaded the Soviet Union in June 1941 and the Canadian Communist Party joined the Canadian war effort, a number of former Universal Athletic Club instructors enlisted and became physical fitness instructors (interview with Fred Kaczor). After the war, the ULFTA (renamed the Association of United Ukrainian Canadians) received a number of gymnastic groups. Along with the Finnish clubs, these programmes flourished until the 1970s, when most of the leaders retired and there was no one else to take their place, their children having gone over to mainstream clubs and agencies. Very few of the post-World War II Ukrainian and Finnish immigrants to Canada were interested in building socialist organisations (interview with Alex Hunnakko).

The Universal Athletic Clubs were never resumed. Once the Soviet Union joined the IOC's Olympics (first competing in 1952), the Communist Party of Canada lost interest in a distinct sport movement.

Conclusion

In terms of the opportunities it provided, the Canadian worker sport movement must be considered a success. Participants overwhelmingly remember their activity as rewarding and enjoyable. For those where the programme was combined with other social activities and continued throughout the year, worker sport was not just recreation, but a way of life. The clubs encouraged many who were not previously engaged in sport or physical activity, especially girls and women, and provided a supportive environment for immigrants and socialists, who were often ridiculed or ostracised in mainstream clubs. Participants of all ages and abilities recall having mastered skills they never thought possible, a tribute to the movement's emphasis on leadership training, skill development, and the instructors it attracted and developed. Several other measures suggest a high standard. CASF and FCASF athletes competed with distinction when they entered mainstream events, and Finns such as Leo Rolninen (javelin, 1948), Roy Pella (discus, 1952), and Bill Heikkila (javelin, 1968) represented Canada at the Olympics. Several of the movement's outstanding leaders made important contributions to other areas of Canadian sport. Fred Kaczor and Em Orlick, who led the WSAC team to the Soviet Union in 1935, played major roles in promoting Olympic gymnastics in Canada. In 1982, Orlick was given an R. Tait McKenzie Honour Award by the Canadian Association for Health, Physical Education, and Recreation for his contribution to gymnastics (Salmela & Salmela, 1984). Heikkila, perhaps the last great athlete developed by the FCASF, was, in the late 1980s, the national javelin coach for the Canadian Track and Field Association and a consultant for Sport Canada.

However, as a political movement designed to recruit foot soldiers for the revolution by breaking the bourgeoisie's hold on workers through sport, it clearly failed. Although successful clubs like the Winnipeg and

Montreal WSAs and political campaigns like that against the 1936 Olympic Games earned the movement considerable visibility, the effective membership never extended appreciably beyond the closely knit immigrant and communist communities in which it was founded. Few WSAs actually attempted to penetrate the established sport clubs to turn their members to the WSAs or to sign up workers at plant gates, as the YCL urged; those who did try met with little success. Nor did the WSAs try to transform themselves into a militant revolutionary arm of the party. Even when they assisted with political rallies, their chief interest was the chance to perform, not the possibility that they might be deterring the party's political opponents from mounting an attack. The late Robert Wheeler observed that the worker sport movement was caught up in an agonising dilemma. If it gave too much emphasis to the political questions that grew out of its existence as an alternative culture, it risked losing those members, even socialists, who participated primarily for the opportunities it provided to engage in sports. If it completely ignored the political questions, it risked losing its identity as an oppositional movement (Wheeler, 1978). The ultimate disappearance of the Canadian movement was in part a consequence of its failure to resolve this dilemma.

Even if the leaders had been more sensitive to the intrinsic attractions of "sport for sport's sake," the conditions they faced were never favourable. The Canadian Communist Party was the only party of the left to attempt to build socialist cultural organisations, and it never achieved the status of a major party. The trade unions, even those the party organised in the 1930s and 1940s, had little time for worker sport. More significantly, the Canadian movement faced escalating capitalist cultural integration on all fronts. As S. Ewen (1976) has so ably demonstrated, during the 1920s and 1930s, more and more sectors of capital embraced the strategy of creating consent through consumerism and advertising. It was a period when the new technologies of radio and the motion picture developed new audiences for the drama and the spectacles of sport entrepreneurs. In 1936, for example, 6 million Canadians—one third of the entire population—were said to have tuned into a playoff game of the National Hockey League, the binational cartel that would soon extend its control over all hockey in Canada, even that under the jurisdiction of the Canadian Amateur Hockey Association. Worker sport was a noble undertaking, but perhaps the odds were too great.

References

Avery, D. "Ethnic loyalties and the proletarian revolution: a case study of communist political activity in

Winnipeg, 1923-36," in: J. Dahlie & T. Fernando (eds.), *Ethnicity, Power and Politics in Canada* (Toronto, 1980).

Babcock, R.H. *Gompers in Canada* (Toronto, 1974).

Betcherman, L.-R. *The Little Band:The Clashes Between the Communists and the Political and Legal Establishments in Canada, 1928-32* (Ottawa, 1982).

Clarion. 4 July 1936.

Ewen, S. *Captains of Consciousness: Advertising and the Social Roots of the Consumer Culture* (New York, 1976).

Gruneau, R. *Class, Sports and Social Development* (Amherst, 1983).

Kealey, G., & Palmer, B. *Dreaming of What Might Be: The Knights of Labour in Ontario* (New York, 1982).

Kidd, B. "Canadian opposition to the 1936 Olympics in Germany," *Canadian Journal of History of Sport and Physical Education*, IX (2) (1978), pp. 20-40.

Kolasky, J. *The Shattered Illusion* (Toronto, 1979), pp. 27-47.

Laine, E.W. "Finnish Canadian radicalism and Canadian politics: the first forty years, 1900-1940," in: J. Daihle & T. Fernando (eds.), *Ethnicity, Power and Politics* (Toronto, 1981), pp. 94-112.

Lindstrom Best, V. (ed.). "Finns in Ontario," *Polyphony*, 3 (2) (1981).

Metcalfe, A. "Working class physical recreation in Montreal, 1860-1895," *Working Papers in the Sociological Study of Sport and Leisure*, 1 (2) (1978).

Mott, M. "One solution to the urban crisis: manly sports and Winnipeggers, 1900-1914," *Urban History Review* 12 (2) (1983), pp. 57-70.

Naison, M. "Lefties and righties: the Communist Party and sports during the Great Depression," *Radical America,* 13 (4) (1979), pp. 47-59.

Riess, S.A. "Working-class sports in America, 1882-1920," a paper delivered to the American Historical Association (San Francisco, 1982).

Salmela, S.I. & Salmela, J.H. "Emmanuel Orlick: Canada's gymnastic pioneer," unpublished paper, Départment d'education physique, Université de Montreal (1984).

Toronto Daily Star. 26 November 1934.

Wheeler, R. "Organised sport and organised labour: the worker sports movement," *Journal of Contemporary History,* 13 (1978), pp. 252-265.

Worker. February 1928; October 1928; March 1931; July 1931; March 1932; October 1932; August 1933.

Young Worker. October 1924; February 1925; June 1925; July 1925; October 1926; May 1928; September-October 1928; May 1930; April 1931; May 1931; June 1931; July 1933.

Chapter 10

Hapoel: Israel's Worker Sport Organisation

Uriel Simri

ISRAEL

This country east of the Mediterranean Sea, with its internationally recognised borders established in 1967, covers an area of 20,667 km². In the same year, 2.65 million people lived in Israel.

Zionism, as the wish of Jewish groups for the establishment of a national homestead, was born out of necessity in the face of the swelling tide of anti-Semitism in Europe at the end of the 19th century that led to pogroms in Eastern Europe. The first important success of the movement occurred in 1917 when British Foreign Secretary Balfour, motivated by the hope of greater Jewish backing for the Allied cause, especially from American Jews, wrote to Lord Rothschild declaring the support of his government for "the establishment in Palestine of a national home for the Jewish people." That this was on no account support for a Jewish state that could only be achieved to the detriment of the Arab population became clear when, in 1922, the League of Nations gave Britain the mandate over Palestine. London was only willing to allow entry to Jews wishing to immigrate and to establish a "Jewish Agency" to advise its mandatory power.

The growing bitterness of the native population over the incessant flood of immigrants led to regular bloody clashes between Arabs and Jews after 1929. The suggestions offered by various commissions of experts sent to Palestine were coloured by the momentary political interests of the British. In 1936, for example, there was still talk of splitting the mandate, yet in 1939, on account of the growing German influence in Arab circles, the aim was to create an independent Palestine state. After the war, the British government kept to the latter plan, thus provoking increasing terror from extremist Jewish groups as well as pressure from the pro-Zionist Truman administration.

Consequently, the issue was taken to the United Nations General Assembly that voted, in November 1947, to split Palestine into a Jewish and an Arab state. The Arab world announced at once that it would oppose this decision by force, and the fighting began immediately after the state of Israel was proclaimed on 14 May 1948. The passage of arms produced a clear victory for the Israelis, and the armistice agreements signed in the summer of 1949 left them in possession of all the areas they had so far captured. The remaining parts of the previous mandate were given to the present Jordan.

The Arab world would not accept the existence of a state that had come about by a flagrant violation of the right of self-determination of the indigenous population. This, together with the Israeli refusal to retreat to the borders settled by the United Nations in 1947 and to allow the return of Palestinians who had fled or had been expelled, not only excluded the possibility of a peace agreement that went beyond partial settlements, but also made further armed clashes inevitable. These clashes led to the Israeli-Arab wars of 1956, 1967, and 1973, as well as the invasion of Lebanon in 1982 that aimed to destroy the bases of the Palestine Liberation Organisation (PLO), feared because of its uncontrollable paramilitary activities.

National politics in Israel stood, until 1977, completely under the banner of the *Mapai* (Labour Party), that, as the strongest faction in various coalition governments, was able to nominate the prime minister. Under this leadership, the state followed socialist economic and social ideals. These found particular expression in the development of cooperative villages (*kibbuzim*). The dependence on foreign economic aid that grew with every new rearmament programme pushed socialist concepts more and more into the wings. This loss of profile, the worrying economic development, the deep shock over the relatively poor showing of the Israeli troops in the 1973 war, and the political awakening of conservative oriental Jews—the majority of this population thus far underrepresented in socially and politically important positions—led to the electoral victory of the right-wing coalition under the leadership of the *Likud* party in 1977. Fifteen years later, the population's realisation that the right was incapable of starting serious peace talks with the Arabs brought the parliamentary left, led by the *Mapai*, back into government.

Although the beginnings of an organised worker sport movement in Palestine (Eretz-Israel) date only from the mid-1920s, the sources of the movement were present in the years prior to World War I. At that time, the Maccabi sports organisation existed in Palestine, and it had a socialist ideology. Its statutes banned employers from joining the association, and, when some employers were permitted to join the Petach Tikvan Club—one of Maccabi's largest members—it provoked a split. It is hardly surprising, therefore, that, before the war, Maccabi clubs had an avowed socialist philosophy, particularly in collective settlements.

All the same, the organised-labour sport movement, *Hapoel* (The Worker), only came into existence in 1926 at a time when Maccabi succumbed to right-wing control. When exactly the first *Hapoel* club appeared is under contention; evidently, just such a club had existed for a short time in Tel Aviv in 1923, but the club that formed the basis for the national movement came into being in Haifa in April 1924. The national movement followed 2 years later, and its initial slogan—*"Alafim ve'lo Alufim"* ("Thousands Not Champions")—indicated clearly that *Hapoel* valued mass activity above all else. The only exception was soccer, in which *Hapoel* competed from the very first day of its existence because the British mandatory government had tried to promote the sport and to establish a national soccer association. We, therefore, find *Hapoel* among the founders of such an association in 1928, whereas it avoided contacts with Maccabi in all other sports.

A year after its founding in 1927, *Hapoel* joined the Socialist Worker Sports International (SWSI), but the considerable geographical distance from northern Europe effectively prevented direct international contacts until 4 years later. This took place when *Hapoel* sent an 81-strong delegation to the second Worker Olympics in Vienna in 1931.

Even before 1931, *Hapoel* had arranged two national festivals (1928 and 1930); 780 athletes from 10 clubs took part in the first, and 1,200 athletes from 36 clubs took part in the second.

Because *Hapoel* avoided an emphasis on winning and champions, we find in the first festival only the names of clubs to which the winners belonged, whereas 2 years later the names of winners were added to the list. A reorientation of *Hapoel*'s philosophy came in 1932 when the Maccabi World Union staged the first Maccabiah Games, and *Hapoel* expressed a wish to take part. *Hapoel* was eager to prevent a situation occurring whereby Maccabi would be the only representative of Jewish sport in the diaspora; nonetheless, it did not want to join the Maccabi World Union because it preferred to retain its independence in Palestine. However, the Palestine

At the second international Zionist conference in Basle (1898), Max Nordau coined the phrase "muscular Jewishness" (*"Muskeljudentum"*), following the British notion of "muscular Christianity." The idea to take matters in one's own hands, to not accept any pogrom or latent anti-Semitism, was so popular that in the same year the first Jewish sport club, *Bar-Kochba*, was founded in Berlin. It became the centre of the German-Jewish *Turner* Federation. In 1912, the first Maccabi clubs were founded in Palestine.

The Maccabi World Union (CSR) was founded at the 1921 Zionist World Congress in Karlsbad. It was soon joined by bourgeois-Zionist *Turner* and sport clubs from other European countries. This resulted in the formation of non-Zionist sport organisations, such as *Schild* (Shield) in Germany—which was Jewish-German national by definition and had its basis in the German-Jewish war veterans of World War I—and in nonbourgeois Jewish sport organisations, such as *Hapoel*.

Maccabi rejected *Hapoel* by serving an unacceptable ultimatum on it that *Hapoel* should leave the SWSI; it based its demand on the statutes of the international federations to which Maccabi belonged.

Hapoel's response was to attempt to establish *Hapoel* organisations all over the diaspora. It succeeded in Latvia (1932), Lithuania (1934), and Poland (1925), yet *Hapoel* never managed seriously to rival the well-established Maccabi. Similar attempts after World War II and in more recent times met with failure.

So *Hapoel* had to be satisfied with its own internal events and with participation in SWSI tournaments. As many as 2,500 athletes took part in the third *Hapoel* festival of 1932, after which the worker sport movement in Palestine really flourished. In 1935, *Hapoel* succeeded in attracting as many as 10,000 athletes to its fourth festival, a number that clearly demonstrated that within 9 years it had become the largest sport organisation in the country. It had sent a contingent to the 1934 festival of the Czechoslovak worker sport organisation in Prague; apart from this, no regular meetings with SWSI athletes took place.

Hapoel was also unsuccessful in its attempt to be represented at the second Maccabiah Games in 1935. All the same, the games had repercussions that radically altered the nature of *Hapoel*'s organisation. Following the

Scene from the opening ceremonies of the 10th *Hapoel* Games, 1979.

A markswoman at the *Hapoel* Games. Note the *Hapoel* symbol in the top left corner.

The "Thuatron," *Hapoel*'s national modern dance group.

A mass hike organised by *Hapoel*.

The annual noncompetitive crossing of the Sea of Galilee, organised by *Hapoel*.

Pole jump.

The first Makkabiah in Tel Aviv had participants from 16 countries, the second, in 1935, from 27 countries. The third, planned for 1938, did not take place. The first international Jewish Winter Games took place in Zakopane (Poland) in February 1933; they were retroactively called the first Winter Makkabiah. The second Winter Makkabiah were organised in Banska-Bystrica in February 1936.

second Maccabiah Games, hundreds of skilled athletes remained in Palestine illegally, and many joined the ranks of *Hapoel* once they realised the bourgeois character of Maccabi. Like many others from working-class families, they had belonged to the nonpolitical Maccabi World Union clubs and saw their natural, social home with *Hapoel*.

However, insofar as these athletes had grown up in an atmosphere of competitive sport, they now expected to find—or at least to establish—a similar milieu within *Hapoel*. Their effect on *Hapoel* was so marked that within a few years *Hapoel* had altered its slogan to *"Alafim we' Alufim"* ("Thousands *and* Champions"), meaning that competitive sport was now considered officially as important as mass sport activity. It was not long before *Hapoel* seriously rivalled Maccabi in sport results; in fact, within 15 years it became both the largest and the strongest sport organisation in the country. This ideological *volte face* caused a bitter and protracted debate between the extreme wings of the labour movement, the left accusing the right of neglecting mass activities at the expense of competitive sport. Fifty years later, this dispute still continues. In the spring of 1936, the Arab population of Palestine launched a campaign of political disturbances that were to continue until the outbreak of World War II. The relatively small Jewish population had to defend itself, and, among the Jews, there began a fierce discussion between the labour movement and the right wing about how to react to the problem. *Hapoel*'s reaction to these political developments was to set up the *Plugot Hapoel* (*Hapoel* squads), analogous to the Austrian *Schutzbund*. The squads were under the command not only of the trade unions (the *Histadrut*), like the entire *Hapoel* movement, but also of the official Jewish underground movement (the *Haganah*). The squads were active until World War II, when most of their members were recruited into the British Army. After the war, attempts to revive their activities failed.

Despite the political disturbances in Palestine that greatly restricted sport activities, *Hapoel* did its utmost to maintain contacts with SWSI. For example, it dispatched a delegation to the Worker Olympics in Barcelona in 1936 (the games had to be cancelled at the last moment because of the Franco coup). A year later, in July 1937, *Hapoel* sent a large group, including soccer, basketball, and handball teams, to the third Worker Olympics in Antwerp.

In spite of the troubles, very few contacts developed between the Jewish sport organisations within Palestine (soccer being the only exception). Maccabi continued to do all it could to hamper *Hapoel*'s international relations outside the framework of SWSI, a fact that naturally restricted the worker sport movement that by now was also emphasising competitive sport in its activities. In the winter of 1938-1939, *Hapoel* founded, along with independent clubs not affiliated with Maccabi, the Palestinian basketball and volleyball federations. The volleyball federation gained immediate international recognition because Palestine had not hitherto been represented in the international federation. The basketball federation, on the other hand, ran into difficulties because the basketball section of the Palestinian Amateur Sports Association, which had been set up by Maccabi back in 1931, had already been recognised by the Fédération Internationale de Basketball (FIBA). All the same, *Hapoel* succeeded in gaining provisional recognition of its federation "until the problem ha[d] been resolved." The resolution occurred after the war. All the same, the provisional recognition by FIBA was regarded at the time as an important breakthrough for *Hapoel* into a Maccabi domain.

Paradoxically, the tragedy of World War II caused a further strengthening of *Hapoel*. Palestine was practically cut off from Europe during the war years, and most sport activities in wartime revolved around military teams. These teams did not belong to an international federation, and, for them, there was no difference between Maccabi and *Hapoel*. So the two organisations operated on more or less equal terms between 1939 and 1945. Beyond that, the limited sport activities forced clubs from both organisations to cooperate, often against the express wish of their leadership. Although the mutual boycott still existed on paper, more and more competitions in the various sports were taking place between *Hapoel* and Maccabi. At the end of the war, the picture changed once more; but there was no way back to the pre-1939 situation. An objective analysis would show the further growth and strengthening of *Hapoel* in wartime, largely because the worker sport movement had better means of organisation at its disposal.

Following the war, *Hapoel* became one of the 11 founder-members of the successor to SWSI—the *Comité Sportif International du Travail* (CSIT), established in May 1946. At the first CSIT meeting, *Hapoel* proposed

"There is hardly any worker sport federation in the SWSI which has to overcome as many difficulties as our comrades from the *Hapoel* in Palestine. Far away from their European comrades, entirely depending on their own vigour, they lead an heroic struggle for the spreading of worker sports and by this for the socialist movement. While all other federations of the SWSI can support each other by visits and international competitions, our comrades in Palestine have to depend upon themselves. Only once has it been possible to send an Austrian worker soccer team for some matches with the support of the SWSI. There is a particular lack of technical experts and physical education specialists which can put some proper content into the ever increasing number of members of the *Hapoel*. The main events are *Turnen*, free exercise, track and field, and swimming. The great enthusiasm with which our comrades in Palestine are following the SWSI could be observed by their strong participation in the second Worker Olympics in Vienna. This enthusiasm was transferred to their own 3rd Federation Meeting in Haifa, Oct. 21-23, 1932.

Already on the 1st and 2nd October the water events took place. Because of the geographical conditions, there is special emphasis on swimming which is part of the training of all sailors. There were 3,000 spectators at the swimming in Haifa harbour. The swimming basin was enclosed by commercial vessels which also served as stands for the spectators.

The actual meet took place in Tel Aviv in front of 10,000 spectators, which regarded this as a popular festival which included dancing in the streets. 84 percent of the members of *Hapoel* took part. . . . Ben-Gurion, the secretary of the *Histradrath* delivered the final speech and under the singing of the *Internationale* and the *Techezakno* (the hymn of the trade union of Palestine) the last part of the federation meeting was ended. This final manifestation made a big impression on the participants and it showed that the meeting of the *Hapoel* was not only a sports meet but a reunion of all the Jewish workers in Palestine. Aware of the support of all Jewish workers of Palestine *Hapoel* will progress and prosper."

K. Bühren, "Arbeitersport in Pälastina," *Sportpolitsche Rundschau* (Berlin), 6 (1933), 2, p. 30.

that independent worker sport organisations should continue, but that they should try to integrate themselves into the sport activities of their own countries. Contrary to SWSI precedent, CSIT did not try to intervene in the internal sport activities of countries containing its member organisations, so the way was clear for *Hapoel* to continue its own internal sport policies. Internationally, *Hapoel* has continued to play a major part in the work of CSIT.

Another path opened for *Hapoel* in international sport when it affiliated with the World Federation of Democratic Youth, and the federation decided to include sport in its first festival held in Prague in 1947. *Hapoel* sent a large group of athletes to Prague, yet once again ran into opposition from Maccabi. Although the Prague festival was not under the auspices of an international federation to which Maccabi belonged, it was intent on participating out of fear that *Hapoel* would increase in membership and influence. Maccabi, therefore, appealed to the supreme Jewish agencies in Palestine, claiming that, to ensure the strongest possible representation of Palestinian Jewry, its athletes should be part of the delegation sent to Prague. Under pressure from the General Council of Jews in Palestine (*Va'ad Le'umi*), the sport group sent to Prague had to include Maccabi athletes; as a result, they were the only bourgeois athletes to take part in the Prague festival. For the first time, we find the Maccabi movement on the defensive, and this was a sign that *Hapoel* had overtaken its archrival in the quality of its work as well as in numbers.

On 29 November 1947, the United Nations approved the partition of Palestine and the establishment of a Jewish state. On the following day, Arab-instigated political troubles broke out that developed into Israel's War of Independence. Cooperation among all Jews became a necessity; this applied to sport as well. On 30 March 1948, *Hapoel* signed a pact with the Maccabi-led Amateur Sports Federation, according to which no side would boycott the other, and international representation would henceforth include the best athletes of both organisations. Nonetheless, another 3-1/2 years were to pass before the official sport bodies were to be established in the state of Israel.

Israel came into being on 15 May 1948. Yet even during the War of Independence, the structure of the country's future government had been discussed, and that included a ministry responsible for sport. Following a debate within the government about which ministry would be responsible for sport, labour Prime Minister David Ben-Gurion approached *Hapoel* in 1949 to make its recommendations. *Hapoel* subsequently called a special conference that recommended that sport should come under the Ministry of Education and Culture, not the

Ministry of Defence. This was accepted by the government. Ben-Gurion's approach to *Hapoel* and the government's acceptance of its recommendation indicated the status of the worker sport movement in the new state of Israel.

In 1950, the Maccabi World Union staged the third Maccabiah Games, at which the state of Israel was represented, according to the 1948 agreement, by both Maccabi and *Hapoel* athletes. *Hapoel* athletes won 56 of the 85 medals gained by Israel, which demonstrates how strong *Hapoel* had become. At its 25th anniversary in 1951, *Hapoel* was rightfully able to proclaim itself the largest and strongest sport organisation in the country.

The stronger *Hapoel* became, however, the more the bourgeois sport organisations opposed it. Only after the government had threatened, in secret negotiations, to nationalise sport was an agreement between the two rival organisations signed in October 1951, according to which national sport bodies were set up on a basis of parity in representation. Even though by this time *Hapoel* was much larger than Maccabi—and represented an absolute majority of Israel's sport—it was nevertheless content to have gained access to organisations recognised by the international sport federations. Previously, both sides had formed their own national Olympic committees, neither of which was recognised by the International Olympic Committee (IOC). It was only in 1952 that the united National Olympic Committee was accepted by the IOC.

Israeli athletes entered the Olympic arena for the first time at the 1952 Helsinki summer games. Altogether, Israel was represented by 26 athletes, 15 of whom were from *Hapoel*. In subsequent Olympics, *Hapoel* continued to dominate Israel's athletic representation; out of the 192 athletes who represented Israel in Olympic Games up to 1992, as many as 119 were members of *Hapoel*. A similar situation appertains to Israeli teams in the Asian Games, in which Israel participated from 1954 to 1974. Thus, *Hapoel* athletes gained 11 gold, 7 silver, and 8 bronze medals in individual events at the Asian Games, and in the Olympics they gained the best placings among all Israeli athletes; one of the two Olympic medals and 10 of the 13 athletes that placed in the first 8 in their events were from *Hapoel*. On a more sombre note, of the 11 Israeli athletes and coaches murdered during the 1972 Munich Olympics, 9 were members of *Hapoel*.

Hapoel celebrated its 25th anniversary in 1952 one year late. The anniversary coincided with the organisation's fifth festival, renamed the International *Hapoel* Games. Whereas the first four festivals had been national events, the fifth festival was international through the participation of some CSIT associations and a number of Turkish track-and-field

athletes. *Hapoel* was determined to make its games the biggest in the country and a rival to the Maccabiah Games.

The 1952 games were followed by further festivals in 1956, 1961, 1966, and 1971. Since 1971 the games have been held quadrennially, in the year preceding the Olympics. In the 10 International *Hapoel* Games held up to 1992, athletes from over 50 countries on all five continents, including many world and Olympic champions, have taken part. Since 1966, official CSIT championships have become part of these games that also feature folk games and mass activities. Whereas the Maccabiah Games developed into a Jewish national celebration, the *Hapoel* games are both international and the major sport event in the country.

Although the 1951 pact between Maccabi and *Hapoel* was originally for a 3-year period, Maccabi asked in 1954 for a prolongation. *Hapoel*, on the other hand, was keen to scrap the parity representation and hold democratic elections to all sport federations. Because Maccabi refused, it was only in the Israeli Soccer Association that democratic elections were held (1954); Maccabi boycotted this election. Ten years were to pass before democratic representation extended to all Israeli sport federations. Following such elections, *Hapoel* won an absolute majority (as high as 70 percent) in all federations, a position it has maintained to this day.

At the beginning of the 1960s, *Hapoel* launched an assistance programme for developing countries. Athletes from such countries had taken part in the *Hapoel* games and had been impressed by the organisation. Following a number of requests, therefore, *Hapoel* sent specialists to Congo-Brazzaville, the Central African Republic, Cameroon, Chad, and Senegal. The assistance came to an end during the 1967 Six Days' War, when practically all African states severed diplomatic relations with Israel; the one exception was Malawi, which continued to receive sport and physical education assistance.

It may be said that *Hapoel* reached its peak in the 1960s but lost some of its ideological commitment since then. Ideological debate on the organisation's activities has continued, but competitive sport has gradually thrust aside the formerly dominant mass activities. In 1962, it is true, *Hapoel* did exclude boxing from its activities on medical grounds, but, on the whole, competitive sports have dictated the movement's progress. Competition against bourgeois sport organisations has required more and more finance that is available only through the nationalised Sports Betting Board. Inasmuch as bourgeois sport organisations tend to spend these funds on their relatively small number of clubs, *Hapoel* has had to follow suit, mainly at the expense of its mass activities (although this has never been admitted officially). The impact of bourgeois sport on *Hapoel* can also be seen in the readmittance of boxing to *Hapoel* activities in 1984. *Hapoel* simply was reluctant to leave the sport in bourgeois hands, preferring political to medical arguments. Organisationally, *Hapoel* split its directorate of sport activities in 1965 into one department for competitive sport and one for mass activities. This bifurcation did not, however, resolve the problem of mass activities because the division of funding continued to favour competition.

One possible solution to the mass sport problem was to hold mass competitions. Hundreds of teams from various sports were created at workplaces, and special leagues were formed for the teams to compete. The problem was that these activities suited only a certain age group and were, for all practical purposes, restricted to males. Another possible solution was to organise individual mass events in such recreational activities as hiking, cross-country running, swimming, orienteering, and cycling. The number of such events that *Hapoel* organises runs into well over 100 every year, with as many as 10,000 people taking part in the largest of them. All the same, the *Hapoel* member who looks for regular recreation in a *Hapoel* club has found the opportunities more and more limited.

For a long time, females felt neglected by *Hapoel*, and it is true that the organisation plays a much smaller part in Israel's women's sport than it does in men's sport. Over the last two decades, however, the worker sport movement has tried to establish a social women's sport section; these attempts have been unsuccessful, primarily because of the stringent financial allocation to sport. There were no funds marked for women's sport. It has to be admitted, further, that women are little represented in *Hapoel* committees. Often only one woman has been present to represent women's sport.

Over the last two decades, actual professionalism has existed in Israel's top soccer and basketball leagues. This professionalism has been growing rapidly and has now obtruded into other sports, such as volleyball, handball, and table tennis. It has to be said that *Hapoel* has had complete control of all the country's sport federations while this development has taken place. Yet, it has not found the strength to oppose it. *Hapoel* suffers from the situation much more than the bourgeois sport organisations do because it is practically impossible to run trade union worker sport clubs as private businesses. For this reason, there are now fewer *Hapoel* teams in the national soccer and basketball leagues than there used to be.

Despite all the difficulties, *Hapoel* remains Israel's largest and strongest sport organisation—70 years after the founding of its first club. It is perhaps the only worker sport organisation actually controlling its country's sport. This has naturally led to a number of compromises in adjusting to the modern world of sport, yet, despite the problems, *Hapoel* has succeeded in leading Israeli sport in the direction it has desired.

References

This chapter is based on Hebrew literature and primary sources, of which the following are the three most important:

Gill, E. *Sipuro shel Hapoel* (The Story of Hapoel) (Tel Aviv, 1977).

Simri, U. *Ha'chinuch ha'gufani ve'hasport be'Eretz Israel, 1917-1927* (Physical Education and Sport in Palestine, 1917-1927) (Netanya, 1971).

Simri, U., & Paz, I. *30 shnot sport be'Israel* (30 Years of Sport in Israel) (Tel Aviv, 1978).

Appendix A

The Two International Worker Sport Organisations: Socialist Worker Sports International and Red Sport International

Compiled by Franz Nitsch

SOCIALIST WORKER SPORTS INTERNATIONAL (SWSI)

11 August 1912	The Second Socialist International discusses worker sport at a Bureau meeting.
16 August 1912	Survey on worker sport is undertaken among member sections.
10-12 May 1913	First international meeting of representatives of worker sport federations is held in Ghent, Belgium, on the occasion of the Belgian Federation's Festival; representatives open an international office in Brussels.
11 January 1914	Bureau meeting held in Paris, France, calls for an international congress in Frankfurt am Main, Germany, in September 1914.
3-4 August 1914	Further Bureau meetings are planned to prepare for Frankfurt (which was postponed due to the outbreak of World War I).
14-16 August 1919	First postwar meeting is held in conjunction with a conference of Belgian worker athletes in Seraing-sur-Meuse.
5 April 1920	An executive is set up in Seraing, Belgium; it decides to hold an international congress in Paris.
12-13 September 1920	First International Congress is held in Lucerne, Switzerland, and an international worker federation for sport and physical culture (known as the Lucerne Worker Sports International [LSI]) is founded.
24-30 June 1921	Second International Congress of LSI is held during the Czechoslovak Worker Olympiad in Prague.
26-27 July 1922	Second (sometimes called Third) International Congress of LSI is held in Leipzig during the First German Worker Sport Association festival; Congress decides to hold a major international congress every 3 years.

28-29 December 1922	Bureau meeting is held in Cologne, Germany.
5 August 1923	Bureau meeting is held in Zurich, Switzerland.
24-26 April 1924	Bureau meeting is held in Frankfurt; conflict occurs with RSI delegates.
14 September 1924	Bureau meeting is held in Vienna, Austria; RSI is not invited to take part in the First Worker Olympiad to be held in Frankfurt.
31 January- 2 February 1925	Winter Olympiad of the Worker Games is held in Schreiberhau (Riesengebirge, Germany).
22-25 July 1925	First Worker Olympiad takes place in Frankfurt am Main, Germany.
31 October- 2 November 1925	Third International Congress is held in Paris; the organisation is renamed the International Socialist Federation for Worker Sport and Physical Culture.
5-8 August 1927	Fourth International Congress is held in Helsinki, Finland; important organisational changes occur; the central office is transferred from Brussels to Prague. Gellert (Germany) and Deutsch (Austria) were elected new presidents, and Sibala (Czechoslovakia) was elected new secretary general.
7 August 1928	Bureau meeting is held in Brussels; representatives establish separate secretaries for the Germanic (Wildung, Germany), Romanic (Devlieger, Belgium) and Baltic and Scandinavian (Kalnins, Finland) countries.
12-14 October 1929	Fifth International Congress is held in Prague.
24 August 1930	The Women's Commission meets in Leipzig.
5-8 February 1931	Winter sports competition of the second Worker Olympiad takes place in Mürzzuschlag, Austria.
19-26 July 1931	Second Worker Olympiad is held in Vienna, Austria, at the same time as the Socialist International in Vienna.
9-10 September 1932	Sixth International Congress takes place in Liège, Belgium.
6 May 1933	Bureau meeting is held in Prague to consider organisational changes after the destruction of the German worker sport movement.
5-8 July 1934	Third Czechoslovak Worker Olympiad takes place in Prague.
6-7 October 1934	Seventh International Congress is held in Karlsbad (Karlovy Vary), Czechoslovakia.
1 March 1935	First talks between SWSI and RSI occur in Prague.
6 September 1935	Joint meeting of SWSI and RSI is held in Prague.
30 November- 1 December 1935	International conference of SWSI takes place in Prague with guest delegates from RSI present.
28 August 1936	Negotiations occur with RSI in Antwerp, Belgium, on holding a joint Worker Olympiad.
29-30 August 1936	Eighth International Congress is held in Antwerp with 36 delegates from 12 federations and 9 countries present.
18-21 February 1937	Winter sports competition of the third Worker Olympiad takes place in Johannesbad, Czechoslovakia.
25 July- 1 August 1937	Third Worker Olympiad is held in Antwerp.
26-29 May 1938	Ninth SWSI Congress meets in Brussels.

3-5 September 1938	Following the Munich Agreement of September 1938 and the occupation of Czechoslovakia in March 1939, the SWSI has to abandon its Prague office and send its leading members into exile in Great Britain.
7 March 1942	SWSI meets in London on the organisational impetus of the British Workers' Sports Federation and forms a provisional committee of the SWSI in exile.
10-13 October 1945	First postwar conference is held in Paris, summoned by the provisional SWSI committee.
26-30 May 1946	First postwar congress meets in Brussels and forms a provisional committee with new statutes.
1-5 June 1947	International congress meets in Warschau, elects an organisational committee, and makes a new appeal to the USSR to join.
21-23 April 1949	International congress is held in Liège, which forms an executive committee of the remaining worker sport organisations (no communist country affiliated) under the leadership of the Belgian Jules Devlieger as president (he had helped to form the original organisation back in 1913).

RED SPORT INTERNATIONAL (RSI)

19-26 June 1921	First *Spartakiad* is held in Prague after the Czechoslovak Worker Sport Organisation had split into reformist and revolutionary wings.
22 July 1921	Founding congress takes place in Moscow following the founding congress of the Red Trade Union International and in conjunction with the Third Comintern Congress, 22 June-12 August.
29-31 July 1922	Second Congress is held in Berlin, Germany, under Bruno Lieske's leadership.
February 1923	A Central European Bureau is formed in Berlin with Fritz Reussner as secretary.
November 1923	The first issue of the journal *Proletariersport* is published under Lieske's editorship; the journal continued until late 1927.
13-14 July 1924	Large sports tournament is held in Paris (the French worker sport movement had split in 1923 into reformist and revolutionary groups).
13-21 October 1924	Third Congress takes place in Moscow, where they decide to unify worker sport.
February 1928	First Winter *Spartakiad* occurs in Oslo, Norway.
12-22 August 1928	Summer *Spartakiad* is held in Moscow.
31 May-3 June 1929	Fifth Plenary Meeting of the RSI Executive is held in Charkow (USSR); Ivan Scholdak takes over as RSI secretary after Reussner dies.
September 1930	Bureau moves to Berlin headquarters.
October 1930	First issue of *Internationaler Arbeitersport* is published, which continues until January 1933.
November 1930	Conference of European RSI sections is held in Berlin.
7-8 March 1931	The International *Spartakiad* Committee meets in Berlin.
5-19 July 1931	Second *Spartakiad* begins in Berlin, is banned, and continues in Moscow.
16-23 June 1932	*Spartakiad* conference takes place in Moscow.

2-5 December 1932	International Winter Sport Conference occurs in Berlin.
25-26 February 1933	International Conference of Children's and Youth Sports Leaders is held in Berlin.
March 1933	The RSI Bureau transfers from Berlin to Copenhagen, Denmark.
June 1933	The RSI Executive Committee meets in Paris.
August 1933	*Internationale Sportrundschau* is published and continues until late 1936.
2-3 September 1933	International RSI conference is held in Amsterdam, Netherlands.
19-21 May 1934	International RSI soccer conference takes place in Strasbourg, France.
1935	RSI Bureau transfers from Copenhagen to Prague.
7-8 March 1936	Fifth RSI Congress meets in Prague.
25 July- 1 August 1937	Third Worker Olympiad takes place in Antwerp.
June 1938	The last RSI section outside the USSR—the Czechoslovak—is dissolved (it is likely that RSI dissolved itself at about the same time, despite rumours that it continued throughout World War II).

The above chronological history of the two international worker sport associations—the social-democratic and the communist—shows that their activities were concentrated in the period between the two world wars. During this period, relations between them faced three major problems.

First, there were the ideological differences between members that were a result of changes within the labour movement after World War I. The Socialist Worker Sports International reacted to the war with a policy of political neutrality toward all worker parties. Particularly in its founding phase it did all it could to distance itself from the socialist and social-democratic parties. The relationship between worker sport and labour parties was debated in the late 1920s and came to a head in the international worker movement in 1931. Worker athletes in Red Sport International and its various national sections subscribed to the view that worker sport should be put to the service of the proletarian revolution.

Second, varying political outlooks within worker sport led to the founding of two separate international worker sport organisations. Subsequently, the relations between these two organisations were another focal point in the history of worker sport and were debated avidly under the "United Front" rubric between 1921 and 1937-1938. This debate can be divided into the phases corresponding to the international political movements (the Socialist Worker Sports International, on the one hand, and the Communist International, or Comintern, on the other). The extent of their relations varied from concerted efforts at collaboration to deadly rivalry.

Third, there were sporting in addition to the political differences between the two worker internationals. Their approach to the importance of competitive or record-breaking sport within the worker sport movement, as well as sporting contacts with bourgeois teams, varied. After 1933, the Soviet-dominated sport movement advanced the slogan of closing the gap and overtaking the sports performances of the bourgeois countries. This was a slogan the SWSI did not share. Even so, with the acceptance of competitive sports, particularly soccer, by the worker sport movement in the early 1930s, a considerable degree of "sportification" took place. Similarly, while the RSI advocated contacts with bourgeois teams, the SWSI categorically rejected such competitions. However, after losing their German (May 1933), Latvian (August 1933), and Austrian (February 1934) member-organisations, SWSI found it difficult to compete at all. Thereafter it had no option but to be more flexible on contacts with bourgeois clubs.

As the timeline shows, the RSI was dissolved before the beginning of World War II. Its social-democratic rival, however, continued after the war. At that time, it was still uncertain whether international worker sport would rise from the ashes. In fact, the decision-making process lasted until 1949, by which time it was evident that the Comité Sportif International du Travail (CSIT) would play no more than a marginal role in world sport. The future belonged to the international sport federations and the Olympic movement which, for the very first time, were able rightfully to claim to represent all of world sport.

Appendix B

Worker Sport Around the World

Arnd Krüger

This book has traced the development of worker sport between the two world wars in 10 countries and in the two rivaling internationals. These parameters are, of course, far from complete. It could even be argued that for some periods and key decisions we omitted several important countries. However, the number and variety of secondary sources cited in each chapter show that the analysis of the worker sport movement in these countries has been quite disparate.

In addition to the countries listed in the table to the right, Red Sport International had members in the Soviet Union, Argentina, Bulgaria, Canada, Egypt, Italy, Norway, Portugal, Spain, Sweden, and Uruguay. Exact membership figures are difficult to assess. The biggest contingent by far came from the Soviet Union, which Dierker (1990) estimates at 2 million in 1924. The smallest was probably Egypt, which the RSI estimated at 300 members.

The following descriptions give information about worker sport in a number of countries not included in the main chapters.

Alsace-Lorraine

In the border area between Germany and France, the ancient *Lotharingia*, small, separate entities have always existed and been coveted by their bigger neighbours. Located south of Holland, Belgium, and Luxembourg on the Swiss border, Alsace-Lorraine has been German (1871-1918), then French (1919-1940), then German-occupied (1940-1945), and now French again (1945-present). In the German period, worker *Turner* clubs were formed and joined the adjacent German regional association of the Worker

Membership of SWSI in 1931

Country	Clubs	Members
Alsace-Lorraine*	249	13,560
Austria	2,500	293,700
Belgium	421	12,900
Denmark	?	20,000
Czechoslovakia		
Czech	1,220	136,977
German	585	70,730
England	?	5,000
Estonia	29	1,600
Finland	419	30,257
France	138	10,895
Germany	15,730	1,211,468
Hungary	?	1,750
Latvia	94	5,171
Netherlands	76	16,759
Palestine	?	4,250
Poland		
Polish	?	7,000
German	?	938
Jewish	110	4,369
Ukrainian	68	1,925
Romania	?	2,500
Switzerland	289	21,624
United States	12	697
Yugoslavia	?	1,800

Source: *Beckmann's Sport Lexikon* (Vienna: Beckmann, 1933), p. 2077f. *H. Dierker, *Arbeitersport im Spannungsfeld der Zwanziger Jahre* (Essen: Klartext, 1990, p. 256).

Gymnastics and Sports Association (ATSB) as part of the 3rd district of the 10th *Turngau.* By 1908 worker sport in Alsace had become strong enough to form its own district, the 5th. This district had a hard time because the region was highly agrarian and thus was not favourable to any worker organisation (see chapters 1 and 2). Its basis was even smaller because its workers were internationally minded; the German and the French *Turner* clubs absorbed most workers interested in physical exercise and nationalism. There were, however, also the Alsace Union (athletes neither in favour of Germany nor France) and management-sponsored factory clubs, which were far more active than in Germany at the time.

Although Alsace and Lorraine were again French after the Treaty of Versailles in 1919, the worker sport organisation renamed itself in French (FSTA.L.) but stayed separate from the French. The FSTA.L. was among the founding members of the French FST (see chapter 2), but with 13,500 members it was strong enough to stay independent and only loosely affiliated. The FSTA.L. continued to use German and its local (Germanic) dialect in its communication and reproduced the organisational splits of Germany more than those of France.

In 1925 the communist worker sport organization FSGTA.L. took over, but in spite of pressure from Moscow it remained part of the SWSI (see Appendix A) and did not strengthen the French USSGT, which had only 4,000 members at that time, or the RSI. In 1930 the rifts within the worker sport of Alsace (more oriented towards Germany and more procommunist) and Lorraine (more oriented towards France and more prosocialist) became stronger.

Finally, after the Nazi take-over in Germany in 1933 and the dissolution of the German worker sport organisation on the one hand and the French Popular Front policy on the other, all of the worker sport of Alsace-Lorraine eventually joined forces with the united French FSGT in December 1934.

References

Kedroff, General. "The Divisionist Activities of the Social-Democrats and the Tactics of the RSI," *Central lecture of the 5th Plenary Session of the Executive Committee of the RSI, May 31 1929.*

Strauss, L. "Le sport travailliste français pendant l'entre-deux-querres," in: P. Arnaud (ed.), *Les origines du sport ouvrier en Europe* (Paris: L'Harmattan, 1994), pp. 193-218.

Wildung, F. *Handbuch des Arbeiter-Turnerbundes* (Leipzig: Backhaus & Diettrich, 1911).

Argentina

The Argentinian sport movement was relatively small and mostly restricted to the British-oriented upper classes until the 1920s. By that time soccer was spreading through the working class. In 1929, the worker sport section of the RSI was split by the social democrats, who set up their own worker sport movement. Neither faction achieved much success. Instead, Argentinian Peronism created a national enthusiasm by combining a national populism with socialist ideas. No room remained for a split in the sport movement. Argentina also began to have international athletic success. It placed second in the football World Cup in 1930 and had its first Olympic champion in marathon running in 1932. By luring the best working-class athletes into the middle class with attractive financial rewards, Argentina followed the British example (see chapter 6).

References

Romero Brest, E., Dallo, A. & Silvestri, S. "Los Deportes y la Educacion Fisica en la Republica Argentina," in: H. Ueberhorst (ed.), *Geschichte der Leibesübungen,* vol. 6 (Berlin: Bartels & Wernitz, 1989), pp. 846-888.

Die Spaltungstätigkeit der Sozialdemokratie und die Taktik der RSI (Moscow, 1929), Arbeitararkivet, Helsinki.

Baltic States

The Baltic States (Estonia, Latvia, Lithuania) only started to enjoy independence in modern times after World War I ended. (See chapter 3 for a discussion of worker sport in the Baltic States before 1919.) The Estonian worker sport movement was slow to start. After 10 years the Estonian Central Federation of Sport Federations (ESK), which also served as the Estonian National Olympic Committee, had only six member federations—soccer, team handball, track and field/weightlifting/wrestling, water sports, winter sports, and tennis. Its biggest successes came in the 1936 Olympics, where Kristian Palusalu won gold medals in both Graeco-Roman and free-style wrestling. The Estonian worker soccer federation started in 1927, had 15 clubs, and played its own national championship. The Estonian Worker Sports Federation (ETL) started in 1929 and immediately joined the SWSI, although the group never had more than 1,500 members. ETL refused to follow SWSI orders and continued to compete with the Soviet Union and RSI clubs. Its main international competitors were, however, the other Baltic States and Finland. The development of TUL (see chapter 4) was important because the languages of Estonia and Finland are similar, while other countries in the same area speak quite differently.

With the Hitler-Stalin Pact of 1939 Soviet leadership took over Estonia and its sport movement. Both could only reestablish themselves in 1990.

By contrast, Latvia (2 million inhabitants in 1933) had a well-developed sport system that also contained a social-democratic worker sport organisation (SSS). The SSS was founded in 1921 and had over 5,000 members. Riga, the Latvian capital, was a very sporting city; it contained four German sport clubs in which the sizable German minority met. Its bourgeois sport had already played an important role in imperial Russia. Latvians won 34 times at the Second All-Russian Olympic Games in Riga in 1914.

The SSS joined the SWSI in 1922 and played a conservative role in it. The SSS had difficulties at home because it followed SWSI rules and refused to compete against the USSR. This policy led to a split in worker sport; the trade unions started their own sport sections and competed across the border. The SSS retaliated by joining the bourgeois Latvian nationalistic forces and agitating against the Russian-dominated trade unions.

Latvia also was swallowed by the USSR following the Hitler-Stalin Pact of 1939. Soviet national teams made particular use of Latvian basketball players for their national teams. Latvia remained under Soviet rule until 1990, when it again started its own sport movement.

There are no reports of a worker sport movement in Lithuania. The Lithuanian sport movement was incorporated into the RSI in 1940 following the Soviet invasion and gained independence only in 1990.

References

Beckmann. *Sport Lexikon* (Vienna: Beckmann, 1933).
Sendlak, P. "Leibesübungen und Sport in der Sowjetunion," in: H. Ueberhorst (ed.), *Geschichte der Leibesübungen*, vol. 4 (Berlin: Bartels & Wernitz, 1972), pp. 64-133.
Die Spaltungstatigkeit der Sozialdemokratie und die Taktik der RSI (Moscow, 1929), Arbeitararkivet, Helsinki.

Belgium

In Belgium the first socialist workers' *Turner* federation was founded in 1904. Belgium became instrumental in forming the SWSI in Ghent in 1913, as the small trilingual (German, Dutch, French) country had already solved for itself many of the problems of competitions across German and French borders. The cooperation of Kleinhof (Germany), Laine (France), and Bridoux (Belgium) as of 1910 can be seen as the root of the LSI/SWSI. During World War I the national workers' *Turner* federation terminated its activities, but many of the clubs continued in spite of the war. This continuity resulted in more members when the federation restarted in 1919. The federation remained a driving force behind the LSI/SWSI, which had Belgian board members throughout its existence.

In addition, there was a seperate Belgian Worker Football (Soccer) Federation that had an another 7,500 members in 200 clubs, so that Belgian worker sport had a total of over 20,000 members. Worker football was organised as a section of the Belgian Socialist Youth Committee (CCJS) because it was considered an important activity to strengthen the adherence of youth to the Socialist Party and trade union activities. These organisations and the international SWSI all had their offices in the Trade Union House of Brussels.

What eventually became the Belgian Socialist Workers Federation for Physical, Sport, and Moral Education (CCEP) again played a primary role for worker sport when it staged the third Worker Olympiad in Antwerp from 25 July to 1 August 1937. This competition, considered a protest of the Nazi Olympics 1 year before in Berlin, hosted 20,000 athletes—many of them from the RSI. The socialist workers had invited their communist counterparts to participate in these games under the name of the Popular Front.

In the interest of better performances Belgian worker sport started to specialise their athletes as early as 1927. The third Worker Olympiad was considered a success because many athletes, particularly Russian, gave international caliber performances. Belgian worker sport ended in 1940 under German occupation and restarted in 1945. Today the CCEP has more than 150,000 members and is mainly a socialist sport-for-all organisation. When international worker sport restarted in May 1946 in Brussels, the board, now known as the *International Committee of Socialist Workers Sport* (CSIT), was again under Belgian influence.

References

Box, E. & Tolleneer, J. "Hinter unserer Olympiade steckt ein anderer Gedanke. Die III. Arbeiter-Olympiade 1937 in Antwerpen," in: *Sozial- und Zeitgeschichte des Sports*, vol. 2, 1988, pp. 28-42.
Deveen, M. "Comité Sportif International du Travail,"

in: Societé Française de Sociologie du Sport (ed.), *Sports et Societés contemporaines* (Crétail: Bardet, 1984), pp. 387-396.

Nitsch, F. "Die III. Arbeiter-Olympiade 1937 in Antwerpen," in: *Sozial- und Zeitgeschichte des Sports*, vol. 2, 1988, pp. 10-27.

Verhaegen, M. "Belgien," in: H. Ueberhorst (ed.), *Geschichte der Leibesübungen*, vol. 5 (Berlin: Bartels & Wernitz, 1976), pp. 122-150.

Bulgaria

The Bulgarian Communist Party was founded by Dimitri Blagoev as early as 1891, and the communist gymnastics club, *Boetz* Sofia, was established by 1900. In 1907 the first social-democratic worker youth gymnastics club, *Mladez,* was founded as part of the socialist youth movement and followed the German gymnastics model (see chapter 1). They also participated in the fight against national chauvinism during the Balkan War and World War I. After the Russian Revolution they followed Soviet ideas very closely (see chapter 3). The Bulgarian Communist Youth Organisation became a founding menber of the RSI in 1921.

As Bulgaria is closely related to Russia culturally and linguistically, it followed the Soviet models in every aspect and participated in the international RSI activities. The *Komsomol* organisations founded sport sections called *Spartak*. Zonkov (1976) claims that there were several hundred sections by 1922, staging massive *Spartakiads* in almost all provinces. On 9 June 1923, RSI athletes were among the most active fighters against the fascist coup. For 8 years worker sport could only exist undergound or hidden in bourgeois sport organisations, but in 1931 a new government permitted it again to some extent. A Bulgarian team went to the 1931 *Spartakiad* in Berlin (which did not take place) and participated in the RSI conference. In 1934, they introduced a badge (*Ready for Work and Defence*) that followed the Soviet example. But in 1935 the total fascist takeover outlawed communist-oriented sport again.

During the fascist period the German model strongly influenced Bulgarian sport. The main organiser of German sport, Dr. Carl Diem, spent 3 months in Bulgaria to bring socialist sport into line. Under the Hitler-Stalin Pact of 1939 the *Spartak* Moscow soccer team toured Bulgaria and was welcomed enthusiastically. These ties were rapidly cut again when Germany went to war against the USSR in 1941. As of September 1944, after the liberation, sport was again under the influence of the USSR.

References

Petrova, N. "Das Wesen der politischen Aspekte der Körperkulturentwicklung in Bulgarien in der Periode zwischen dem Ersten und dem Zweiten Weltkrieg," in: M. A. Olsen (ed.), *Sport and Politics 1918-39/40* (Olso: Universitets-forlaget, 1985), pp. 163-179.

Vassilev, B. "Le développement social et le mouvement sportif ouvrier en Bulgarie au cours du xxe siècle," in: *Sport et développement social au xxe siècle* (Paris: Ed. Universitaire, 1969), pp. 90-96.

Zonkov, V. "Bulgarien," in: H. Ueberhorst (ed.), *Geschichte der Leibesübungen*, vol. 5 (Berlin: Bartels & Wernitz, 1976), pp. 379-398.

Czechoslovakia

Czechoslovakia was considered the third strongest social-democratic worker sport organisation after Germany and Austria. It was, however, divided along ethnic lines into separate Czech and Slovak sections and into a third German-speaking section. The Germans lived mostly along the northern and eastern borders and in the capital of Prague.

The Federation of Czechoslovak Worker *Turner* Clubs (DTJ) was founded in 1903 and become a founding member of the SWSI. In 1920 the DTJ had 1,565 clubs totalling 224,000 members when it broke into a social-democratic section (which kept all the property) and a communist section. By 1930, 1,220 clubs with 137,000 members were social-democratic and 120,000 were in the communist Federation of Worker *Turner* and Sports Clubs (FDTJ). The division between these two factions and their fierce fight determined much of the relationship between SWSI and RSI. In June 1921 Prague saw two different worker sport competitions (Olympics)—one social-democratic, the other communist—each drawing 100,000 spectators. The government was not so broadly supportive; it backed the DTJ and outlawed the FDTJ. To counteract the government's ban, the communists started to work underground by 1924 to achieve a wider membership (e.g., the *Spartakus Boy Scouts*). SWSI (Sibala) and RSI (Aksamit) both had Czech secretary generals. When German and Austrian worker sport was banned in 1933 (see chapters 1 and 5), the DTJ became the strongest worker sport organisation in the SWSI—strong enough to have the seat in Prague—while the FDTJ was the strongest outside the USSR in the RSI.

Every major multisport event with many participants from abroad was called *Olympics* at the time. The Prague

Socialist Olympics of 1921 had 22,300 participants, the Socialist Olympics of 1927 had 30,100, and the third Socialist Olympics from 4-9 July 1934 had 34,900 participants from 14 different countries (60,000 in the major parade). There were as many as 120,000 spectators at the final manifestation, an estimated total of 1 million (as many as the 1932 Los Angeles Olympics). Many considered the Prague Czechoslovak Socialist Olympics the high—and final—point of the SWSI, as these masses still excluded the communist RSI, which was invited to join in the international Worker Olympics in Antwerp in 1937.

RSI and SWSI both boycotted the 1936 Olympics. Even though Soviet and other RSI groups participated in the Antwerp Worker Olympics of 1937, the FDTJ was the only communist organisation that was explicitly excluded. The DTJ also had member clubs in Germany, France, and North America at this time.

The first worker *Turner* club in the old Austro-Hungarian Empire was formed in Eichward in Bohemia in 1889. Prior to World War I the German-speaking worker sport clubs were a section of the Austrian worker federation (see chapter 5). When Bohemia and the rest of Austria split up in 1908, Bohemia decided to become District 16 of the German *Arbeiter Turner-Bund* (ATB) (see chapter 1).

After World War I the German Worker *Turner* and Sport Federation in Czechoslovakia (ATUS) became an independent organisation and a founding member of the SWSI. These shifts of affiliation and the somewhat isolated situation helped ATUS to become one of the best organised groups of worker sport in the world. In addition, by 1924 an independent communist Worker Sport and Culture Federation (ASK) of about 14,000 members had split off and become a section of the Czech RSI. In 1929 there was another split—the ATUS (opposition) split off in Reichenberg to try to unite social democrats and communists in the German-speaking *Sudelen* area again.

When worker sport in Germany was banned after 1933, the German-speaking groups in Czechoslovakia provided a new base of operation for worker sport emigrants of all backgrounds. The seats of Aussig and Prague provided opportunities to print propaganda. From there, the local Friends of Nature and the bicycle riders of the *Solidarität* helped to bring socialist propaganda leaflets back across the German border, particularly into Saxonia. They continued these activities until 1938 when German forces occupied first the *Sudetenland* and later all of Czechoslovakia, banning all worker organisations. Many of the communists, particularly those of German descent, were deported and killed.

After World War II Czechoslovakia was forced to become a Soviet ally. The new united sports federation, CSTV, ended the rivalry between the different national, religious, and political divisions. After the downfall of the USSR in 1989, the national divisions broke out again. As the German *Sudenten* minority had been driven out mainly to West Germany in 1945, the country split up into separate Czech (capital Prague) and Slovak (capital Bratislava) Republics. The two unified sport federations maintain a strong socialist tradition, but separate socialist sport federations have not been started anew.

References

Beckmann. *Sport Lexikon* (Vienna: Beckmann, 1933).
Kratky, F. "Tschechoslowakei," in: H. Ueberhorst (ed.), *Geschichte der Leibesübungen*, vol. 5 (Berlin: Bartels & Wernitz, 1976), pp. 311-328.
Ullmann, A. "Der Arbeiter-Turn- und Sportverband," in: R. Jahn (ed.), *Sudetendeutsches Turnertum*, vol. 1 (Frankfurt/M: Heimreiter, 1958), pp. 271-297.
Wagner, J.F. "Prague's Socialist Olympics of 1934," *Can. J. History of Sport*, vol. 23 (1992), pp. 1-18.

Denmark

The Danish Worker Sport Federation (DAI) and the Danish Worker Soccer Federation were founded in 1929. Both joined the SWSI. Because most of the country was agricultural, both organisations placed their centers in big cities, particularly Copenhagen and Odense. Just like the Danish bourgeois sport, they were influenced by the developments in Sweden (see chapter 7) and Germany (see chapter 1). Surrounded by powerful neighbours, the Danish people maintained their national identity through their particular form of gymnastics. Since the government subsidised all sports, there was little need for a communist (sport) movement as an opposition. When Germany invaded in 1940, the worker sport movement was outlawed. It was restarted after the war and joined the CSIT. Today the CSIT has more than 50,000 members and emphasises sport for all and workers' culture.

References

Beckmann. *Sport Lexikon* (Vienna: Beckmann, 1933).
Berggren, F. & Worm, O. "Dänemark," in: A. Krüger (ed.), *Leibesübungen in Europa I* (London: Arena, 1985), pp. 27-47.
Berg-Sörensen, I. "Dänemark," in: H. Ueberhorst (ed.), *Geschichte der Leibesübungen*, vol. 5 (Berlin: Bartels & Wernitz, 1976), pp. 84-99.

Krogshede, K. *Idraet. Vor Tids store Folkeopdrager*, 2 vols. (Odense: Arnkrone, 1943).

Trangbaek, E. "Danish Olympics. What's so Danish About the Danish?" Paper at the 1995 NASSH conference, *International Journal of the History of Sport*, 13 (1996).

Egypt

The Egyptian Union of Sport Clubs was founded in 1910 and began providing the athletes who participated in the Olympic Games in 1912. Angelo Bolonaki, a Greek residing in Alexandria and the longest-serving International Olympic Committee member (1910-1963), was the driving force. In 1929 two worker sport clubs existed and together had over 300 members. Both clubs had a basis among railroad workers and were affiliated with the RSI. No exact dates about their integration into the mainstream bourgeois sport movement are known. When the Egyptian government sponsored the formation of the National Olympic Committee in 1934, national federations already existed for 14 sports. The whole Egyptian sport movement was particularly influenced by the British.

References

Fadali, M.M. "Historical Development of Physical Education in Egypt," in: H. Ueberhorst (ed.), *Geschichte der Leibesübungen*, vol. 6 (Berlin: Bartels & Wernitz, 1989), pp. 241-260.

Informationsbulletin der Roten Sportinternationalen. Moscow, No. 25 (July 4, 1929).

Hungary

Despite its small size, Hungary has had a great deal of success in the Olympic Games. In 1898 the first Hungarian worker cycling club *Velocitas* Budapest was founded. The Workers and Physical Culture Clubs (MTE) became members of the first SWSI in 1913. While worker sport was diminished during World War I in Germany and Austria, it actually increased in size in their ally Hungary. After the war, the movement split into two groups: a more radical one—Kiraly became a founding member of the RSI—and a social-democratic one that stayed an active member of the SWSI. In spite of a government that became increasingly fascist, the social-democratic worker sport movement was permitted to stay. It was, however, losing its young membership; all youth under

age 21 had to become members of the state youth *Levente*. More and more factory clubs were established, which also reduced the influence of the worker sport movement. After World War II Hungarian sport followed the Soviet model and—building on their strong tradition—was again very successful. With the downfall of the socialist system in 1989, unified sport that included elements of the socialist tradition was maintained.

References

Kutassi, L. "Sportpolitik in Ungarn zur Zeit des Horthy-Regimes. 1919-1944," in: M.A. Olsen (ed.), *Sport and Politics 1918-39/40* (Oslo: Universitets-forlaget, 1985), pp. 180-186.

Ueberhorst, H. & Kutassi, L. "Ungarn," in: H. Ueberhorst (ed.), *Geschichte der Leibesübungen*, vol. 5 (Berlin: Bartels & Wernitz, 1976), pp. 329-346.

Italy

Mainstream Italian socialism had resented sport as a waste of time and as "a way of the capitalists to lead the proletarian youth away from the course of the class struggle," concluded the 1901 Socialist Youth Congress in Florence. The same congress decided that membership could not be held simultaneously in a socialist and a sport organisation since they were mutually exclusive. A vote of the central socialist organisation was against any sport as late as 1909. In spite of this ruling, an interregional conference of the worker sport clubs took place under Austrian influence in Trieste in 1911. A Socialist International Sport Circle had existed in Trieste since 1904, and continued until 1914, under the influence of Austro-Marxism (see chapter 5). From here the word spread. The *Ciclisti Rossi*, the red bicycle squads, followed the lead of the Clarion in England (see chapter 6) and the *Solidarität* in Germany (see chapter 1), combining the spread of propaganda leaflets with physical exercise.

After the First World War, the leading socialist thinker Antonio Gramsci favoured sport. He saw professional sports like football as part of the class struggle from above and the possibility to break into bourgeois hegemony, a term he used that has since spread into current political thinking. Mass participation for him also meant liberation.

Attilio Maffi became the leader in the new APEF (*Associazione proletaria per l'educazione fisica*) and tried to put this notion into action. He thought the Communist Party's lack of interest in youth sport activities had been a political error—one he tried to correct. Gramsci succeeded in turning around the political stance of the Italian socialists and of the youth organisation in 1921. Belloni of the Italian Communist Party (PCI) became a founding member of the RSI and a member of its executive board. With Mussolini's fascist coup of 1926 worker sport dissolved, just like the other socialist organisations. However, many of the red athletes and organisers continued in the *Dopo Lavoro* leisure-time movement. In 1948, the Communist Party was cofounder of the *Union Italiano di Sport Populare* (UISP), which has developed into a strong national sport-for-all organisation that still exists today.

References

Fabrizio, F. *Storia dello sport in Italia. Dalle società ginnastiche all'associazionismo* di massa (Florence: Guaraldi, 1977).

Krüger, A. "Sport im faschistischen Italien (1922-1933)," in: G. Spitzer & D. Schmidt (eds.): *Sport zwischen Eigenständigkeit und Fremdbestimmung. Festschrift für Prof. Dr. Hajo Bernett* (Bonn: P. Wegener, 1986), pp. 213-226.

Mereu, G. *Sport e Politica: Rappresentazioni e Pratiche Sociali in una Rivista di Inizio Secolo.* (Diss. Roma [Fac. Sociologia] La Sapienza, 1992).

Pivato, S. "Socialisme et Antisportisme. Le 'cas' Italien (1900-1925)," in: P. Arnaud (ed.), *Les origines du sport ouvrier en Europe* (Paris: Hermattan, 1994), pp. 129-139.

Rossi, L. "Attilo Maffi e la gimnastica proletaria," in: A. Noto & L. Rossi (eds.), *Coroginnica*, vol. 1 (Rome: Meridiana, 1992), pp. 136-140.

Japan

Industrialisation came late to Japan. The basis for trade unions was only established in 1896 with the *Rodokumiai-Kiseikai* (Union to Achieve Trade Unions). Its first sport festival (also in 1896) was outlawed by the police, but a sport meeting in which all 1,000 workers of one printing shop—including management and owners—participated was not. This success led to a basic split between social democrats in favor of company sport and the radical left, which acted against oppression, military preparation, and indoctrination through company sport by preparing its own separate system.

Left-wing intellectuals favoured western sports as a means of modernisation and democratisation. Their journal entries show that they were open to questions of sport. The first *Spartakiad* in Moscow (1928) particularly impressed them. In 1932 the Japanese Federation of Proletarian Cultural Organisations (KOPF) founded the Proletarian Sport Federation of Japan, which joined the RSI and was immediately outlawed by the Japanese government. Nevertheless clandestine activities were possible on a small scale until the beginning of World War II. No opposition activities are reported during the war.

In 1965 SHINTAREN, the New Japanese Union for Physical Education and Sport, was founded under influence of the Socialist Party. The union was able to expand as more cities came under socialist influence. Today it has more than 50,000 members and is an associated member of the CSIT.

References

Karaki, K. "Arbeitersport und Arbeitersportbewegung in Japan. Die neu gefundene Vergangenheit," in: *Sozialund Zeitgeschichte des Sports*, vol. 2, 1988, pp. 74-84.

Sasajima, K. "History of Physical Exercises and Sport in Japan," in: H. Ueberhorst (ed.), *Geschichte der Leibesübungen*, vol. 4 (Berlin: Bartels & Wernitz, 1972), pp. 191-226.

The Netherlands (Holland)

The Netherlands has a long sporting tradition for all social ranks. Long before Holland participated in the Olympics for the first time in 1900 people enjoyed games such as road bowls and sports such as long-distance ice skating on a wide scale. During the 1920s Dutch society began to fragment (*Verzuiling*). The separations were so strong that distinct Catholic, Protestant, bourgeois, and socialist organisations were found in all spheres of cultural life, including sports. The Dutch Worker Sport Federation (NASB) was founded in 1926. The group immediately joined the SWSI and had 17,000 members by 1931. NASB was not very popular with the Socialist Party because they feared sport would distract youth from the proletarian struggle. In 1936 the NASB reached the largest audience when it concentrated on the boycott of the Berlin Olympics. Its exhibition and conference, *Olympics Under a Dictatorship*, combined for a short time the interests of the Dutch intellectuals with worker sport.

The NASB was dissolved by 1940 during German occupation but was restarted as the Netherland Cultural Sport Federation (NCS) in 1945. By this time it had given up its insistence on separate competitions. Today NCS is an affiliated member of the general sports governing body, has over 40,000 members, and emphasises sport for all and traditional nonprofessional games.

References

Crum, B. "Niederlande," in: A. Krüger (ed.), *Leibesübungen in Europa I. Die Europäische Gemeinschaft* (London: Arena, 1985), pp. 169-183.

de Wolf, L. *Sport Encyclopaedie* (Amsterdam: Breughel, 1951).

Dona, H. *Sport en socialisme. Geschiedenes van de Nederlandse Arbeidersportbond. 1926-1941* (Amsterdam: s.p., 1981).

Lommen, N. "Niederlande," in: H. Ueberhorst (ed.), *Geschichte der Leibesübungen*, vol. 5 (Berlin: Bartels & Wernitz, 1976), pp. 100-121.

Swijtink, A. *In de pas. Sport en lichamelijke opvoeding in Nederland tijdens de Tweede Wereldoorlog* (Haarlem: De Vriesborch, 1992).

Poland

Modern Poland became an independent country only after World War I. Before then it had been divided between Russia, Austria, and Prussia. The first worker sport clubs were founded in the Austrian industrial parts of Silesia: *Sila Teschen* (1908) and the Worker Sport Club Krakow (1910). Worker sport spread out across the industrial parts of Poland. In 1925 four different national organisations were founded that reflected the territorial and ethnic difficulties of the young nation: the ATSB of Poland for the German minority, the Jewish Federation of Physical Education in Poland (SRWFJP), the Ukrainian Federation of Worker Sport and Physical Culture (HLR), and the Polish Worker Sport Federation (ZRSS). All joined the SWSI and soon formed a loose, cooperating *Kartell*. The HLR soon became the biggest organisation (152 clubs) and was disbanded by the Polish government. But the group reorganised and had 68 new clubs by 1932.

Two other groups made things even more complicated: the Free City of Danzig (at the German-Polish border) had a separate worker sport federation (ATSV), and the Poles in Germany also founded their own worker sport federation (ZPRKS) in 1930. Under the Silesia rules of minority rights for Germans in Poland and Poles in Germany ZPRKS was the only worker sport federation allowed to exist after the Nazi take-over of 1933 (see chapter 1). ZPRKS even increased in size and importance because many German workers joined. Eventually it contained 24 clubs. All of this growth ended with World War II.

Under Soviet dominance a different national Polish organisation of worker sport (ZSRR) was established in 1944. With the socialist take-over in 1948 the ZSRR became the basis for the new Central Committee for Physical Education and Sport of the Polish government. After the redemocratisation of Poland in 1989 the sport structures were maintained in a unified sport federation.

References

Beckmann. *Sport Lexikon* (Vienna: Beckmann, 1933).

Liponski, W. *Humanistyczna Encyclopedia Sportu* (Warsaw: Sport i Turystyka, 1987).

Woltmann, B. "Polnische Arbeitersportvereine in Deutschland," in: H.J. Teichler (ed.), *Arbeiterkultur und Arbeitersport* (Clausthal-Zellerfeld: DVS, 1985), pp. 118-127.

Wroczynski, R., Laskiewicz, H. & Hadzelek, K. "Polen," in: H. Ueberhorst (ed.), *Geschichte der Leibesübungen*, vol. 5 (Berlin: Bartels & Wernitz, 1976), pp. 418-436.

Romania

Even before formation of the Romanian state in 1861 physical education and *Turnen* were practiced in *Siebenbürgen*, the border area to Hungary that had a strong German minority. At the turn of the century, Romanian sport was in the process of incorporation, but the state did not participate in the Olympic Games until 1924. In the Carpathian Mountains the socialist group Friends of Nature organised and built their first houses in 1919. The Romanian worker sport organisation (USSMR) was founded in 1927 and immediately joined the SWSI. Although the group quickly had 2,500 members, the numbers stagnated. This halt in growth mainly occurred because the organisation acted in concert with the bourgeois government to suppress the left-wing (communist) trade unions and reduced its recruiting prospects. The country actively supported professional sports (two European champions in professional boxing). The boxers' success showed the working class how to improve their lot through sport. After the fascist take-over in 1940 all worker sport ceased to exist. With Romania's liberation in 1944 a new communist worker sport organisation (OSP) was formed that cooperated closely with the trade unions and the government. In spite of political dependence on the USSR, Romania was able to maintain a relative independence from its Soviet neighbour with regard to sport.

After the end of the socialist and nationalistic Ceauçescu government in 1989, the country's government support for sport was drastically reduced, but its infrastructure was maintained.

References

Beckmann. *Sport Lexikon* (Vienna: Beckmann, 1933).

Gasch, R. "Rumänien," in: Id. (ed.), *Handbuch des gesamten Turnwesens*, vol. 2 (Vienna: Pichler, 1928).

Ghibu, E. & Todan, J. "Rumänien," in: H. Ueberhorst (ed.), *Geschichte der Leibesübungen*, vol. 5 (Berlin: Bartels & Wernitz, 1976), pp. 399-417.

Die Spaltungstätigkeit der Sozialdemokratie und die Taktik der RSI (Moscow, 1929), Arbeitararkivet, Helsinki.

Switzerland

Already in 1838 the first Swiss worker *Turner* club had been founded in Geneva (Grüliverein). By 1874 worker sport started to spread all over Switzerland, forming the oldest national worker sport organisation in the world as the Swiss Worker *Turner* Union (SATB). The SATB connection with the bourgeois *Turner* clubs was relatively close; many of the instructors and coaches received their training in the same institutions. The SATB also was federally subsidised because of its work in the physical preparation of youth. The actual split came during a widespread strike in 1909 where bourgeois and worker *Turners* were on opposite sides of the barricades.

The Friends of Nature (founded in 1905) stayed independent and followed the German (see chapter 1) and Austrian (see chapter 5) models. A worker Touring (bicycle) Federation was founded in 1916 along the lines of the German *Solidarität*. Under the strong influence of sport (particularly football and skiing), the *Turners* eventually renamed themselves as SATUS (Swiss Worker *Turner* and Sport Federation). SATUS was a founding member of the SWSI in 1913 and provided the facilities for the reestablishment of worker sport in Lucerne in 1920 after the First World War.

In 1937 SATUS favoured physical preparation for national defence, which helped end the split in Swiss sport in 1939. SATUS became a member of the Swiss General Sports Federation (SLL) and has remained as an independent organisation ever since. Its successful youth programmes have been heavily subsidised by the federal government, and money from the *Toto* football pools has paid for their facilities. Emphasising sport for all and hiking, it is still the only sport club in some industrial communities.

References

Burgener, L. "Schweiz," in: H. Ueberhorst (ed.), *Geschichte der Leibesübungen*, vol. 5 (Berlin: Bartels & Wernitz, 1976), pp. 265-284.

Burgener, L. *Sport-Schweiz. Geschichte und Gegenwart* (Solothurn: Habegger, 1974).

Dannenmaier, B. *Die Geschichte des schweizerischen Arbeiter-Turn- und Sportverbandes (SATUS) von ihrer Grüdung im Jahre 1874 bis zu seinem 100 jährigen Bestehen im Jahre 1974* (Dipl. DSHS Cologne, 1974).

Pieth, F. *Sport in der Schweiz. Sein Weg in die Gegenwart* (Olten: Walter, 1979).

United States

The Labour Sports Union of America (LSU) was formed in 1927 by old Wobblies, socialists, and communists. In 1928 the communists expelled all others and affiliated with the RSI in 1929. The LSU formed soccer leagues to recruit members of recent European extraction and basketball leagues to recruit the young. It was especially active in the iron belt (an area characterised by a diverse population of blue-collar workers in northwestern Pennsylvania and northern Ohio). It advocated sport-for-all activities and competed with the Young Men's Christian Association (YMCA) for use of local sports facilities.

In 1932 the LSU staged a counter-Olympics in Chicago to the games held in Los Angeles and was active in the campaign to ban American participation in the 1936 Olympics in Berlin. In both cases it was only moderately successful. The LSU drew relatively small numbers of participants and spectators to its meet and, although it helped raise the issue of racial inequality in Germany, it could not stop American participation in Berlin. In its campaign for equal rights for African-American athletes it did not compromise—banning any worker sport clubs that discriminated. However, with the marginal position of communists and socialists in America the boycott did not have any long-term effect.

References

"Aus Amerika," *Informationsbulletin der RSI*, no. 25 (July 1929).

Baker, W.S. "Muscular Marxism and the Chicago

Counter-Olympics of 1932," *Int. J. Hist. Sport*, vol. 9 (1992), pp. 397-410.

Krüger, A. *Die Olympischen Spiele 1936 und die Weltmeinung. Ihre außenpolitische Bedeutung unter besonderer Berücksichtigung der USA* (Berlin: Bartels & Wernitz, 1972).

Naisson, M. "Lefties and Righties: The Communist Party and Sports During the Great Depression," *Radical America*, vol. 13 (July 1979), pp. 47-59.

Uruguay

Winning the 1924 Olympic gold medal in soccer gave Uruguayan sport considerable emotional importance in that small South American country. Uruguay staged the first soccer World Cup in Montevideo in 1930, which its national team also won. In this climate of sporting enthusiasm the Uruguayan socialists realised that a separate sport organisation would be useful for spreading its ideological stance. With the railway workers as its basis, a Red Sport Federation was founded and sent a team to the 1928 *Spartakiad* and the fourth RSI Congress. Very little is known today about the activities of this organisation.

References

"Internationale Einheit des Arbeitersports," *Circular Letter Rote Sport Internationale*, 1931, No. 1, p. 7.

Morales, F. "Historia del Deporte del Uruguay," in: H. Ueberhorst (ed.), *Geschichte der Leibesübungen*, vol. 6 (Berlin: Bartels & Wernitz, 1989), pp. 978-987.

Yugoslavia

Prior to World War I, the first worker sport clubs were founded under Austrian influence (see chapter 5). These clubs included Friends of Nature (Sarajevo, 1905), Football Club (Zagreb, 1908), *Hajduk* Split (Sarajevo, 1912), *Anarh* Split (1913), and others. The Russian Revolution was welcomed by many Yugoslavian workers because it happened in a slavic country. Emotion from the revolution resulted in a strong worker movement after 1918. The worker movement did not, however, lead to a strong worker sport movement because sport facilities were very limited. Even with a lack of facilities, there were many different worker sport clubs.

Although a central worker sport organisation was only built in 1926, separate clubs joined the SWSI in 1921 and others the RSI in 1922. Soccer was particularly strong. *Hajduk* Split (still one of the best soccer clubs) never founded its own league, but rather competed with the regular bourgeois clubs. Worker sport had a hard time trying to unite the many different ethnic groups among Yugoslavian workers in a newly formed state. Serbian, Croatian, Slovenian, Bosnian, Montenegrinian, and other workers already had their own *Sokol* organisations and *Turner* clubs. The bourgeois government tried to prohibit the openly communist organisations but permitted social-democratic ones, which meant that Yugoslavian teams participated in all Worker Olympiads. With the fascist coup of 1928 a state sport movement was installed that eventually prohibited all worker sport organisations and brought everything into line with the Italian fascist model. When Yugoslavia liberated itself from fascism and German occupation at the end of World War II, the old worker sport traditions were built up again, but they stayed an integral part of the general Olympic movement.

After the death of Marshal Tito, the architect and then president of modern Yugoslavia, and the end of "strategic" neutrality between the two power blocs after 1989, Yugoslavia fell apart in a lengthy civil war. Although the old suprastructure of Yugoslavia still exists in 1996, there are now separate sport organisations in the independent countries of Slovenia, Kroatia, Serbia, and Bosnia. All maintain an integral worker sport tradition inside their national sport governing bodies.

References

Bjeloborodov, S. "Der Arbeitersport in Jugoslawien unter den Bedingungen der Arbeiterselbstverwaltung," in: A. Krüger & J. Riordan (eds.), *Der internationale Arbeitersport* (Cologne: Pahl-Rugenstein, 1985), pp. 103-109.

Krüger, A. "The influence of the state sport of fascist Italy on Nazi Germany. 1928-1936," in: J.A. Mangan & R. Small (eds.), *Sport-Culture-Society* (London: Spon, 1986), pp. 145-165.

Radan, Z. "Sport und Politik in Jugoslawien 1918-1941," in: M.A. Olsen (ed.), *Sport and Politics 1918-39/40* (Oslo: Universitets-forlaget, 1986), pp. 187-196.

Stepisnik, D. "Jugoslawien," in: H. Ueberhorst (ed.), *Geschichte der Leibesübungen*, vol. 5 (Berlin: Bartels & Wernitz, 1976), pp. 347-368.

Index

North London Workers Union Team, 99
Norway
  description of, 132
  economic development of, 132, 133
  labour movement in, 132, 136
  trade unionism in, 133, 139
  worker sport movement in, viii, 131-142
Norwegian Trade Union Congress, 139
Nothilfe, Norway, 133, 136
Norwegian National Federation of Sport (NFS), 133, 136-141
Nudists, in Germany, 10, 12, 19
Ny Dag (New Day), 122

O

Obukhov Works *druzhiny,* 46
Olsen, 133
Olsson, Knut, 128
Olympic Games
  in 1924, 178, 180
  in 1948, 79
  in Amsterdam (1928), 62
  in Antwerp (1920), 146
  in Berlin (1916), 8
  in Berlin (1936), 19, 20, 34-35, 63, 72, 76, 120, 121, 128-129, 136, 139, 150, 155, 172, 175
  boycotts of, 60, 63, 120, 121, 128, 175
  democratisation of, ix
  German participation in, 8, 14, 17
  in Helsinki (1952), 40, 41, 79, 164
  in Helsinki (summer, 1940), 77
  in Moscow (1980), 22, 41
  in Munich (1972), 164
  in Paris (1900), 122, 177
  purpose of, 30
  Soviet participation at, 64, 155
  in Stockholm (1912), 70, 122, 176
  worker sport opposition to, vii, viii, ix
Open-air movement, 112
Orekhevo-Zuyevo Worker Sports Club, 46
Orienteering, in Israel, 165
Orlick, Em, 155
OSP worker sport federation, Romania, 178

P

"Pageant of Universal October" (1927), 56-57
Palestine Liberation Organisation (PLO), 158
Palestinian Amateur Sports Association, 162
Palmer, B., 145
Palusalu, Kristian, 172
Paris Soir (newspaper), 32
Pascot, "Kolonel," 38
Pekkala, Eino, 72
Pella, Roy, 155
Pépin, Edmond, 30
Petach Tikvan Club, 159
Petites A's, France, 29, 31
Physical fitness, in the United Kingdom, 109
Plugot Hapoel (*Hapoel* squads), 162
Podvoisky, Nikolai, 49, 61
Poland, worker sport movement in, 178
Polish Worker Sport Federation (ZRSS), 178
Populaire, Le (newspaper), 31, 32
Popular Front

in France, 32, 33, 34, 35, 38-39, 40, 172
in Spain, 35
in Sweden, 120, 127-129
and 1937 Worker Olympiad, 173
Prévost, Jean, 37
Proletarian Cultural and Educational Organisation, 56
Proletarian Sport Federation of Japan, 177
Proletkultists, 56-57, 60
Puchler, Josef, 89

Q

Quisling, Vidkun, 132

R

Racial discrimination, vii, viii, 41, 179
Ramadier, 40
Ramblers' Rights Movement, 112
Rambling
  in Austria, 84, 87, 89
  in Czechoslovakia, 175
  in Germany, vii, 10, 19, 22, 84, 87
  in the United Kingdom, 99, 107, 109, 111, 112, 113
Rambling Federation, United Kingdom, 107
Rassemblement Sportif International, 32, 34
Red Sport Federation, Uruguay, 180
Red Sport International (RSI)
  formation of, 45, 104
  history of, 169-170
  influence in Argentina, 172
  influence in Bulgaria, 174
  influence in Canada, 149, 150, 152
  influence in Czechoslovakia, 174, 175
  influence in Egypt, 176
  influence in Finland, 72
  influence in France, 31, 32, 33, 39, 172
  influence in Germany, 14, 16, 19, 20
  influence in Italy, 177
  influence in Japan, 177
  influence in Lithuania, 173
  influence in Norway, 136, 137
  influence in Soviet Union, 45, 60-64
  influence in Sweden, 119, 120, 122, 128
  influence in the United Kingdom, 105
  influence in the United States, 179
  influence in Uruguay, 180
Red Sports Day, in the United Kingdom, 111
Reichssportführer, 19
Renger, Annemarie, 22
Renner, Karl, 82, 84, 86
Renoir, Jean, 38
Republican Defence League. *See Schutzbund* (Defence League), Austria
Reussner, Fritz, 14, 61, 126
Road bowls, in the Netherlands, 177
Rodokumiai-Kiseikai (Union to Achieve Trade Unions), Japan, 177
Rolninen, Leo, 155
Romania, worker sport movement in, 178-179
Rostov Worker Boxing Club, 46
Rothschild, Lord Lionel Walter, 158
Rousseau, Lucienne, 34
Rousseau, René, 33, 34, 39-40
Rowing

in Finland, 69
in Norway, 137, 138
in the Soviet Union, 56
Russenfimmel (Russomania), 19

S

Sailing, in Finland, 69
Samuelson, Oskar, 119
Scandinavia, worker sport movement in, viii, 117-129, 131-142
Schild (Shield), Germany, 159
Schonerer, Georg Ritter von, 83
Schuster, H., 6
Schutzbund (Defence League), Austria, 87, 89, 91
Second Congress of the Third International (1920), 49
Second International, 30
Seelenbinder, Werner, 19-20
Seitz, Karl, 86
Semashko, Nikolai, 52, 54
Serbia. *See* Yugoslavia
Seventh Congress (of the Comintern), 154
SFIC, 28
SHINTAREN (New Japanese Union for Physical Education and Sport), 177
Shooting
  in Austria, 87
  in Finland, 69
  in Norway, 138
Sila Teschen, Poland, 178
Sinfield, George, 105, 107, 111
Sixth Congress (of the Comintern, 1928), 63, 153
Skiing
  in Canada, 148-149
  in Finland, 69
  in Norway, 137, 138
Slalom, in Norway, 137
Slovakia. *See* Czechoslovakia
Slovenia. *See* Yugoslavia
Soccer (football)
  in Argentina, 172
  in Austria, 87, 89
  in Canada, 149, 154
  in Denmark, 175
  in Estonia, 172
  in Finland, 72
  in France, 32, 34
  in Germany, 8, 16, 19
  in Israel, 159, 162, 164, 165
  in Norway, 137, 138
  in Russia, 46
  in the Soviet Union, 49, 56, 60, 63
  in Sweden, 128
  in the United Kingdom, 99, 101, 102, 105, 107, 110, 111, 112
  in the United States, 179
  in Uruguay, 180
  in Yugoslavia, 180
Social Democratic Labour Party, Russia, 53
Social Democratic Party
  in Austria (SPÖ), 82, 83-84, 86-87, 94
  in Canada, 146
  in Finland (SDP), 68, 73, 76, 77, 79

About the Editors and Contributors

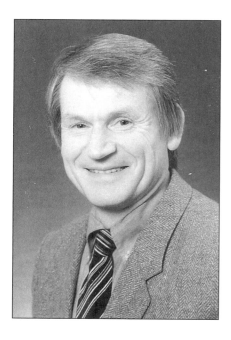

Arnd Krüger, PhD, one of the leading international sport historians, is a professor at the Institut für Sportwissenschaften, Göttingen, Germany. He was the first chairman of Sport Science at the University of Göttingen to become dean of the School of Social Sciences.

Dr. Krüger holds positions in many international sport science organizations, being chairman of the European Committee of Sport History, vice president of the International Olympiade Union, and coeditor of the *International Journal of the History of Sport*. He has also been on the editorial boards of the *International Journal of Comparative Physical Education and Sport*, *Olympika* (Olympic Yearbook), and *Leistungssport* (a German coaching bimonthly).

As a decorated track-and-field athlete, Dr. Krüger has been the German national champion in various events on 11 separate occasions. He earned a track scholarship from UCLA and was a member of its 1967 team that held the world record in the distance medley relay. He also made it to the semifinals in the 1500 meters at the 1968 Olympics.

Dr. Krüger earned his PhD in modern and medieval history from the University of Cologne, Germany, in 1971.

James Riordan, PhD, a leading international sport historian and the author of several books on communist sport, is head of the Department of Linguistic and International Studies at the University of Surrey, Guildford, U.K.

Dr. Riordan is vice president of the International Sports and Physical Education History Association and a member of the editorial boards of *World Physical Education Review*, *Leisure*, the *Journal of Sports History*, and *Sociology in Sport*.

As a student, Dr. Riordan played soccer for Moscow *Spartak* from 1962 to 1965. He was the first westerner to play for a Soviet soccer team.

Dr. Riordan earned his PhD from the University of Birmingham in 1975 and was awarded an honorary doctorate by the University of Grenoble for his contributions to sport history.

The late **Stephen Jones**, PhD, was a lecturer in the Department of Economics and Economic History at Manchester Polytechnic, England.

Bruce Kidd, PhD, is a professor of sport history at the University of Toronto, where he is chairman of the Department of Physical Education. Kidd is also chairman of the Canadian Olympic Academy.

Reinhard Krammer, PhD, is a research fellow at the Institute of Social Research in Salzburg, Austria.

Leena Laine, lic. phil., is a research fellow of the Finnish Society of Physical Education and Sport. She is currently working on her PhD at the University of Stockholm.

William Murray, PhD, is a senior lecturer in French history at La Trobe University at Bundoora in Victoria, Australia.

Franz Nitsch, PhD, is head of the Social Sciences Division at the German College for the Blind in Marburg.

Rolf Pålbrant, PhD, is a lecturer in history at Uppsala College, Sweden.

Rolf Pfeiffer, author of the histories preceding each chapter, is a research fellow at the History Department of the Philipps-University, Marburg, Germany.

Uriel Simri, PhD, has retired as director of media studies and professor of sport history from the Wingate Institute for Physical Education and Sport in Netanya, Israel.

Gerd von der Lippe, PhD, is an associate professor of sport studies at Telemark University in Bø, Norway.

Other Sport History Resources

David K. Wiggins, PhD, Editor
1995 • Paper • 352 pp • Item BWIG0520
ISBN 0-87322-520-1 • $24.00 ($35.95 Canadian)

This book brings to one volume 19 essays representing some of the best sport history research in the field today. *Sport in America* helps fill the gaps in American sport history literature and provides a balanced perspective by presenting a variety of approaches to historical research.

This anthology is designed to supplement the most widely used sport history texts and to provide a valuable reference for sport history specialists.

Written by distinguished scholars, these articles explore the changes and patterns of American sport over the past 400 years. Learn about topics ranging from the changing attitudes toward health and exercise to southern backcountry gouging matches and the importance of recreational and sporting activities for slaves.

Gertrud Pfister, Editor
1995 • Paper • 120 pp • Item JSSR04-01
Individuals—$15/issue ($20 Canadian);
Institutions—$29/issue ($39 Canadian)

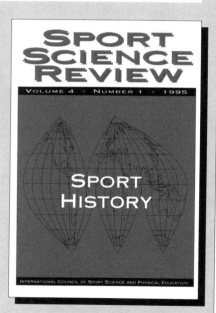

In this issue leading sport history scholars examine the interrelationship between National Socialism, images of the body, and gender ideology; the social and cultural history of the "racial" body; and the relationship between body and dance. *Sport Science Review* publishes two major international reviews each year of important new achievements in the sport sciences.

Contents

"Dance is Body"—The Body as Main Element of a Theory of Dance, *Gabriele Klein* • The "Racial" Body and the Anatomy of Difference: Anti-Semitism, Physical Culture, and the Jew's Foot, *Patricia Vertinsky* • Gender, Body Culture, and Body Politics in National Socialism, *Gertrud Pfister and Dagmar Reese* • Images and Politics of the Body in the National Socialist Era, *Thomas Alkemeyer* • Body, Soma, and Nothing Else?: Bodies in Language, *Henning Eichberg*

Prices subject to change.

Human Kinetics
The Information Leader in Physical Activity
http://www.humankinetics.com

2335

To place an order: U.S. customers call **TOLL-FREE 1-800-747-4457.**
Customers outside of U.S. use the appropriate telephone number/address shown in the front of this book.